# Ice Blink

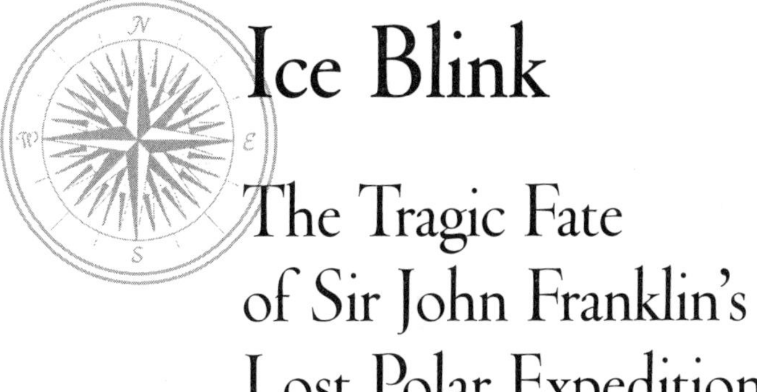

# Ice Blink

## The Tragic Fate of Sir John Franklin's Lost Polar Expedition

Scott Cookman

John Wiley & Sons, Inc.

New York • Chichester • Weinheim • Brisbane • Singapore • Toronto

This book is printed on acid-free paper. ∞



Published by John Wiley & Sons, Inc.
Published simultaneously in Canada.



*Library of Congress Cataloging-in-Publication Data:*

Cookman, Scott.
Ice blink : the tragic fate of Sir John Franklin's lost polar expedition / Scott Cookman.
p. cm.
Includes bibliographical references (p. 233)
ISBN 0-471-37790-2 (cloth : alk. paper)
1. Franklin, John, Sir, 1786–1847. 2. Northwest Passage—Discovery and exploration. 3. Arctic regions—Discovery and exploration. I. Title.
G660.C66 2000
919.804—dc21 99-047620

Printed in the United States of America

10 9 8 7 6 5 4 3 2 1

*For my sister, Constance Lee Cookman, who in her losing struggle with cancer displayed the same sublime courage and grace as the gallant officers and men of the Franklin Expedition*

*Ice blink*—the name nineteenth-century sailors gave polar mirages, caused by light reflected off the pack ice.

# Contents

# Preface

I didn't encounter the ghost of Sir John Franklin until I went north. In the summer of 1988, a bush plane dropped me at a remote outpost cabin in northern Ontario. My purpose was two weeks of solitude and fishing, nothing else. But in my backpack was a book I'd picked up, literally at the last minute, entitled *Frozen In Time* by Dr. Owen Beattie and John Geiger. It was the first account I'd ever read of the 1845–1848 Franklin Expedition disaster—the disappearance of the largest, best-equipped expedition England ever sent in search of the Northwest Passage. In the years that followed, I read dozens of equally fascinating accounts, but Beattie and Geiger's book first opened the door on the Franklin mystery for me and suggested that its solution was still waiting to be found.

What triggered the disaster—the deaths of Sir John Franklin and all 128 of his officers and men—will always be open to debate. Yet arguably, the most abundant and tangible evidence available for reconstructing Franklin's voyage and the events that led to its doom doesn't lie in the Arctic. It lies in British Admiralty records, made firsthand and documented at the time. These provided a comprehensive look at Franklin's ships, the men manning them, their clothing, stores and provisions, rationing plans, and a wealth of other details. Since the expedition was completely self-contained, its survival—or death—hinged wholly upon what it took into the Arctic. But the records also revealed a paper trail implicating a cause and a culprit behind the tragedy that followed. In ferreting out these records, I'm indebted to two exceptionally capable researchers accredited by the United Kingdom's Public Records Office (PRO): Robert O'Hara, accredited PRO military and naval researcher, and Lydia Amey, accredited PRO naval researcher. Thanks must also be given to the librarians at the Public Records Office, Ms. Eleanor Heron at the National Maritime Museum, and Ms. Philippa Smith at the Scott Polar Research Institute. In evaluating the thesis suggested, I'm especially grateful to Dr. David L. Swerdlow, Medical Epidemiologist, Foodborne and Diarrheal Disease Branch at the Centers for Disease Control and Prevention.

Lacking original source narratives left by the expedition itself—in the form of messages, diaries, or log books yet to be found, or other such undiscovered "smoking guns"—reconstructing the events of Franklin's voyage is a delicate, demanding exercise in "fill-in-the-blanks." Fortunately, there is no shortage of contemporary accounts of polar voyages tracking the route of Franklin's. Through the eyes of these men we can experience, as nearly as possible, what Franklin's men did. Likewise, contemporary accounts detailing the agonies of polar manhauling, snow blindness, frostbite, starvation, and scurvy also paint a vivid picture of the ordeal that must have been endured by Franklin's crews. A listing of the sources of these accounts can be found in the bibliography; they are all fascinating and highly recommended reading.

As general reference relating to cannibalism practiced by the Franklin survivors, the expert forensic findings presented by Dr. Owen Beattie in *Frozen In Time* and various periodicals, and those reported by Anne Keenleyside in *Arctic Magazine* must be fully and gratefully acknowledged.

The encouragement of my parents, Jane and Leon Cookman, also helped immeasurably in completing the book. Few parents, I think, understand a son quitting a well-paid career in advertising to take up the dubious path of the pen.

Lastly, I must freely acknowledge the unfailing support of my co-author: a black Lab named Kelly, who was there at the inception of the book on Hematite Lake in Ontario and patiently under my desk in the years it took to complete it. Interestingly, the Franklin Expedition embarked a dog named Neptune on its voyage. If it served them half as faithfully as Kelly has me, then "man's best friend" is the least tribute that can be paid.

# CHAPTER 1
# The Epitaphs

*By Admiralty Order, 18 January 1854: It is directed that if they are not heard of previous to 31 March 1854, the Officers & Ships companies are to be removed from the Navy List & are to be considered as having died in the service. Wages are to be paid to their Relatives to that date; as of 1 April 1854, all books and papers are to be dispensed with.*

—Admiralty Order No. 263

The only thing Sir John Franklin left behind were two faded ship's muster books. He sent them back from Greenland on July 12, 1845, just before his entire expedition—the largest, best-equipped England had ever sent in search of the Northwest Passage—disappeared in the Arctic.

By Admiralty regulation, the muster listed "the Names of all Persons forming the complement of the ships, with particulars." By twist of fate, this accounting proved the epitaph of Franklin and every man aboard.

William Orren's was typical. The paymaster simply listed him *AB,* or able-bodied seaman, aboard Franklin's flagship HMS *Erebus.* He was thirty-four that summer. He gave his birthplace as Chatham, Kent, near the mouth of the River Thames. He signed on with the expedition and appeared for duty the same day—March 19, 1845—exactly two months before it sailed.

Orren was either eager to get back to sea or, more likely, to collect the higher pay the Royal Navy offered for "Discovery Service." His previous posting had been the Woolwich dockyards, where

Received in Office 14 Augt. 1845

Entered 18

MUSTER BOOK

OF

HER MAJESTY'S SHIP

Erebus

Commencing 1 May
Ending 30 June } 1845.

Officers and Ships Company are to be considered as having died in the Service & their Wages are to be paid to their Relatives to 31 March 1854—

*Final Muster Book, HMS* Erebus  Sent back from Greenland just before the expedition vanished, this was its last communication with the outside world. The scribbled Admiralty notation—written more than ten years later—sealed its fate. "*Officers & Ships Co. are to be considered as having died in the service and their Wages are to be paid to their Relatives to 31 March 1854.*" (Public Records Office, London, England) skeleton crews manned a mothball fleet of ships laid up "in ordinary," or out of service. He'd been in the navy for fifteen years. His "first entry" was recorded at age nineteen, when he signed aboard the HMS *Swan*. He must've been a rather dull-witted fellow or happy being a simple jack tar, because in all those years he never advanced a grade in rank.

The muster book shows 16 shillings (worth about U.S. $55 in 1998 values)[1] deducted from his pay for tobacco, slop (heavy) clothing, and a horsehair mattress. This wasn't much; an experienced sailor, his seabag must have been ready. Offsetting the deductions was two months' advance pay—10 pounds and 4 shillings (about U.S. $688 today). At a time when a common laborer made 18 pounds a year ($1,210 U.S.), this was quite a windfall.

The paymaster counted the coins out to him at pay parade—ten gold sovereigns and four silver shillings—and by tradition placed them on top of his outstretched cap. Knowing he was bound for three years in the Arctic, with no ports of call or chance to spend it, the money was probably gone before he was—most of it gone on gambling, rounds of gin (a penny a glass), and prostitutes (sixpence for a "knee trembler" in an alley) before sailing.

Nothing more was ever heard of Able-Bodied Seaman Orren, or of Sir Franklin himself for that matter. Their names—and 127 others—were checked off in the muster books in 1854. On each page, an Admiralty clerk repeatedly made the same notation: "See Memo in Red Ink on Muster Table." There the clerk inked a single sentence:

> "Officers & Ships Co. are to be considered as having died in the service and their Wages are to be paid to their Relatives to 31 March 1854."

Thus the Admiralty closed the book on the Franklin Expedition—the greatest disaster in the history of polar exploration and one

[1] Based upon the Bank of England's "Equivalent Contemporary Values of the Pound," one pound in 1845 would be worth about 42 pounds in 1998 or approx. U.S. $67 at current exchange rates.

that rocked Victorian England to its core. Franklin and the rest—129 hand-picked officers and men—were written off with no more explanation. Indeed the Royal Navy, stunned by the dimensions of the catastrophe, had no explanation to offer. Its most advanced, expensive, and sophisticated technology had inexplicably failed; its finest, most qualified personnel had inexplicably failed. It was as if Apollo 11, confidently embarked for mankind's first lunar landing, had disappeared on the dark side of the moon.

The shock was devastating, the failure to find a reason for it humiliating. The navy simply closed ranks and officially, bureaucratically, put an end to the whole affair.

For the families of the men who perished, the "Wages to be paid to their Relatives" were little comfort. The men had been missing for nine years before the Admiralty reckoned them dead, during which their loved ones had been living on nothing but hope. As the clerk forcefully underlined, they would be compensated no longer.

The cause of the disaster was never determined.

The Franklin Expedition remains one of the most enduring mysteries in the annals of exploration. Something—or someone—turned the greatest Arctic expedition of its time into the greatest Arctic tragedy of the age.

What, or more intriguingly, who was responsible will always be open to debate. But an answer to the expedition's fate lies, riddle-like, in its story.

# CHAPTER 2

# Messages from the Dead

*Around the cairn a vast quantity of clothing and stores of all sorts lay strewed about, as if at this very spot every article was thrown away which could possibly be dispensed with.*

—Capt. F. L. M'Clintock, RN, on visiting Victory Point, King William Island, in 1859

On May 5, 1859, Royal Navy Lieutenant William Hobson staggered from the pack ice of the Arctic Ocean onto one of the loneliest places on earth. Lying in the heart of the Arctic archipelago, King William Island was almost 1,200 miles from the nearest whaling station in Greenland and nearly 900 miles from the northernmost Hudson's Bay Company outpost in all Canada. It was entombed in sea ice for up to nine months a year and almost perpetually cloaked by fog. But Hobson was grateful to reach it at all.

He could scarcely walk. His legs were swollen twice their size and the pain in his joints was excruciating. His skin was like dough, hemorrhaging brown and purple wherever it was touched, his gums bled and he could not shake the awful chill: signs he knew full well meant scurvy.

His party—two sleds, four seamen, an Eskimo named Christian, and seven dogs—had left the steam-schooner *Fox* thirty-four days earlier. It was one of three sledge parties from the *Fox* scouring the Arctic moonscape that spring for signs of the missing Franklin Expedition. King William Island was one of the last, most forbidding places to look.

Hobson was no stranger to the hardships of Arctic sledging. In the two years the *Fox* had been beset in Bellot Strait, some 200 miles to the north, he'd led countless sled parties searching for Franklin. But he had never gotten used to it. Few men ever did. As Captain Henry Kellett, another Royal Navy veteran of man-hauling sleds in the Arctic, described the experience: "I have been a long time at sea and seen varying trying experiences, but never have seen such labour before and misery after. No amount of money is an equivalent. Men require much more heart and stamina to undertake an extended (sled) travelling party than to go into action."

But a month into the search mission, Hobson was convinced it was the worst he'd ever experienced. Ironically, it was the fine, clear weather—cloudless skies and a cutting north wind—that made it so bad. Since leaving the ship, the temperature had averaged a bone-numbing 30 degrees below zero. Every man had frostbite; he could see it growing on their faces like a cancer. The cheeks turned an odd scaly gray, almost reptilian, as the flesh froze, but he could at least watch for that and warn a fellow. That didn't frighten him half as much as their feet. A man who couldn't walk, couldn't haul. Almost from the moment he pulled his icy boots onto his feet in the morning, he lost all feeling in them. It was the same with the rest. As they walked, he constantly called out, "How are your feet?" If a man complained more than usual, they'd halt, remove the man's boots, and take a look.

Thomas Blackwell, the ship's steward, was in the worst shape. His feet were as white as two lumps of ice and just as cold. By turns, every man in the party warmed them with their bare hands. As circulation returned, huge blisters formed, as if his feet had been severely scalded. Getting his socks and boots back on caused him agony and he limped as he walked, but there was nothing for it. The frost-burned parts swelled grotesquely, turned black as the tissue died, and made a terrible stink in the tent at night. Hobson knew there was no saving the black parts. If they got back to the ship, the surgeon would only be able to slice or hack the dead flesh away and hope no contagion spread. Hobson expected that.

Among the other cruelties of Arctic sledging, the men burned as they froze. The brutal glare of the sun reflected off the ice not only blistered their faces, it sunburned the inside of their nostrils, the undersides of their eyelids, even the roofs of their mouths as they gasped for breath. The thirst was altogether overwhelming. Though he tried to stop them, Hobson could not prevent his men from eating snow. It didn't slake their thirst; it only made them colder.

The men's only relief was three days of foul weather. A ferocious southeast gale pinned them in their brown Holland tent and wolfskin sleeping bags. But although they were spared hauling the sleds on frostbitten feet under the sun, they could still not escape the cold. It remained 18 degrees below zero. Frost a half inch thick built up on the inside walls of the tent. Their breath rose in a crystalline pall that fell back like snow. The sleeping bags froze into body casts. When the storm stopped, the men did not have to be ordered to march, no matter how painful their feet. They were anxious to move so they could generate warmth in their bodies again.

Crossing Rae Strait, some 50 miles of jumbled pack ice separating King William Island from the mainland, almost broke them completely. Pressure ridges up to 40 feet high blocked the way. Paths had to be hacked up the jagged slopes with pickaxes before the sleds—one hauled by the men and one by the dogs, each sled weighing 800 pounds—could be dragged forward. Leads—lanes of open water veining the pack—appeared without warning. These blocked their advance, forced long detours, and threatened their return. It was sometimes necessary to travel 5 miles to advance one. The crossing took nearly a week.

When Hobson reached the ice-littered shore of King William Island, he was 200 miles or more from the ship. He couldn't be sure. Squarely atop the magnetic North Pole, his compass was useless. Half his provisions—canned pemmican, ship's biscuit, tea, and rum calculated to last eighty-four days—were gone. The split codfish carried to feed the dogs was completely exhausted. Once ashore, he shot the weakest animal to feed the rest, and went on.

To make matters worse, he could hardly see. Two hundred miles above the Arctic Circle, the sun shone almost eighteen hours a day and left him and nearly everyone else snow-blind. Everything was white, brilliant and dazzling, without a particle of shade. Even wearing colored snow goggles, he felt a dull aching in his eyes that grew in intensity until it felt "as if someone had thrown a handful of sand into them." The landscape before him tinged pink, then blood red until his eyes watered so constantly he could barely see at all.

Still, atop a point on the island's northwest coast, he was sure he saw something. But even through the naval telescope, he couldn't make it out. He made for it nonetheless. The closer he got, the more fantastic it appeared. He glassed it again and pulled up short. It wasn't an "ice blink"—one of those damnable Arctic mirages. Above the sea stood a 6-foot-tall chinked stone cairn. Around it, piled in heaps 4 feet high, was a surreal hoard of discarded clothing, blankets, mattresses, and other debris.

Hobson was flabbergasted. He counted four iron boat's stoves, with kettles and pans stacked nearby as if they'd just been left. A bewildering assortment of tools—adzes, awls, mallets, mattocks, pick-axes, shovels, and saws—were scattered everywhere. Rope, chain, sail cloth, iron barrel hoops, lightning rods, even brass curtain rods, poked out of the snow. There were stacks of rusted meat tins and bottle fragments bearing the Royal Navy's broad arrow mark. The evidence was overwhelming. It could only be Franklin.

With urgency, he tore down the cairn. At its base, in a carefully sealed tin, was a single sheet of standard Admiralty record paper. Printed in six languages, it directed: "WHOEVER finds this paper is requested to forward it to the Secretary of the Admiralty, London, with a note of the time and place it was found."

Through tearing eyes, he made out two messages inked on the paper. The first was prosaic. It gave a position fix of the Franklin Expedition 12 years earlier and was noteworthy only for its optimism:

> 28 of May 1847. HM Ships *Erebus* and *Terror* wintered in the ice in Lat. 70-05′ N. Long. 98-23′ W. Having wintered in 1846–47 at Beechey Island in Lat. 74-43′-28″ N. Long. 90-39′-15″ W., after

> having ascended Wellington Channel to Lat. 77, and returned by the west side of Cornwallis Island. Sir John Franklin commanding the expedition. All well. Party consisting of 2 officers and 6 men left the ships on Monday 24th May 1847.—Gm. Gore, Lieut., Chas. D. DesVoeux, Mate.

In his hand, Hobson held the only written record of the Franklin Expedition ever found. If his hopes were buoyed by it, they were just as quickly crushed. There was a second message inked around the margins of the first—by a hand shaking with cold or terror. Dated eleven months later, it reported catastrophe:

> April 25th, 1848—HM's Ships *Terror* and *Erebus* were deserted on 22nd April, 5 leagues N.N.W. of this, having been beset since 12th September 1846. The Officers and crews, consisting of 105 souls, under the command of Captain F. R. M. Crozier, landed here in Lat. 69-37′-42″ N., long. 98-41′ W... Sir John Franklin died on 11th June 1847; the total loss by deaths in the Expedition has been to this date 9 officers and 15 men.
>
> —James Fitzjames, Captain HMS *Erebus*
> —F. R. M. Crozier, Captain and Senior Officer
>
> And start tomorrow, 26th, for Back's Fish River.

In the eerie, never-ending twilight of that Arctic evening, Hobson was sick. Over eleven years had passed since the last message was left. By that time one-fifth of Franklin's party was already dead, including over one-third of its officers. No polar expedition had ever suffered such appalling losses. The prospect the survivors faced—a 900-mile march inland—was unthinkable. It was clear to Hobson that there was no hope of finding anyone alive. If he found anything, he was certain it would only be bodies.

He followed the ice-foot along the shore, the route he guessed the survivors had taken. To avoid snow blindness, he largely marched during the brief hours of semidarkness. His eyes improved, but the scurvy redoubled. The first of his teeth fell out. His mouth was so bubbled with lesions he could no longer eat the flintlike ship's biscuit. Blood seeped from the hair follicles on his head and spontaneous hemorrhages purpled his skin. He traced the coastline for

H. M. S.

Commander.

WHOEVER finds this paper is requested to forward it to the Secretary of the Admiralty, London, *with a note of the time and place at which it was found*: or, if more convenient, to deliver it for that purpose to the British Consul at the nearest Port.

QUINCONQUE trouvera ce papier est prié d'y marquer le tems et lieu ou il l'aura trouvé, et de le faire parvenir au plutot au Secretaire de l'Amirauté Britannique à Londres.

CUALQUIERA que hallare este Papel, se le suplica de enviarlo al Secretario del Almirantazgo, en Londrés, con una nota del tiempo y del lugar en donde se halló.

*Expedition's Last Record* Found by Hobson on King William Island, it shows an "All Well" message left in May, 1847, and around the margins another dated April, 1848—reporting the desertion of both ships, death of Franklin and twenty others, and 105 survivors desperately headed inland. (National Maritime Museum, Greenwich, England) another 45 miles, some of the time obliged to ride in the sled like an invalid.

As the spring temperatures warmed, the men's misery increased. The shore ice turned to meltwater and slush, soaking them to the bone and leaving them every bit as cold as before. Dense fog blinded them as much as snow glare. The remaining food—pemmican consumed cold—did them little good.

About May 11, fully ready to turn back, Hobson made a most bizarre discovery. Even in the fog, and at a distance, it was instantly recognizable. Above a broad bay on the island's west coast, a lone ship's boat lay drawn up on shore. Coming closer, he saw it was mounted atop a solidly built oak sled. From its length, he reckoned it to be a pinnace (a small, sail-rigged boat) that could only have come from *Erebus* or *Terror.*

Despite the agony of walking, Hobson was among the first to reach it. In the bottom of the boat, amidst snow-covered debris, lay two grinning skeletons. The bones of one, partly devoured, were jumbled in a pile in the bow. The other, warmly clothed and undisturbed, was sprawled under the boat's after-thwart. Beside it were five gold watches and propped nearby were two double-barreled shotguns—one barrel in each loaded and primed. Neither body could be identified, but twenty-six pieces of silverware, bearing the personal crests of Franklin and nine other officers, were found. Some loose tea and 40 pounds of chocolate, in one-ounce foil-wrapped squares, constituted the only provisions.

In wild confusion in the bilge, Hobson found a dizzying variety of equipment and personal possessions. There was heavy wool and canvas clothing, eight pairs of boots, a pair of hand-worked slippers, silk seamen's handkerchiefs, towels, bits of soap, combs, and a toothbrush. In addition, there were boat's stores: nails, saws, files, knives, sailmakers' palms, two rolls of sheet metal, a canvas boat cover, paddles, a collapsible mast, and sails.

Six books—five Bibles and *The Vicar of Wakefield*—were also discovered, but no journals. Every item of clothing was searched, but no messages were found. There was no indication whatever of the terror that had overtaken these men or where the rest of them had gone.

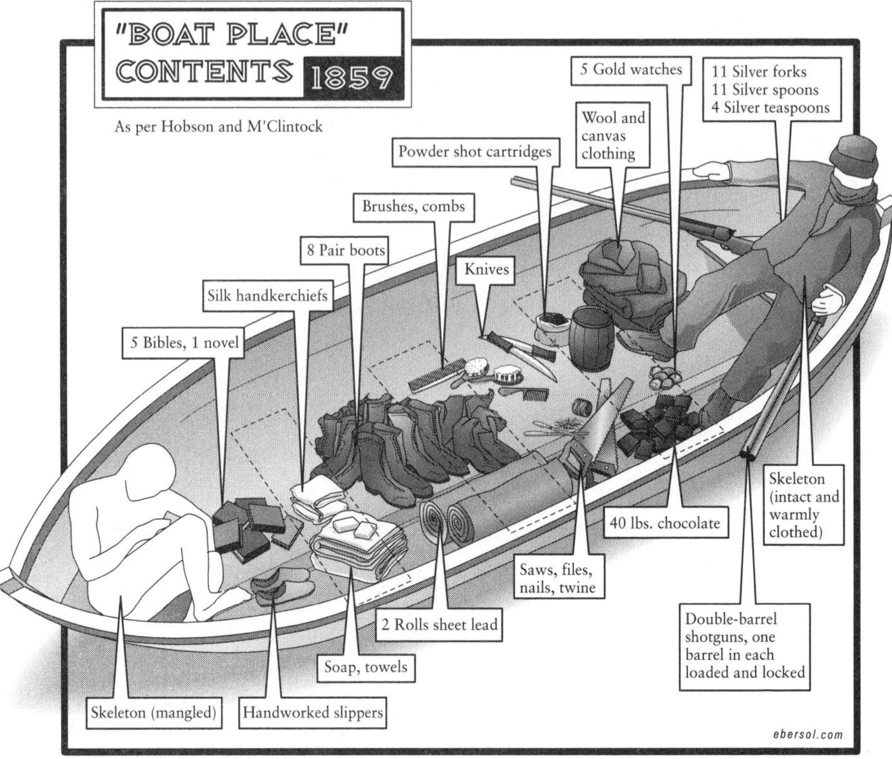

(Illustration by Rob Ebersol)

Oddly, the sled was pointed northeast—back to the cairn where the ships' stores had been abandoned, not toward Back's River where the survivors had been headed. Stranger yet was the position and condition of the corpses. They lay a full 25 feet apart—not what one would expect of desperate men huddling together for warmth. The skeleton in the bow was mangled, its bones disarranged as if devoured by something or, more chillingly, someone. All the warm clothing, weapons, watches, and silver plate were heaped around the intact skeleton in the stern. Hobson shivered at the implications.

He made no attempt to bury the corpses. The ground was too frozen and they all lacked the strength. The boat and its contents would be its own monument. Though he did not know it, scattered underfoot, beneath the snow, were the bones of fourteen other men searchers would find years later. Ominously, most of them were long bones—meat-rich arms and legs—scoured with parallel knife marks, clear signs the flesh on them had been meticulously carved away. The skulls later found were stripped of their jaws, the quickest, easiest route to get at the protein-rich brains inside. None of the bones under Hobson's freezing feet were complete skeletons; universally, they consisted of body parts—the fattest, most easily butchered and portable body parts.

Pitching their tent, Hobson's party encamped for the night. Some tea with the last of the rum lulled him into a nightmare sleep. Like the forever-sleeping skeletons not more than 6 yards away, he knew full well what was in store for them if they did not make for the ship soon. He had found what he'd been sent to find—at least all that was left. He could do no more.

By late June, near dead from scurvy and dragged in a sled by his companions, Hobson was back aboard the *Fox*. In September, still not yet recovered, he was back in London with the gruesome news. Both ships lost. Sir John, eight other officers, and fifteen men confirmed dead. The other 105 souls mentioned in the expedition's last message had vanished entirely. Then the Arctic drew a curtain over the tragedy.

For his discoveries, the Admiralty promoted Hobson commander. He never speculated on his findings; he certainly didn't speculate on the almost certain probability of cannibalism. That was unspeakable. The messages and mute testimony of the dead were enough. They were more than enough for Hobson. Though he remained in the navy, he never volunteered for Arctic service the rest of his days.

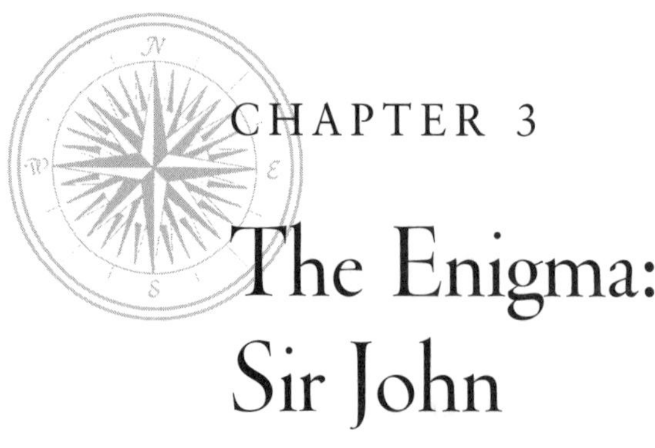

# CHAPTER 3

# The Enigma: Sir John

*Just as they were setting sail, a dove settled on one of the masts, and remained there some time. Every one was pleased with the good omen . . .*

—Eleanor Franklin (Franklin's daughter), on the Franklin Expedition's departure

If the difference between success and failure in human endeavor hinges upon leadership, the Franklin Expedition was the most egregious failure in the annals of English exploration. Sir Robert Falcon Scott, failing to beat Roald Amundsen to the South Pole in 1912, froze to death with four companions. Sir John Franklin failed to find the Northwest Passage in 1845–1848 and perished with 128 officers and men. No English explorer, before or since, lost more.

By any measure, John Franklin appeared eminently qualified to command England's largest, best-equipped expedition to force the Northwest Passage. He'd made three Arctic voyages, fought in three wars, explored the South Seas, and been knighted. He was no stranger to hardship, horror, or outright disaster. He had survived all three.

Born in Spilsby, Lincolnshire—he'd been at sea his whole life. He was twelve when he first shipped out with an uncle. At fifteen, he entered the Royal Navy as a midshipman, or Volunteer/First Class. This seems unusually young today, but for its time it wasn't; in fact, for suitable young gentlemen it was something of a fast career track.

Midshipmen had only to serve a six-year apprenticeship before recommendation for a lieutenancy; boatmen on the River Thames had to serve an eight-year apprenticeship.

Franklin's family was well connected, which, in the Royal Navy, advanced his "interest" considerably. He was well educated. The Admiralty mandated that a Volunteer/First Class "must not be under twelve years of age. He must be in good health, fit for service, and able to write English correctly from dictation and be acquainted with the first four rules of arithmetic, reduction and the rule of three." Not many high school graduates today meet those qualifications.

His practical education was quickly and brutally broadened. At fifteen he was aboard the HMS *Polyphemus* at the Battle of Copenhagen and watched Admiral Nelson blow the Danish fleet to splinters. It was to have a lasting effect on him. Though he was to fight again, he remained a pacifist for the rest of his days. He was a man who, according to contemporaries, "wouldn't harm a fly, saying there was room in the world for both," a man "who when a flogging was ordered, trembled from head to foot."

At seventeen, as surveyor (chartmaker) aboard the sloop HMS *Investigator,* he got his first taste of the rigors of "Discovery Service." Serving under his cousin, the master hydrographer Captain Matthew Flinders, he voyaged to Australia. Young Franklin assisted in charting the Great Bight and the Gulf of Carpenteria, and participated in the first circumnavigation of Australia, which proved it to be a continent. He learned a great deal about mapping and a great deal more about the meaning of "Discovery Service."

Scurvy, the vitamin C deficiency disease, killed many of his shipmates. The *Investigator,* worn out and leaking uncontrollably, was abandoned. The HMS *Porpoise,* her replacement, grounded on the Great Barrier Reef and was pounded to pieces. While Captain Flinders made a 1,200-mile open-boat journey for help, Franklin and the shipwrecked survivors barely subsisted on ship's biscuit, whelkfish, and land crabs. Rescued, he embarked for home on the schooner HMS *Cumberland* but, on landing at French-held Mauritius in the middle of the Indian Ocean, discovered war had broken out between France and England and was briefly imprisoned.

*Captain Sir John Franklin (1786–1847)* The expedition's commander, a somewhat rusticated hero who had not seen the Arctic for almost twenty years. It would be his third and final attempt to find the Northwest Passage. He was, in all likelihood, the first officer to die. (National Maritime Museum, Greenwich, England)

The Australian expedition, like almost every other in his life, had mixed triumph with tragedy.

Barely nineteen, Franklin was plunged back into the gore of combat. At Trafalgar, as signals officer on the HMS *Bellerophon* ("Billy Ruffian" to her crew), he saw thirty-three of his forty fellow officers killed or horribly wounded. Franklin wasn't scratched. Ten years later, serving in the invasion fleet carrying General Sir Edward Pakenham's army from Jamaica to America in the War of 1812, he was slightly wounded at the Battle of New Orleans.

All these were career-making events. Copenhagen was an audacious victory. At the turn of the nineteenth century, going to Australia was akin to going to the moon. *Bellerophon* was the most heavily engaged ship at Trafalgar, fighting five enemy vessels single-handed. At New Orleans, over 2,000 Englishmen were shot down in less than an hour (including Pakenham, whose corpse was pickled in a hogshead of rum for the voyage home).

Yet in spite of being in the thick of things, with abundant opportunity to distinguish himself, Franklin didn't stand out. So far as is known, he led no daring "cutting out" operations or boarding parties, never volunteered for any "forlorn hopes." He was simply not the warrior type. As a naval surveyor, he charted coastlines and anchorages—a tedious job of sounding depths, calculating currents, and figuring tides. As a signals officer, he dealt with the fastest, most advanced nautical codes of the day, not combat. Neither specialty led to quick promotion in war, far less in peacetime.

Franklin followed orders, did his duty, and "got on" well with nearly everybody. But at age thirty-three, after seventeen years in the navy, he was still a lieutenant, without a ship of his own. By comparison, Lord Nelson commanded a frigate at twenty, a "first rate" at twenty-two, another at twenty-seven, and a 64-gunner at thirty-five. Lt. William Owen, who served with Franklin in the *Investigator,* won his captaincy at twenty-six and later command of two ships and the Great African Survey. Lt. Price Cumby, Franklin's fellow lieutenant aboard *Bellerophon* at Trafalgar, took command when Captain John Cooke was killed and fought the ship so courageously (simultaneously engaging the enemy ships *Aigle, Monorca, Bahama, Swiftsure,* and *San Juan Nepomuceno*) that he was made a captain at twenty-eight. Franklin languished.

Finally, in 1818, he was given command of "a paltry gun brig" named the HMS *Dorothea,* but not a captaincy. He served under Captain David Buchan, commanding HMS *Trent,* on another "Discovery Service" expedition—an attempt to reach the North Pole.

This was his indoctrination in the perils of Arctic voyaging. It was also his first encounter with Sir John Barrow, the cadaverous Second Lord of the Admiralty and the man who would send him north four times.

The expedition came to nothing. North of Spitzbergen, the ships encountered permanent pack ice. Lt. F. William Beechey of the *Trent* described the encounter: "The brig, cutting her way through the light ice, came in violent contact with the (pack). In an instant, we all lost our footing, the masts bent with the impetus and the cracking timbers from below bespoke [immense] pressure."

The ships followed twisting, ever-narrowing leads into the pack. "The channels by degrees disappeared," wrote Beechey, "and the ice, with its accustomed rapidity, soon became packed, encircled the vessels and pressed so closely upon them that one boundless plain of rugged snow extended in every direction."

Attempts to warp the ships through the pack seemed, at first, to succeed. In fact, the southward drift of the ice actually carried them backwards. After four futile forays trying to penetrate the ice, Buchan beat a hasty retreat—so hasty that Barrow never entrusted an expedition to him again.

The lesson wasn't wasted on Franklin. Whenever he got his chance, there would be no turning back. When the chance came, it very nearly cost him his life. It cost nine other men theirs. Ironically, it was this fiasco, Franklin's 1819–22 overland Arctic expedition, that made him famous. The fact that Barrow picked him to lead it in the first place was no great endorsement. It was a minuscule naval survey party: just Franklin (still a lieutenant), two midshipmen, a surgeon, and one able-bodied seaman as an "attendant" (servant). The expedition involved no ships whatever and minimal expense so, in Barrow's estimation, entailed negligible risk. Lt. Franklin was ordered to take his party overland deep into Canada's Northwest Territory, hire some canoes and paddlers, and do some mapping.

With his four Englishmen, seventeen French-Métis voyageurs (expert canoemen, most of whom were mixed-blood Native Americans), three voyageur's wives, and three of their children in tow, he departed Fort Providence on Great Slave Lake in early August 1820.

His plan was to ascend today's Snare River, cross over to the headwaters of the Coppermine River, descend to its mouth on the shores of the Arctic Ocean, follow the coastline eastward in search of the Northwest Passage, and return. The fact that this involved paddling and portaging over 1,200 miles through some of the most unforgiving wilderness in the world did not seem to trouble him much. He had been given his chance.

Governor Sir George Simpson, head of the Hudson's Bay Company, who had agreed to support the expedition, didn't think much of it. No light judge of character, he was blunt in his estimation of Franklin: "Lieut. Franklin, the Officer who commands the party, has not the physical powers required for the labor of moderate Voyaging in this country; he must have three meals per diem, Tea is indispensible, and with the utmost exertion he cannot walk Eight miles on one day."

Indeed, Franklin set out like an unprepared summer camper. By his own admission, he embarked with only ". . . two casks of flour, 200 dried reindeer [caribou] tongues, some dried moosemeat, portable [dried] soup and arrowroot, sufficient in the whole for ten days' consumption [for his entire party]." He naively presumed that a band of Chippewyan natives hired at Fort Providence (a chief named Akaitcho, two guides, and seven hunters) could feed them all. Ten days later, the hunters having found no game, the food was gone. Franklin's fishing nets produced only "4 carp." The hungry voyageurs "broke into open discontent" and refused to continue unless they were fed.

Franklin threatened to ". . . inflict the heaviest punishment on any who should persist in their refusal to go on." He was saved making good on this completely hollow threat (his Englishmen were outnumbered five-to-one, after all, and couldn't go anywhere without the voyageurs) only when the Chippewyan hunters providentially arrived with the flesh of two caribou. Hunger, which was to stalk the expedition all of its days, was momentarily kept at bay. But it was, to say the least, an inauspicious beginning.

Less than three weeks out of Fort Providence, at a lake above the headwaters of the Snare River, even this shaky beginning came to an end. By Franklin's calendar it was only August 19 and, in his mind, the height of the summer voyaging season. Despite the scarcity of food, he was determined to press ahead, straight across the height of land and down the Coppermine to the frozen ocean. Akaitcho, the Chippewyan chief, was operating on an entirely different calendar. He pointed out the falling leaves and told Franklin winter was near and it was too late in the season to proceed. He said that eleven days' travel would put them north of the treeline, out in the "barren lands," with no protection from the weather or wood for fires. He said descending the Coppermine would consume forty days more, that the caribou had already left the river for the winter, and food would be impossible to find in the "barren lands." Akaitcho concluded that if Franklin wanted to go on, he was a dead man. Franklin replied the Englishmen had "instruments by which we could tell the state of the air and water" and that winter was not "so near as he [Akaitcho] supposed." The chief threw up his hands and said that "as his advice was neglected, his presence was useless, and he would therefore return to Fort Providence with his hunters." Franklin, as completely dependent upon the Chippewyans for food as he was upon the voyageurs for transport, had no choice but to "reluctantly" halt for the winter. He had not reached the Coppermine, much less descended it. In fact, he had traveled only seventeen days from Fort Providence and had already exhausted all his provisions and experienced two near mutinies.

Eleven days later, true to Akaitcho's prediction, the temperatures turned freezing. Franklin put his voyageurs to work building a "dwelling house" for the Englishmen. It was fully 50 feet long by 24 feet wide—to house the five of them. It took a month to complete. When it was finished, the voyageurs were allowed to build their own cabin: 34 feet long by 18 feet wide for all seventeen men. Franklin christened this "establishment," two crude log cabins and a log storehouse, Fort Enterprise. About this time, Franklin's two midshipmen fell in love with a sixteen-year-old Chippewyan girl called "Green Stockings" and challenged one another to a duel over her. To prevent bloodshed, Franklin sent one back to Fort Resolution for supplies.

By December (about the time he would have been returning from the Arctic Ocean, if Akaitcho hadn't stopped him from going) the outside temperature plummeted to 57 degrees below zero. Even in the Englishmen's commodious cabin, the thermometer (by Franklin's careful calculation placed some 16 feet from the blazing fireplace) showed 15 degrees below zero. During the winter the voyageurs were constantly employed in cutting and hauling wood, ice fishing, and hunting (which quickly exhausted the slim supply of ammunition Franklin had brought). In contrast, Franklin passed the time like a proper English gentleman: writing in his journals, reading, walking "for a mile or two on the river," and "occasionally paying the woodmen a visit." That winter their only food consisted of "the carcasses of a hundred deer, together with a thousand pounds of dried meat and suet . . . varied twice a week by fish and occasionally by a little flour, [without] vegetables of any kind."

In early June 1821, having received some supplies from Fort Providence, Franklin set off once again for the Coppermine River, his voyageurs hauling canoes on sleds over still unmelted snow and ice. It was July—after hauling the sleds 117 miles—before the ice in the river finally went out, allowing them to float the canoes. By the end of that month, paddled and portaged by his voyageurs, Franklin finally reached the river's mouth and what he called the Hyperborean Sea [Arctic Ocean], 334 miles from Fort Enterprise. He pushed east through the ice-dotted waters of Coronation Gulf, Bathurst Inlet, and coasted the shoreline of the Kent Peninsula, doggedly mapping over 300 miles of the North American coast.

In fact, he was too determined. Pressing forward, expecting daily to find the Northwest Passage, he waited until the end of August to turn back. By that time the food was almost gone, the first snow began to fall, the men were broken, the birchbark canoes were wrecks, and it was far too late to return to Fort Enterprise safely.

Winter overtook Franklin on September 7, 1821, in the "barren lands" that Akaitcho had warned him about. Three feet of snow fell, the Englishmen's instruments showed temperatures of 20 degrees F, and every ounce of food had been consumed. The party was reduced to subsisting on "tripe de roche"—an edible, but nauseating lichen growing on rocks—and the boiled leather uppers of their shoes. Suffering exposure, exhaustion, scurvy, and starvation, several voyageurs collapsed on October 4, unable to walk. Dr. John Richardson, Franklin's surgeon, one of his midshipmen (Robert Hood), his seaman (John Hepburn), and one voyageur volunteered to remain behind with them and catch up. Franklin, confused, weak, and seemingly out of control of the deepening disaster, agreed. At the same time, he ordered his other midshipman, George Back, and three voyageurs to make for Fort Enterprise to bring back food. Franklin and the rest of the voyageurs would attempt to follow. Thus the party dissolved into three groups, each out of touch, none able to help the other. Franklin's decision would bring death to each.

Midshipman Back's party left a scurvy-stricken, starved voyageur to freeze to death in its wake. Franklin's party left three starved voyageurs behind. Dr. Richardson's party experienced far worse, after it left behind the voyageurs the group had been caring for. Richardson, Robert Hood, the midshipman, and John Hepburn, the seaman, accompanied by a voyageur named Michel Teroahaute, staggered on across the tundra. Michel, however, managed to somehow bring them meat that he claimed "he had found from a wolf which had been killed by the stroke of a deer's horn." They ate it greedily. But as Dr. Richardson later related, he "became convinced, from the circumstances, the details of which may be spared, that it [the meat] must have come from the body of Belanger or Perrault [the voyageurs abandoned on the march]."

Ten days later, while Richardson and Hepburn were gathering tripe de roche, a gunshot rang out. On running back to camp, they found midshipman Robert Hood dead "from a shot that had entered the back part of his head and passed out of the forehead, and that the muzzle of the gun had been applied so close as to set fire to the nightcap behind." Michel, holding a loaded pistol, claimed it was an accident. Richardson and Hepburn were convinced, as they later reported, that the man was plotting to kill and cannibalize them as they suspected he may have done with Belanger and Perrault. As soon as he got the chance, Richardson walked up to Michel and shot him in the back of the head. Oddly, when Richardson and Hepburn reached Fort Enterprise to rejoin Franklin and his starving companions, they appeared far stronger than anyone else: far stronger than men who had been surviving on a diet of rock lichens alone. Whether Englishmen had resorted to cannibalism was never discussed. Dr. Richardson's account was accepted.

Franklin and the rest were rescued only after Midshipman George Back made a perilous trek on snowshoes to bring back some Hudson's Bay Company Indians (including Akaitcho) with help. In terms of loss of life, the expedition had been an unmitigated disaster. Nine of the twenty-one men who had left Fort Enterprise never returned. Two had been murdered. Leadership had been nowhere in evidence, and discipline had plainly evaporated.

Ironically, Franklin returned to England to great notoriety—the intrepid explorer of the "frozen regions" who survived because he "ate his shoes." The sudden fame, curious in light of the fact that it was Franklin's naïve and overconfident decisions that nearly exterminated the expedition, changed him forever. At last he was promoted to captain and, for his discoveries, made a Fellow of the Royal Geographical Society. Also, at thirty-seven, following a prolonged, awkward engagement that contained about as much heat as afternoon tea, he finally wed Eleanor Anne Porden. He quickly fathered a daughter, who was named after his wife. Just seventeen months later, Captain Franklin was given another chance at finding the Passage and Eleanor Porden Franklin was dead of tuberculosis.

Six days before her death, he departed, as ordered, on his second overland Arctic expedition. Barrow had, for the first time, seen his mettle. If Franklin could cheaply chart the North American coastline for him and fire public imagination about the Passage, he reckoned it a bargain. The men he'd lost on the 1819–1822 voyage—more than any previous Royal Navy Arctic expedition—were of no consequence. Only one was English; all the rest were Frenchmen, métis, or Indians.

On his 1825 expedition, Franklin took English seamen, not capricious French voyageurs. He took stout-built wooden boats, not flimsy birchbark canoes. And he took plenty of food and recruited plenty of Indians to hunt. The fact that English seamen were nowhere near the equals of voyageurs made no matter. The fact that wooden boats were heavy, ponderous, and a galaxy less maneuverable and portageable than canoes made no difference. It was an all–Royal Navy show. He had Barrow's confidence and another crack at discovering the Passage.

He had also learned a thing or two about politics and the dangers of sharing the spotlight. He singled out George Back, whose heroic snowshoe trek had saved him and his companions. Back was a dashing, impulsive, womanizing, hard-drinking rakehell (fathering at least one child, perhaps more, at Fort Enterprise) itching for fame. The plodding, sober, evangelical, but equally fame-hungry Franklin found Back's ambition threatening. "You know I could have no desire for his company," he wrote Dr. John Richardson, his surgeon on the Coppermine trip, "but I do not see how I can decline it, if the Admiralty press the matter, without being of great disservice to him, and publicly making an exposure of his incapacity in many respects." This was the pot calling the kettle black, but Franklin was adamant: Back was not going. Lt. A. Bushnan would go as assistant surveyor. While the expedition was fitting out however, Bushnan died of typhoid fever and the Admiralty apparently did press the matter. Franklin reluctantly took Back along, taking pains to keep him more or less in the background. The expedition would be Franklin's and his alone.

The 1825–1827 voyage was eminently successful. Franklin mapped another 600 miles of Arctic coastline west of the Mackenzie River. East of the river, the redoubtable Dr. Richardson mapped over 1,000 miles of previously unknown coast. Franklin lost not a man and was—to the English world at least—but one final piece away from solving the puzzle of the Passage.

It was the zenith of his career, certainly his life. He came back to England a bona fide hero. In quick succession, he married one of his dead wife's closest friends, Jane Griffin (the vivacious, intellectual, decidedly feminist thirty-six-year-old daughter of a wealthy silk weaver); was knighted by King George IV; was awarded the Gold Medal of the Geographical Society of Paris; and was given command of HMS *Rainbow,* a 26-gun frigate in the Mediterranean (a choice posting). At forty-one, he had finally made his mark.

At that point however, his career stalled. The Admiralty, after eight failed attempts to find the Passage in a decade, planned no more. The great surveys charting Africa and Australia were complete. There were no great wars to fight, no continental blockades to maintain. In short, there was no employment and the Royal Navy suffered drastic cutbacks. Ships were laid up and thousands of seamen discharged to shore. Hundreds of officers were put on half pay and Franklin was left a suddenly notable chap with nothing notable to do.

After three years in the Mediterranean, he returned to England and requested a new assignment. The strong-willed Lady Franklin evidently propelled him. "You will fancy, my dearest," he wrote her after petitioning the First Lord of the Admiralty for a post, "that your shy, timid husband must have gathered some brass on his way home or you will be at a loss to account for his extraordinary courage . . . because I know you would have wished me to do so."

Evidently, he'd asked for a big assignment. Pointedly, the Admiralty didn't grant it. In fact, it didn't give him anything to do. He sat "on-the-beach," on half pay, for two years. At age forty-nine, he was offered the governorship of Antigua but refused it, perhaps because both he and Lady Franklin hankered for a suitably higher post, one that would again take him north into the limelight.

He sat "on-the-beach" another year. Finally at age fifty, he was offered the governorship of Van Diemen's Land—present-day Tasmania. It was a bitter choice. Van Diemen's Land was a penal colony—about as far away from England, the Northwest Passage, and any chance of influence or recognition as Franklin could have imagined. Nonetheless he accepted it, probably because it was doubtful he'd be offered another such job if he refused, and more probably because life on half pay had become a hardship. He served a miserable seven years there—the worst years of his life.

The colony consisted of 18,000 convicts, the worst from England's jails. It was run by a murky colonial cabal who profited hugely from free convict labor. Lt. Barlatier Demas, a French naval officer who visited the island during Franklin's tenure, was taken on a tour of the place. The memory never left him.

On the Tasman Peninsula, the narrow neck of which was guarded by a cordon of savage dogs, chained muzzle to muzzle, Demas found a high-walled prison filled "with the dregs of England's criminals; they represent the basest human depravity." He was shocked to discover that, not only was there another prison for women, but a children's prison, too. "I saw there one unhappy child," he wrote, "whose crime had been to steal a few bunches of onions." The children, like the adults, labored under an enforced system of total silence with "grim-looking constables walking around with whips in their hands."

Demas was shown convicts in harness dragging wagons in place of horses, building roads to nowhere, draining swamps for no purpose. At the colony's coal mine—"worked by the government which sends there the worst scoundrels from its gaols"— he saw firsthand how cheaply convicts' lives were valued. "The pit (mine) is a hundred and forty yards deep," he wrote, "and the day I was there, two men were drowned in an unexpected flash flood underground."

He found the whole island "everywhere heavily guarded by sentinels [and] police posts that mount a continuous surveillance." Any prisoner, adult or child, who violated any rule, went to a lightless solitary cell. For more severe infractions, the prisoner was shackled to a stone block by a 6-foot chain and set to breaking stones from first light until it was too dark to see. Chained out in the open, without shade from the sun or protection from rain and cold, the punishment lasted for seven days; few prisoners endured it more than once. Escape attempts were brutally punished. Demas watched a recaptured inmate strung up in chains and given ninety lashes "heavily laid on" with a nine-tailed leather whip.

This was the world of John Franklin, the "man who wouldn't harm a fly." Every year 3,000 new convicts—men, women, and children—were delivered to him in chains. He superintended the deaths of thousands due to the climate, hardship, tropical disease, and tuberculosis. He also watched helplessly as native aborigines perished almost to extinction from European diseases.

Franklin did his level best to improve things, lobbying for more humane treatment of convicts and aborigines alike. He established a small college (for the colony's young gentlemen only) and a scientific society. Devoutly religious, he ordered strict observance of the Sabbath, urged temperance, and tried to police the endemic drunkenness, whoring, and gambling in Hobart Town, the capital. Lady Franklin, assertive and generations ahead of her time, was much behind these initiatives.

But the gentlemen of the colony, who prospered handsomely from inmate labor, dispossessing the natives, and fleecing sailors in the grog shops and fleshpots of Hobart Town, found the Franklins' measures threatening. Governors usually took their share of the colony's profits and kept their mouths shut; they didn't interfere with the colony's business. Using nefarious means, the colony's gentry rallied for Franklin's recall.

The man who'd survived shipwreck on the Barrier Reef, the broadsides of five enemy ships at Trafalgar and near death in the Arctic, didn't survive their attack. He wasn't up to it. As a contemporary noted: "Chicanery made him ill and so paralyzed him that when he had to deal with it he was scarcely himself." In short order, he fell victim to the pettiness and intrigue of the Colonial Office, finally suffering the indignity of recall.

During these dark days, there were only three bright moments. In 1829 and 1839, the colony was visited by the French explorer Captain Jules Dumont D'Urville, whose expeditions charted much of the South Pacific and penetrated the south polar ice pack to discover the Antarctic continental land mass. The two immediately hit it off. Like Franklin, D'Urville had begun his career as a surveyor and hydrographer, served in the Mediterranean (where on the island of Melos he secured for the Louvre an armless, yet astonishingly beautiful statue later famous as the Venus de Milo), coasted Australia, and had himself experienced career eclipse and life ashore on half pay. He was an ardent student of natural history and science, and a member of the Geographical Society of Paris, whose gold medal Franklin proudly wore. He was only four years younger than Franklin; it would be hard to imagine contemporaries who shared more. D'Urville's bracing accounts of his Antarctic voyages temporarily washed the stink of Van Diemen's Land from Franklin's nostrils.

In 1840, the English Antarctic expedition led by Captain James Clark Ross and Commander Francis Crozier called at Hobart Town. Franklin discovered he had perhaps even more in common with his younger countrymen than D'Urville. All three men had made voyages in search of the Northwest Passage. All three were intimates of Sir William Parry, England's most celebrated Arctic explorer. All shared the same passion for voyages of exploration.

Sir John and Lady Franklin insisted they make the Governor's House their residence during their stay. In turn, Captain Ross invited Franklin to inspect his ships—HMS *Erebus* and HMS *Terror.* Unlike any ships Franklin had ever seen, they had been specially modified for polar service. Indeed, their sole purpose was for voyaging in the ice. They were tailor-made for the one thing Franklin still dreamed about: a voyage north. Though he could not have guessed it, he would eventually come to know both vessels as well as he knew himself. But the visit was all too brief. Ross and Crozier sailed off toward Antarctica and fame. Franklin ignominiously sailed for home.

When he got back to England, he was fifty-seven, bald, overweight, and entirely without prospects. For another two years, he remained ignored, idle on half pay, pestering the Admiralty for an assignment. It was then that Sir John Barrow plucked him from obscurity for consideration to command the greatest expedition Victorian England ever dispatched in search of what Franklin had always sought—the Northwest Passage.

Cruelly, he was considered only after three other officers refused the job. Franklin (more especially Lady Franklin) politicked hard for the post, but neither this nor his previous Arctic qualifications assured his assignment. Barrow considered him only because no other suitable candidates presented themselves.

When the Admiralty asked Sir William Parry's opinion of Franklin, his recommendation was tepid, to say the least. "He's a fitter man than any I know," responded Parry. "If you don't let him go, the man will die of disappointment." Unconvinced, the Admiralty voiced concern about his age, pointing out he was sixty. Franklin assured them he was only fifty-nine, though his birthday was but a month away. And so his appointment was finally approved by the Lord Commissioners.

Franklin—an old man for his day, with a once shiny but tarnished reputation, who had not seen the Arctic in nearly twenty years—was given his third chance to find the Passage.

# CHAPTER 4

# The Passage

*Nature can be conquered, if we can but find her weak side.*

—James Watt, inventor of the steam engine

In 1845, finding a navigable route over the top of the world, a shortcut between the Atlantic and Pacific, seemed not only possible but inevitable. The more pressing question was who would find it first.

The Hudson's Bay Company explorers—Peter Dease and Thomas Simpson—had charted the North American coastline eastward almost to the point where the elder Sir John Ross's independent westward expedition had been stopped by ice. Only a few hundred miles in between remained unmapped. If there was a Northwest Passage, it would certainly be found there.

Sir John Barrow, the Second Secretary of the Admiralty, was convinced of its existence. It was, in fact, his obsession. In the previous two decades he'd dispatched eight Royal Navy expeditions—by land and sea—to find it. Piecing the parts of a gigantic, geographical jigsaw puzzle, they'd managed to fit together a fairly comprehensive outline of the Arctic.

Exploiting this work (in what Barrow clearly viewed as poaching on the navy's franchise), the Hudson's Bay Company and Felix Booth, the gin merchant who had sponsored Ross's expedition, had come very close to completing the puzzle. But one piece remained to be placed. Once it fit, England's 300-year search for the Passage would be crowned with success.

At age eighty-two, Barrow knew full well that the 1845 expedition was his last chance to achieve the prize of a lifetime. He did not intend to let it fall to anyone but himself and the Royal Navy. He especially did not intend to let it fall to French and Indian half-breeds of the Hudson's Bay Company or self-promoting liquor distillers. He planned to grab it in an audacious coup de main that would demonstrate to the world the dominance of England's navy, science, and technology. Not incoincidentally, it would also demonstrate that there was a new aristocracy emergent in the Industrial Age—one bestowed not by title or wealth, but earned through initiative and energy. As much as the Passage, this aristocracy of the mind, of ability, was the legacy Barrow wanted to leave behind.

His whole life John Barrow had worked ceaselessly to escape what he had been born—a common North countryman from a dot of a village called Dragley Beck in Lancashire. Though he had been Second Secretary of the Admiralty for forty years—serving eleven First Lords, he wasn't a naval officer. Beyond a brief voyage as a youth, working on a whaler in Greenland waters, he had no seagoing experience. He started out clerking, Cratchit-like, in a dingy Liverpool ironworks. He had little money, no connections and, as a lowly clerk, could scarcely claim status as a "gentleman." But he was both tireless and ambitious, with a unique talent for recognizing opportunity and a tenacious way of grasping it.

He quickly parlayed his aptitude for figures into a job teaching mathematics in Greenwich. To supplement his meager earnings, he tutored on the side and, quite suddenly, his whole destiny changed. One of his pupils was the wayward son of Sir George Staunton, and by dramatically improving the boy's grades he won Staunton's interest. As a reward, Staunton got him a job as household comptroller for Lord Mcartney, who had just been appointed England's first ambassador to China. With the rest of Mcartney's household, Barrow was packed up and taken east. It was his attachment to Mcartney that won him a highly placed sponsor. He never afterward forgot how the system of "interest" worked. He would later attach himself to Lord Melville and eventually to King William IV, bettering his station with each.

But Barrow—emphatically—was no sycophantic dunce. Brilliant, his talents were encompassing and his rise rapid. Still in his twenties, he learned to speak fluent Chinese (Mandarin, Wu, and Cantonese) and quickly became Mcartney's interpreter and expert on Chinese affairs.

At thirty-three he was in Africa, negotiating a peace between the Boers and Zulus. At thirty-seven, still juggling figures, he was the Cape Town Colony's auditor-general. And at the almost unprecedented age of forty-one, he was appointed Second Secretary of the Admiralty by Lord Melville, though his critics, jealous of his advance, said he acted as if he were First Secretary.

Despite his almost complete lack of naval experience, he proved exceptionally capable in the post. A year after his appointment, the Royal Navy won the most complete sea victory of its era at Trafalgar. He established the first schools for naval architecture, engineering, and gunnery. He brought the navy's first steamships into service, adopted propellers, and experimented with iron ships.

Recognizing the importance of steam power, he gave engineers officer's rank (though they still had to mess separately; greasy, coal-dusted coveralls and "mechanics" weren't welcome among gentlemen officers in the wardroom). At the same time, he abolished the antiquated Navy Board, streamlined the Victualling Department, and rejuvenated the whole navy.

Barrow was not merely a facile administrator. After his navy wiped out the last vestige of French sea power at Lissa in 1811, he waged five wars. Under his watch, he fought America to a standstill in 1812 (ravaging Chesapeake Bay, burning Washington, and very nearly capturing Baltimore), subdued the Algerian pirates in 1816, and sank a sixty-ship Ottoman fleet at Navarino in 1827 (the last great sea battle fought under sail). During the Opium Wars of the 1830s, the Royal Navy decimated the entire Chinese fleet in half an hour; seized Hong Kong, Canton, and Nanking; and won $6 million in gold in reparations. In 1840, the English fleet leveled Acre, driving the Egyptians out of Syria.

These and other actions opened ports to English trade worldwide. Just as importantly, by Barrow's design, they established a strategic network of coaling stations that gave the Royal Navy the ability to project its power on a global scale.

But exploration was Barrow's greatest passion. He established a special corps of naval surveyors and commissioned specially built survey ships. It was John Barrow who sent Ross, Parry, Franklin, and Back (all of whom would be knighted for their services) to chart the Arctic. It was Barrow who dispatched Buchan to the North Pole. It was Barrow who sent William Owen on the Great African Survey to map the continent's coast.

The voyage of the *Beagle*—with an unknown naturalist named Charles Darwin aboard—was Barrow's idea. So was the voyage of James Clark Ross to the Antarctic, to penetrate the Ross Ice Shelf and open the door to the South Pole. More than any other man of his time, Barrow helped map the ends of the earth.

His achievements were by no means limited to Admiralty matters. He earned a doctorate in literature and was a prolific author. He somehow found time to write three biographies (the first, a flattering account of Lord Mcartney, his primary sponsor), as well as books about China, Africa, and the Arctic.

Forty years of unbroken success in almost every endeavor had brought him to the apogee of his life in 1845. At the very crest of it lay the Passage. He reached for it with every resource at his disposal. Like everything else in his life, he did it exceedingly well.

He planned the thing on a grand scale. The expedition was to be the largest and best-equipped ever mounted to seek the Passage: two ships, 24 officers, and 110 men supplied with every necessity for three years. It was perhaps the most technologically advanced mission of the mid-nineteenth century—the Apollo program of its day. The ships were revolutionary: locomotive-powered, iron-plated, driven by retractable screw propellers, steered by retractable rudders, and ingeniously steam-heated throughout. They were equipped with desalinators to produce fresh water, newly invented canned food to prevent scurvy, daguerreotype cameras to document the triumph, and many other equally radical innovations.

Since any delay endangered Parliamentary funding (discovery expeditions of such magnitude weren't cheap), Barrow also moved with urgency. Miraculously, he somehow planned, organized, outfitted, and provisioned the entire enterprise in just three months.

His biggest problem was finding an officer to command it. His first choice, Sir William Parry, who'd led three voyages seeking the Passage, declined. His second choice, Sir James Clark Ross, perhaps the best-qualified polar explorer of the day and only recently returned from his epic Antarctic expedition, had promised his new wife he would accept no more such assignments. Barrow's third choice was Commander James Fitzjames, who, though without any Arctic experience, had worked with the steam engines upon which Barrow pinned the expedition's hopes. But the Admiralty refused his appointment; at age thirty-three he was considered "too young."

Another eminently sound choice wasn't even considered. Captain Francis Rawdon Moira Crozier had successfully completed five Arctic voyages and done outstanding service as Sir James Clark Ross's second-in-command on the Antarctic expedition. But he was Irish and common.

Barrow needed a name for his venture, someone with what impresarios call "marquee value," to fire public imagination and Parliamentary support. The only man who fit the bill was the last man he wanted—Sir John Franklin. Franklin was a bona fide, if somewhat rusticated, hero, a Knight Companion of the Bath. Yet his uncle and cousin were distinguished Royal Navy officers and his wife's family connections were strong. What's more, he was English, Anglican, and a proper gentleman.

Barrow, of course, knew all this. He'd sent the man north three times, after all. He was well acquainted with his capabilities and shortcomings, which was why he hadn't given him an important assignment in sixteen years. Franklin lacked the stature of Parry, the dash of Ross, and the youth of Fitzjames. Worse, he suffered from habitual bad luck. He had been part of the Buchan fiasco. There had been that disastrous business on the Coppermine expedition, and the perfectly dreadful mess he had made in Van Diemen's Land.

But in this instance, Barrow found himself beaten at his own game by the well-placed, vivacious Lady Franklin. She lobbied relentlessly on her husband's behalf, writing letters to every "interest" she could think of. She petitioned the influential presidents of the Royal and Geographical Societies, the navy's Arctic Council, the Lord Commissioners of the Admiralty, members of Parliament, everyone. By the time she finished, the president of the Geographical Society was telling the press, "The name of Franklin alone is, indeed, a national guarantee."

Barrow didn't share the opinion, but without time or alternative, needing the backing of those in high places, he had no choice. He reluctantly recommended Franklin for the top command, but took pains to limit his role to more or less of a figurehead. Indeed, down to almost every detail, it was Sir John Barrow's expedition, not Franklin's. He picked the ships. He appointed their captains. He even wrote the sailing instructions himself.

While he publicized scientific studies as a major goal of the expedition, privately they were nothing of the kind. Barrow's object was to find and force the Passage at all speed. Nothing else mattered.

# CHAPTER 5
# Two Ships

*There can be no objection with regard to any apprehension of the loss of the ships or men.*

—Sir John Barrow

The ships Barrow assigned Franklin were the space shuttles of their day; built to go, quite literally, where no ships had gone before. Coincidentally, they were the same vessels Franklin had inspected during his last, grim days in Van Diemen's Land.

HMS *Erebus* and HMS *Terror* were so-called bomb ships—shore bombardment vessels designed to withstand the crushing recoil of 5-ton mortars firing 13-inch shells packed with 200 pounds of explosive. As such, they were built extraordinarily strong out of English oak, with ribs and beams up to 1½-feet square. To provide a stable gun platform, they had a wide beam, bluff bows, and essentially flat bottoms, offering plenty of cargo space once their mortars and shell rooms had been removed. This combination of strength and capacity made them well suited for long journeys amidst pounding ice.

Both ships were already famous for their 1839–1843 Antarctic voyage, planting the English flag farther south than man had ever been. *Terror* was doubly renowned. In 1836 (under the irrepressible George Back) she had survived an Apollo 13–type ordeal in the heart of the Arctic. Stove in by pack ice, she was tossed like a toy upon an iceberg—"on an icy cradle," Back reported—completely out of the water. Left rudderless and practically dismasted, she somehow managed to get off and, shipping water that at times almost overmastered the pumps, managed to make it home before being beached on the Irish coast. Consequently both vessels were great favorites with the public and symbols of national pride, which, among their other attributes, made them ideal for Barrow's purpose.

*Erebus* was a Hecla class bomb ship, the largest and last purpose-built bomb vessel commissioned by the Royal Navy. Launched at Pembroke Dockyard in 1826, she was the biggest ship Barrow had sent in search of the Passage—some 372 tons, 105 feet long with a 29-foot beam. *Terror* was an older (launched 1813), smaller Vesuvius class bomb ship of 326 tons, 102 feet long with a 27-foot beam. (Among its other distinctions, *Terror* had participated in the attack on Ft. McHenry in the War of 1812; so the "bombs bursting in air" in the "Star-Spangled Banner" quite likely came from *Terror.*)

Although they had demonstrated their capability on previous expeditions, Barrow had the ships completely refitted and equipped with Victorian England's latest technology. To render the vessels all but indestructible in the ice, he strengthened them to truly Herculean proportions. Their bows were reinforced internally with a maze of beams, cross beams, and diagonal beams to bull through the polar pack. A London reporter marveled that the result was "a mass of timber about eight feet thick." For added protection, the bows were armored for 20 feet back from their stems with inch-thick rolled and tempered plates of sheet iron.

To resist the constrictorlike pressure of the pack, which could amount to hundreds of pounds per square inch, Barrow took special precautions. The ships' sides, 3 inches of English oak, were "doubled" with two layers of African oak, each 1½ inches thick, wrought diagonally against one another for even greater strength. This in turn was overlaid with two layers of Canadian elm, each 2 inches thick, wrought diagonally against the African oak. This amounted to five belts of timber fully 10 inches thick.

The ships' decks and bottoms were also reinforced. The upper decks were "doubled" with 3 inches of Canadian fir wrought diagonally over the original planking. Two layers of African oak, each 1½ inches thick, were laid over the already built-up bottoms, rendering them even more formidable than the sides—seven belts of solid oak some 13 inches thick.

*Model of* Erebus A purpose-built bomb vessel, *Erebus* was originally designed as a stable platform for 5-ton mortars hurling 300-lb. shells at shore fortifications. As such, she was built extraordinarily strong with plenty of stowage space belowdecks for ammunition. These attributes made her ideal for Discovery Service in the ice. (National Maritime Museum, Greenwich, England)

The ships' wooden knees, the vital supports that secured their beams to their sides, were replaced with massive cast-iron ones. Channels, stout wooden winglike projections extending 2 feet from the topsides, were installed to prevent rising ice from climbing the ships. The gunwales were raised for the same purpose.

In addition to cork insulation against the cold, the ships were fitted with internal heating systems, an unheard-of advance at the time. Tubular boilers conveyed steam in 11.8-inch-diameter pipes all around the lower deck to warm the officers' cabins and mens' berthing spaces. All hatches were "doubled" against the cold. All ladderways were double-doored to prevent frigid air from entering the vessels.

Perhaps the most radical improvements—the ones Barrow felt would give the expedition the ability to force the Passage regardless of ice and weather—were the ships' power and propulsion systems.

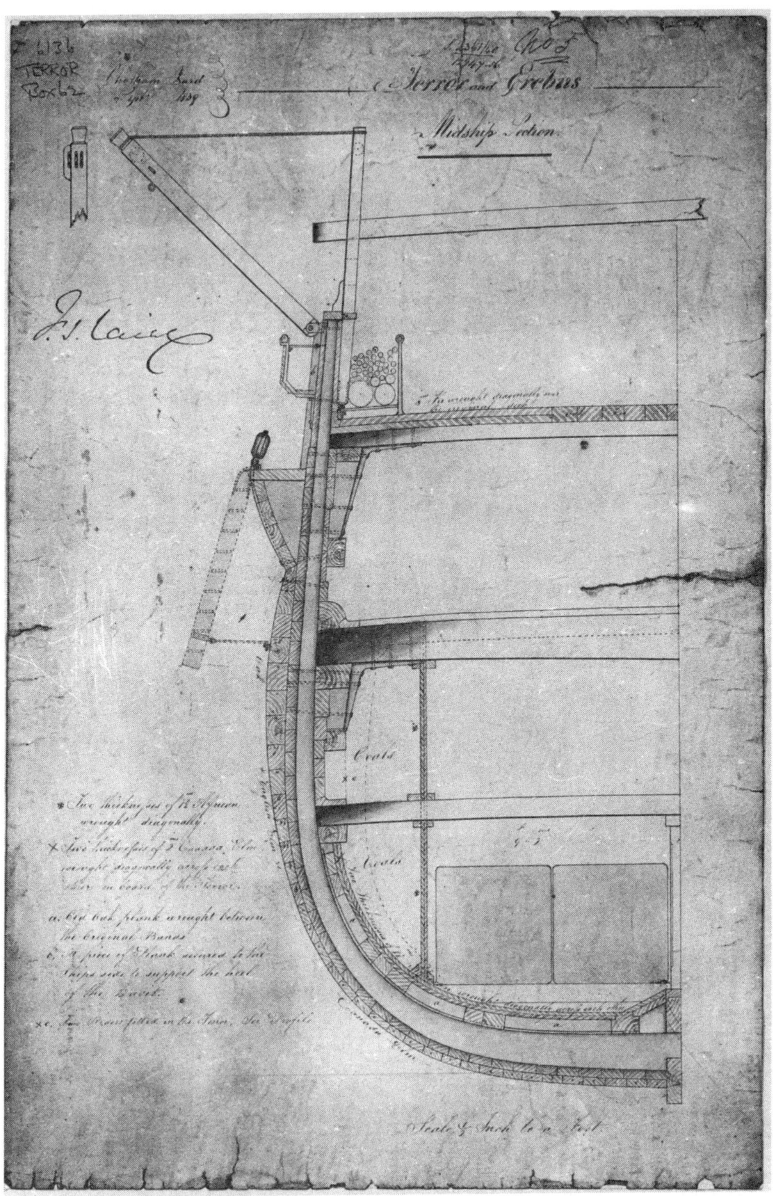


Erebus *and* Terror: *Midships Section* Massive reinforcements were made to protect the vessels from the ice: 10 inches of oak and elm planking on the sides, 13 inches on the bottom, iron knees, and doubled deck planking. Note: coal "sleeves" built into her sides and the upper deck stowage racks for spare masts and yards. (National Maritime Museum, Greenwich, England)

He fitted them with auxiliary steam engines, retractable propellers, and detachable rudders. Impervious to ice and independent of wind, the vessels could move at will. Franklin had but to find the Passage. Technology would take him through.

*Erebus* was quickly fitted with a converted 15-ton, 25-horsepower steam locomotive from the London & Greenwich Railway. *Terror* was equipped with a smaller 12-ton, 20-horsepower railroad locomotive. Both were mounted in the afterholds, entirely below the waterline, for protection. Ingenious elbowed, telescopic exhaust funnels cranked up and down to carry smoke and cinders away from flammable sails and tarred rigging.

At a time when steam-powered ships were a relatively recent advance, Barrow went further. Instead of paddle-wheel propulsion, vulnerable to attack by the ice, he proposed installing even more advanced screw propellers. These were truly new, largely unproven, and openly criticized by many in the navy itself. In fact, Sir William Symondes, Surveyor of the Royal Navy, contended that "Even if the propellor had the power of propelling a vessel, it would be found altogether useless in practice, because the power being applied to the stern, it would be absolutely impossible to make the vessel steer."

Barrow determined to prove him wrong. In March 1845, as the expedition was fitting out, he staged a tug-of-war pitting two otherwise identical ships against one another. The steam frigate HMS *Rattler,* with a propeller, was lashed stern-to-stern with her sister steam frigate the HMS *Alecto,* equipped with conventional paddle wheels. Equal steam was laid on and each tried to pull the other backwards. It proved no contest. *Rattler* dragged *Alecto* handily in her wake at 2.7 knots. The questions of power and steerageway—and the efficacy of Barrow's judgment—were at once resolved.

Even more radical than the propellers themselves was the fact that they were retractable. A 32-foot shaft, connected to the driving wheel of the locomotive, turned a twin-bladed propeller 7 feet in diameter. When the ice was bad or the winds favorable, the propeller could be detached from the shaft and hauled up into an iron well on the orlop deck, completely safe and out of harm's way. The ships' all-important rudders were also detachable. In minutes, the crews could withdraw the pintles (metal pins) from the gudgeons (metal rings fixed to the ships' sternpost) and haul the rudder clear of any threatening ice.

To fuel the engines, sleevelike coal bunkers were built along the port and starboard sides of the ships. Stocked with about 90 tons of coal, at a maximum cruising speed of 3 to 4 knots, this gave the ships a range of about 2,800 nautical miles under power alone. Burning some 2 to 3 tons of coal a day allowed thirty to forty-five days' steaming time and considerably more if, as expected, the vessels relied primarily on sail and employed the engines intermittently to pick a path through the ice. Time enough, Barrow hoped, to get the ships through the Passage in the summer season.

In event of calamity, Barrow provided for that as well. Each vessel was "equipped with boats which were to be of sufficient capacity to carry all of the crew if the vessel was lost." HMS *Terror* carried no fewer than nine for her complement of sixty-four.

None of these modifications enhanced the ships' sailing qualities. Bomb vessels were short, stubby, and monstrously heavy to begin with. With tons more timber and iron plate added, and tons of locomotive gear straining the afterholds, they sat dangerously low in the water. All this made them ponderously slow sailers and, essentially being shore vessels, their sea-keeping ability was notoriously bad.

But indestructibility and dependability in the ice, not speed on the high seas, was the reason Barrow assigned Franklin these vessels. With their redundant hulls, steam and sail propulsion, retractable propellers and rudders, internal heating systems, and desalinators, each was a completely self-contained, self-propelled, and self-sufficient module.

When Barrow had finished with them, there were no stronger-built, more advanced ships on the planet.

# CHAPTER 6
# Specters

*The legs, thighs and arms are the first parts to be attacked. The parts affected become insensible, blackish and, when one touches them, there remains a hollow such as one would make in a piece of dough.*

—Sir de la Potherie

Of all his concerns about the expedition's well-being, two specters haunted Barrow most: starvation and scurvy.

Starvation stalked every Arctic expedition; not because food ran out during the necessarily long voyages, but because up to half of it was lost to rampant spoilage or vermin. Salt, the primary preservative of the time, could retard but not prevent food going bad. Not even polar cold could stop it. Where men could live, mold, mildew, fungus, rats, roaches, and weevils could live just as well and sometimes far better.

A typical Admiralty report on the state of provisions remaining aboard the *Lady Franklin* and *Sophia,* after only eighteen months in the Arctic searching for Franklin in 1850, indicates the pervasiveness of the problem. All the ships' biscuit, flour, and barley was found "Mildewed and damp." The salt beef and salt pork were "Discolored, stinking and unfit." Raisins were "Mouldy, unfit for service," the tea "Musty, to be destroyed," and peas "Mildewed and unfit."

Losses to spoilage were exceeded only by those caused by the bane of every Arctic expedition—rats. Elisha Kane, an American navy officer who also participated in the search for Franklin, was emphatic: "They are everywhere . . . under the stove, in the steward's lockers, in our cushions, about or under our beds. If I was asked what, after darkness, cold and scurvy, are the three besetting curses of our Arctic sojourn, I should say RATS, RATS, RATS."

More specifically, these were brown or Norway rats. Nocturnal, they thrived in polar darkness and proliferated aboard ship, breeding up to thirteen times a year, producing up to twenty-two young in each litter. If *one* pair of mating rats was aboard and bred a rather nonamorous six times a year, producing half-sized litters of eleven or so each time, they would've numbered over 4,000 by the end of the second year. By the end of the third year, if enough food was available, they could have conceivably numbered over 100,000.

These armies of ravenous rodents, who must gnaw constantly to keep their sharp, extremely fast-growing teeth in check, bored through barrels, planking, even lead plate in search of food. Whenever they reached it, they fed gluttonously, leaving nothing but fetid droppings and leptospirosis, salmonella, rat bite fever, typhus, and the plague.

The loss of food to spoilage and vermin often forced polar expeditions to starvation rations long before the provisioning plans called for any reduction. But starvation at least was insidious, slow-moving, and understood. It was less evil than its more frightful twin, scurvy.

Scurvy was incredibly pernicious and widespread in the nineteenth century. Whole populations were laid low. At times as much as one-third of the Royal Navy was debilitated by it. Arctic expeditions, lacking fresh meat and vegetables for years at a time, were especially susceptible. It's a particularly ugly disease caused by a lack of vitamin C. Its root name, *skarve,* literally translates as "disgusting" or "contemptible."

Its onset is remarkably swift and, untreated, its course unrelentingly fatal. The symptoms usually appear after six to eight weeks on a diet of all-salt provisions devoid of vitamin C. For reasons still largely unknown, blood vessels begin to rupture. At first, blood weeps spontaneously from follicles of the victim's body hair, especially the head. Then hemorrhages and livid red blotches mushroom all over the body. Any bump, bruise, or exertion results in more internal bleeding. Any wound, even a minor scratch, will not heal. In short order the limbs, most particularly the legs, swell, and an excruciating rheumatoidlike pain wracks the joints. The skin loses its elasticity and becomes doughlike. The gums redden, recede, and blacken until teeth loosen and fall out.

The cumulative effects are revolting. The victim's body grows bloated, misshapen. There is anemia and overwhelming weakness. The skin turns jaundiced and yellow, covered with ever-growing purplish-brown ulcers oozing blood and pus. Without vitamin C, there is no stopping it. The hemorrhaging continues, and the likelihood of infection spreads. The body's immune system is breached, leaving it vulnerable to a plethora of supervening diseases. Within weeks, the victim is incapacitated; within months, he dies.

Barrow clearly meant to defeat the threat these twin scourges posed to the expedition, but faced a dilemma. The ships not only had to carry enough food to feed the crews for three years—no mean feat considering a great deal of stowage space for victuals was now filled with steam engines and coal—but it had to somehow be made impervious to spoilage to forestall starvation, yet somehow kept fresh to prevent scurvy.

In recently invented canned meats and vegetables, he found a solution. Soldered in airtight tins, safe from damp and vermin, precooked, canned food was warrantied to remain fresh for years. The recent Antarctic expedition had, in fact, carried quantities of tinned meats and vegetables and suffered almost no scurvy at all. So Barrow ordered Franklin's ships supplied with over 45 tons of fifteen varieties of canned food in rigorously specified 1-, 2-, 4-, 6-, and 8-pound canisters. There were seven kinds of fresh meat—boiled mutton, roast mutton, roast beef, seasoned beef, veal, ox cheeks, and beef with vegetables—amounting to more than 15 tons in all. There were 12 tons of vegetable soup, meat soup, and concentrated gravy, plus 9 tons of freshly canned potatoes, carrots, parsnips, and mixed vegetables.

Neither Barrow nor anyone else at the time understood why, or which, fresh meats, fruits, and vegetables prevented scurvy. It wasn't until vitamins were discovered in 1912 and deficiency diseases diagnosed in the 1930s that anyone did. But many an expedition near

No. LVI.

Her Majesty's Ship *Erebus*
*Woolwich* the *11th* day of *March* 184*5*.

DEMAND for PROVISIONS and VICTUALLING STORES for the use of Her Majesty's Ship above-mentioned, to complete her to *1092* Days, for her Complement of *70* Men, for *Foreign* Service.

| Species of Stores. | Quantities. Remaining on Board. | Required to be Supplied. | Denomination. | In what Casks or Packages required. | Remarks. |
|---|---|---|---|---|---|
| Biscuit | | 17.640 | Pounds. | Tin cases | All to be square Biscuit |
| ~~Beer~~ Flour in lieu of Bread | | 58.800 | Gallons. | Casks | |
| Spirits, concentrated | | 2388 | Gallons. | Water tight Casks | |
| Wine, ~~Red~~ Preserved Potatoes | | [illegible] | Gallons | | |
| Wine, White | | | Gallons. | | |
| Beef | | 2048 | 8 lb. pieces. | Casks | water tight |
| Pork | | 4095 | 4 lb. pieces. | " | |
| Flour | | 10.920 | Pounds. | " | |
| Suet | | 1536 | Pounds. | " | |
| Raisins | | 512 | Pounds. | " | |
| ~~Currants~~ Preserved Vegetables | | ~~8190~~ | Pounds. | Cases | |
| Peas Split | | 2730 / 195 | Bushels. | Casks | |
| Oatmeal | | 85 | Bushels. | " | |
| Sugar | | 4165 | Pounds. | " | |
| Chocolate | | 4444 | Pounds. | " | Do. |
| Tea | | 1194 | Pounds. | Cases | " |
| Vinegar | | 682 | Gallons. | Casks | Do. |
| Tobacco | | 3568 | Pounds. | " | " |
| Lemon Juice | | 4444 | Pounds. | In 5 Gall: Kegs | Do. |
| Sugar for ditto | | 4444 | Pounds. | Cask | Do. |
| Soap | | 1444 | Pounds. | " | " |
| Preserved Meats, including Soup and Bouilli | | 16.384 | Pounds. | Cases | " |
| Soup, Common, equal to | | 10.920 | Pints. | | |
| Soup, Concentrated | | | Pints. | | |
| ~~Canvass~~ Pickles | | 4444 | ~~Ells.~~ | In 10 Gall: Kegs | water tight |
| ~~Water Casks~~ Scotch Barley | | 1248 | ~~Tuns.~~ | Casks | Do. |
| Cranberries | | 1365 | | In 5 Gall: Kegs | Do. |

Approved, *(Signed) C. H. Osmer* Paymaster and Purser.

To *(Signed) John Franklin* Captain.

*The Captain Supt*
*Deptford.*

Office, day of 18 .

The above Demand duly entered,

Approved,

Clerk.

*Victualling List, HMS* Erebus The immense quantity of provisions embarked is evident. Goldner's treacherous canned foods (bottom), source of the expedition's woes, amounted to almost 14 tons alone. (Public Records Office, London, England) death from scurvy found such diverse things as fresh-killed caribou, fresh-caught salmon, boiled spruce needles, even seaweed had a remarkable effect.

In fact an effective preventive, lemon juice, had been prescribed by the Royal Navy's Dr. James Lind as early as 1747. He took six pairs of scurvy-riddled sailors and fed them six different "cures." Five of these (cider, vinegar, seawater, diluted sulphuric acid, and a garlic-mustard paste) proved worthless. But the sixth, two oranges and a lemon every day, had "sudden and visible good effects . . . these [fruits] they eat with greediness." Within a week, the sailors eating them had recovered.

Still, it took the Royal Navy almost fifty years to adopt lemon juice as a specific measure against the disease. By the 1840s, however, an ounce of lemon juice, leavened with an ounce of sugar, was regulation issue to every man daily. The expedition was supplied over 9,000 gallons of it. But as Barrow knew firsthand, even this wasn't proof against the disease. Of the fatalities suffered on previous expeditions he'd sent searching for the Passage, all had been caused by scurvy. So in addition to the canned food, he had the ships loaded with more antiscorbutics: 5 tons of pickled cucumbers, cabbages, onions, and cranberries, and over 2 tons of dried split peas. Smaller amounts of Normandy pippins (dried apples), dates, and canned milk were also taken as further insurance against scurvy.

Yet these amounts were dwarfed by the vast quantity of provisions carried to prevent starvation. Fully 68 tons of flour and 17 tons of premade ship's biscuit were issued. As a precaution against spoilage, the biscuit was packed in specially made tin cases to keep it free from the black-headed weevils that infested it when packed in canvas bags or wooden casks. The expedition also shipped over 4 tons of salt pork, a favorite of the lower deck, and more than 7 tons of salt beef, laid up in casks filled with brine. A supply ship that accompanied the expedition to Greenland carried a dozen live cattle to provide fresh meat, known to prevent scurvy.

Crammed aboard the ships were also nearly 12 tons of sugar, 5 tons of oatmeal, and over 4 tons of chocolate. Barrow included luxuries as well: 3½ tons of Virginian and Brazilian tobacco in carrot, twist, and plug for smokers and chewers; a ton of East Indian tea; a half ton of raisins; and a half ton of hot English mustard, along with quantities of white pepper and vinegar.

The quantity of alcohol supplied, over 4,500 gallons of concentrated West Indian rum, appears staggering. Stored in jugs in the Spirit Room, it was rated from 130 to 140 proof. Yet considering the three-year length of the voyage and the daily issue (one gill or about ¼ pint, cut with ¾ pint of water), it hardly seems excessive. Over 1,000 barrels of beer and Burton's ale was also shipped for issue to the crew. For the sick, for whom rum was thought harmful, there were 200 gallons of French brandy and 200 gallons of port wine and white wine.

For its time, this was a remarkable variety of food for common seamen. In fact, Barrow had provided them with a diet far healthier than what they had in civilian life.

The poor in England subsisted largely on gruel (made from barley or oats), an abundance of stale bread, onions, potatoes, and occasionally bacon. In place of butter, they ate cheese (a lower-class favorite) and fish, because it was cheaper than meat. Since fuel was expensive and ovens more so, the average laborer's family had one hot meal a week, usually on Sunday when they took their suppers to the local baker's to get them cooked.

The middle-class diet was more substantial, but relentlessly monotonous. It consisted primarily of mutton (old, rather tough sheep's meat) and ham and bacon, which were cheap to raise, easy to cure, and kept well. To these were added potatoes and a very few vegetables, mostly cabbage, beets, and parsnips.

No one drank water, because it was rightly presumed to be impure and unsafe (the great London cholera epidemic of 1854 was traced to a single public water pump). Owing to high import duties and the East India Company's virtual monopoly, tea was too expensive for most. Beer, stout, ale, and porter quenched the thirst of the poor; gin and rum were the favored spirits. Only the wealthy could afford wine.

Compared to their contemporaries ashore, able-bodied seamen in the Franklin Expedition—thanks to Barrow's foresight—ate and drank quite well. Contrary to myth, a seaman wasn't surviving on weevil-filled hardtack and putrid water. On "Discovery Service" to the polar regions, he was living high on the hog.

On a typical Monday, he got 1 pound of bread (fresh-baked if the weather and seas permitted the cook a galley fire, premade ship's biscuit if it did not). He was issued 1 pound of salt pork or beef and ½ pound of canned potatoes. He also got 2 ounces of raisins, 2 ounces of pickled vegetables, 2 ounces of suet, 2 ounces of chocolate, 1½ ounces of sugar mixed with 1 ounce of lemon juice (against scurvy), ¼ ounce of good tea, plus vinegar, mustard, salt, and pepper for seasonings, and some oatmeal or Scotch barley. Then, of course, there was the 1 gill of concentrated rum issued every day at noon.

In all, this constituted about 3 pounds of food a day, discounting the rum, tea, seasonings, and liberal 1 ounce of tobacco issued daily. Not bad, when at home a fellow was lucky to get a stale end of bread, bowl of gruel, and some oysters. Based on today's National Outdoor Leadership School's (NOLS) bulk rationing system, which judges 2¼ to 2½ pounds of food per day sufficient for "very strenuous wilderness activity," it was more than ample.

What's more, it was a lot less monotonous fare than most of the population got ashore. The Admiralty built considerable variety into its polar victualling plans. On Mondays, a man could count on getting salt beef and potatoes. Tuesdays, any one of six kinds of canned meat and canned vegetable soup. Wednesdays, fat-rich salt pork boiled with split peas. Thursdays, another kind of canned meat made different with the addition of canned carrots, parsnips, or mixed vegetables. Fridays, it was salt beef again, livened up by the cook with pickles, cabbage, or onions. Saturdays salt pork and split peas were repeated, but as this was always a favorite of the men, it was done on purpose. Thursdays and Sundays were "flour days"; the cook would make up pudding or duff, dappled with raisins, cranberries, or dried apples, as well as serving canned meat, vegetables, and concentrated gravy.

Officers, of course, fared even better. They enjoyed fresh eggs from two coops of laying hens on each vessel. While they lasted, they had beef tongues; by regulation a ship's captain was allotted forty-eight. They also had calves' heads, Westphalia ham, rashers of bacon, and corned beef. Rather than the plain canned soups issued the crew, they had mock turtle, oxtail, and mulligatawny. Other officers' fare included hard cheeses like double Gloucestershire, Cheshire, and cheddar; vermicelli and macaroni; rice; pickled tripe; salted salmon, herring, cod, and smoked Findon haddock; pickled rhubarb, gooseberries, cherries, and plums; tinned tapioca; raspberry, strawberry, and black currant jam.

The gustatory differences didn't end there. Instead of the unrefined brown muscavado sugar given the men, officers enjoyed white Barbudian loaf wrapped in delicate indigo paper. In addition to the vinegar, salt, pepper, and mustard given the crew, they had an amazing selection of spices and condiments: curry, cayenne pepper, ginger, fennel, cloves, mushroom sauce, mint, horseradish, chilies, capers, Spanish olive oil. "Fine tea," not coarse, and "fine coffee" as well.

While the men had to be content with their rum, officers were free to indulge themselves from a well-stocked storeroom and personal stores. Most began their day with the "forenoon stand easy," when, at about 11 A.M., they slipped below for their first drink of the day. Thereafter they would "freshen the hawse," taking two or three nips of rum after a spell on deck.

With meals, they invariably drank claret (Bordeaux) with beef—the only proper drink for gentlemen. The stewards served them sherry with soup; hock (a white wine from Hockheim in Germany) with pork; port with cheese; and Madeira or Tokay (a sweet, white Hungarian wine) with dessert.

In all, the Franklin Expedition was the most lavishly provisioned Arctic voyage England ever assembled. On full allowance, free of scurvy, it could subsist handsomely and with great variety for a minimum of three years. With judicious rationing, it could easily last five—more than ample time to force the Passage or outlast any conceivable period they might be trapped in the ice.

# CHAPTER 7
# Ships' Commanders

*I have been on half pay with the exception of one year I served with Captain Sir Edward Parry on HM Ship* Hecla *in his attempt to reach the North Pole.*

—Captain Francis Crozier

If Barrow entertained doubts regarding Franklin's age or capabilities as the expedition's titular leader, he had none about the officers he placed in day-to-day command of the ships. He handpicked both of them, and for very different reasons.

At forty-nine, the expedition's second-in-command, Captain Francis Rawdon Moira Crozier, was a completely politically incorrect choice by class-conscious nineteenth-century English standards. He was Northern Irish for one, and Presbyterian, not Anglican, for another, at a time when prejudices ran very deep, especially in the army and navy (Irish Presbyterians were required, by law, to make an oath of allegiance to the Crown). He was an officer, but not an English officer, and certainly not a gentleman in the English sense. He had none of the snobbishly hazy requisites—"breeding," "good family," "social graces," and the rest. He may have worn the crown-and-anchor-topped epaulettes of a captain, but among gentlemen officers, he was considered something less, something decidedly inferior. He was the sort of fellow it was all well and good to serve aboard ship with, but definitely not the sort to bring to the club, to tea, or into polite society. All this was quite obvious and accepted by everybody in nineteenth-century England. A man knew his station and was careful to remember his place. Even common seamen saw Crozier was not a real "toff," as they would say.

At the same time—as the crew recognized, most English officers grudgingly admitted, and Barrow knew full well—Crozier was a blue water man. He may have been "dreadful Irish," coarse as the country he came from, ill at ease in society, and crudely educated (at sea continuously since age thirteen, Crozier had no alternative except to teach himself), but few officers on quarterdeck were his equal. He had been thirty-five years in the Royal Navy, working his way from cabin boy to captain, passing examination after examination, without assistance from special interests. By 1845 he'd seen service aboard tenders, cutters, sloops-of-war, gun brigs, frigates, and ships-of-the-line throughout the Atlantic, Pacific, and Indian Oceans as well as the Mediterranean and North Seas. But Barrow singularly seized upon him for one reason: he had more experience voyaging amongst the ice than almost any man alive.

In 1819, at twenty-two, Crozier had sailed as a midshipman with Captain William Edward Parry's first expedition in search of the Passage, which had come very near succeeding, getting farther west than any other expedition would for thirty years. Under Parry's enlightened leadership (Parry grew mustard greens aboard ship to combat scurvy, published a newspaper, ran shipboard schools, and held theatricals to occupy the men during the long polar night and lost but one of his 94-man crew to disease), Crozier learned a good deal about wintering in the Arctic. Ironically, at almost the same time, Franklin's expedition was literally dying in its tracks on the Coppermine hundreds of miles to the south. At age twenty-four, Crozier sailed again with Parry in search of the Passage and spent another two winters in the ice. At twenty-six, he accompanied Parry once more in pursuit of the Passage, surviving the loss of HMS *Fury* and a precarious return aboard HMS *Hecla*. Five years later, he voyaged a last time with Parry in an attempt to reach the North Pole, achieving a "farthest north" record that would stand for fifty years.

Still not forty, he made a fifth voyage to the Arctic under his former shipmate James Clark Ross. Like himself, Ross had been on all of Parry's expeditions. Ross and Crozier were, in a way, mirror

*Captain Francis Rawdon Moira Crozier (1796–1848?)* The expedition's second-in-command, though he had far more experience in the ice than Franklin (six expeditions to both the Arctic and Antarctic). Northern Irish, Presbyterian, and common, he was passed over. He led the survivors in a desperate attempt to reach safety and was among the last officers seen alive. (National Maritime Museum, Greenwich, England)

images of each other. Both entered the navy about the same time. Both endured the same polar trials, suffered the same privations, and met the same emergencies. Brothers in the ice, each had demonstrated equally remarkable courage, judgment, and ability. In the navy of the time, however, their social stations remained poles apart. Unlike Crozier, Ross was the "right sort"—well-connected, Church of England, English. Consequently, command of HMS *Cove,* on a mission to rescue English whalers beset in Davis Strait, went to Ross. Crozier went as second-in-command.

At forty-two, Crozier was passed over again. Barrow gave command of England's first great voyage to the South Pole, the Antarctic Expedition of 1839, to Ross. Again he took Crozier, his good friend, as second-in-command. They voyaged together for four years, attaining the "farthest south" record of the day. They penetrated what would later be called the Ross Sea, discovered what was later named the Ross Ice Barrier, and what was later christened James Ross Island. Two dormant volcanoes were named *Erebus* and *Terror,* after the ships. Nothing was named for Crozier. In 1843, Ross returned to a knighthood; Crozier, though promoted to captain, was put on half pay.

During the outward and return voyages, the two stopped in Van Diemen's Land. Here Crozier made his first acquaintance with Governor Sir John and Lady Franklin and spent "many enjoyable hours" with them. In truth, it was likely the radiance, charm, and intellect of the ladies of Franklin's household—Lady Jane and Franklin's niece Sophia Cracroft—that captivated him. They were orchids in Sir John's shade. In contrast Franklin himself—in his mid-fifties, dull, ponderously religious, and stagnating in a backwater of the Empire—appeared a man whose career was all but over. Crozier had no way of knowing that within two short years he would be second-in-command under Franklin, headed north.

By all rights, Crozier should have been offered command of the expedition. He was intimately acquainted with both ships. He'd wintered ten years in the ice, north and south. He was younger and fitter than Franklin, his experience was more recent and more relevant. Instead, because of his nationality and social status, he wasn't seriously considered for the top spot, not outwardly anyway.

But Barrow, attendant to every detail, was very much at work behind the scenes. Crozier had stolidly served in all four of Parry's expeditions and ably supported James Clark Ross during the Antarctic voyage. Lacking Parry and Ross, Crozier was the best polar hand he had and Barrow worked diligently to secure him the number two role. Behind Franklin's figurehead, he wanted a well-found ship, a known quantity he could rely upon. He wanted, as Oliver Cromwell once said, "a plain russet-coated captain that knows what he fights for and loves what he knows, than what you call a gentleman and is nothing else." Bolstered by the recommendations of Parry and Ross, he gave Crozier the job. Franklin's name might be a guarantee, as the press was saying, but Crozier's was insurance, gentleman or not.

The assignment did not impress Crozier at all. He saw it for what it was—he was again to hold an Englishman's coat. He had been too long gifted, too often overlooked, and spent far too many irredeemably lonely, introspective years wintering in the ice to see anything else. When the expedition sailed, he was, by one description, "as melancholy an Irishman as I ever saw." None of the real honors of the Antarctic voyage had been accorded him. He faced another three years, perhaps more, of near-solitary confinement in polar darkness and cold. Whether or not the expedition succeeded (and he frankly doubted Franklin's would where the far more capable Parry had failed), made little difference to him. Franklin was to lead; he was but to follow.

To make matters worse, his heart had been broken. Following his return to England from Antarctica in 1843, the forty-nine-year-old bachelor had fallen hopelessly in love. The object of his affection was Sophia Cracroft, Franklin's vivacious and appealing niece, whom he'd met in Van Diemen's Land. Clumsily, for he was thoroughly incompetent about the intricacies of nineteenth-century courtship, he had proposed. Politely, but promptly, his offer of marriage was refused. Miss Cracroft professed her love for his shipmate and closest friend, the newly knighted, socially acceptable Sir James Clark Ross.

The fact that Ross had just wed another must have been particularly painful for Crozier. The social and class discrimination was plain. Even in affairs of the heart, an Irishman, no matter his rank or qualification, was second to an Englishman, whether the latter was married or not. An Irish Presbyterian seeking the hand of an English Anglican lady, no matter how deeply in love he may have been, was no proper match. Even as Sir John's executive officer, considerations of family, station, and status precluded him.

He penned his pain to one of the few who truly knew him. In one of the last letters he sent home, he wrote to James Clark Ross, "In truth I am sadly lonely and when I look back to the last voyage, I can see the cause and therefore no prospect of having a more joyous feeling." Writing to a former shipmate, John Henderson, just eight days before his departure from Greenland, he echoed the feeling. "Living alone," he wrote, "is the great drawback to me, but I know well it cannot be otherwise."

In contrast, Commander James Fitzjames, picked by Barrow to command Franklin's flagship HMS *Erebus,* was ebullient. The opportunity to pocket the Passage was all he wanted—he already had almost everything else. Called "the handsomest man in the navy," he was everything Crozier wasn't. He was young (thirty-three), well-educated, aristocratic, wealthy, of good family, Church of England, fast-rising in the service—and thumpingly, lispingly English to the core.

He was also a documented hero. In 1835, as his ship was fitting out in Liverpool for the Euphrates Expedition (a "Discovery Service" voyage to Mesopotamia), a customs officer had fallen overboard in the face of a gale. Swept away by river currents and an ebbing tide surging at over 4 knots, there was no time to launch a boat to save the man. Fitzjames didn't hesitate. Though "embarrassed by a great coat, hat and a very valuable watch," he plunged overboard and swam to the rescue. Dragged down by his heavy clothes, he still managed to reach the man who "could not swim" and "holding him up by the hair," kept him afloat until a boat retrieved them. For this act the merchants of Liverpool awarded him an engraved silver plate and the Admiralty took notice. But it was not merely these attributes and well-placed, influential "interests" that won Fitzjames's appointment. It was his knowledge of steam.

He had been mate aboard the first Royal Navy steamship to ascend the Euphrates River and had served in steamers on other stations. While none of this duty had taken him anywhere near an iceberg, it all involved making rather long voyages (for the time) under steam. On the face of it, getting a steamer up the Euphrates through a desert doesn't seem to bear any relevance to getting a steamer

*Commander James Fitzjames (1812–1848?)* Called "the handsomest man in the navy," he was very nearly given command of the expedition, but at thirty-three the Admiralty thought him "too young." Oddly, he had no Arctic experience, but he had significant experience with the navy's new steamships. He was alive when the ships were deserted. (National Maritime Museum, Greenwich, England)

through the ice in the Arctic. But the fact is that the river snaked as tortuously through the desert as any path through the pack ice. Its sandbars, submerged snags, and deadwood sweeping downstream were as hazardous in their way as Arctic shallows and ice floes. What's more, no one had ever done it before and Fitzjames had. Working his vessel almost 500 miles upriver against the current—

which, of course, meant largely under steam alone—was, by any measure, considering the cranky and inefficient machinery of the day, a splendid accomplishment. Perhaps more than any other officer in the service, he understood the implications the nascent technology had for the navy and wholeheartedly embraced it.

Fitzjames also had dash, a quality Barrow admired above all others. On the voyage up the Euphrates, he voluntarily led a shore party in pursuit of Bedouin bandits and drove them off despite breaking his leg. Leading another shore party, he was taken prisoner by Bedouins, yet managed to escape. When the expedition's two steamers—HMS *Euphrates* and HMS *Tigris*—were struck by a hurricane at the head of the Persian Gulf, Fitzjames was conspicuous. The *Tigris,* her machinery failing, was lost. "The safety of the [Euphrates]," according to the official report, "is mainly due to the good conduct of Mr. Fitzjames."

In 1841, Fitzjames, only twenty-nine years old, again distinguished himself in the Opium Wars, where he was commended five times. Happily fiddling with another recent invention—rockets—he drove the Chinese army off the heights at Segoan and Tzekee; rocketed them out of Chapoo; served ashore at the battle of Woosung and commanded the navy's rocket brigade at the storming and capture of Ching-Kiang-Foo, where he was severely wounded. Still bandaged, he pluckily attended what amounted to the Chinese surrender—the signing of the Treaty of Nanking. In recognition, he was promoted Commander (at age thirty) and given command of the sloop-of-war HMS *Clio,* serving again in the Persian Gulf. In October 1844, he returned to England and, like so many other promising officers, was put on half pay. Less than five months later, however, he was given what must have appeared to him the chance of a lifetime—a prominent place in Sir John Franklin's expedition in search of the Northwest Passage.

One gets the impression that Barrow selected him almost singularly because of his youthful enthusiasm and modern outlook. He was as much a proponent of steam power as Barrow and had proven, as much as anyone, what it could do. It was a measure of Barrow's belief in steam that, despite Fitzjames's complete lack of polar experience, he was given command of the expedition's flagship.

With the selection of these two officers, Barrow had cagily hedged his bets. Both backed up Franklin, the expedition's figurehead, who had hero status, knighthood, and connections. In Crozier, he had a seasoned ice sailor with years of polar experience. In Fitzjames, he had an energetic young officer on a "fast track" to promotion, who understood the latest technology and how to use it.

Like the redundancy he employed with ships, propulsion, provisions, and outfitting, Barrow left nothing to chance. Any other thing might fail, but the officers commanding Her Majesty's ships would not.

# CHAPTER 8
# Ships' Companies

*The crews are fine hearty fellows, mostly north country men.*
—Commander James Fitzjames, HMS *Erebus*

Most of the officers and almost all the men joined the expedition not for glory or any desire to demonstrate new-fangled technology or explore unknown places, but for a far simpler and sounder reason—the extra money the navy paid for "Discovery Service." And the navy paid a portion of it in advance. For officers ashore struggling along on half pay and sailors, some of whom had been a year or more waiting for a ship, hard cash, especially in advance, outweighed the risks of any hazardous duty afterward.

The Admiralty, legendarily parsimonious, had to open its purse wide to procure volunteers for voyages like this. Everyone in the navy knew that "Discovery Service" involved terrible privations and dangers. Ships were routinely gone for four to five years to the most remote and hostile regions on earth. In the days before the telegraph, once an expedition vanished over the horizon, it was completely on its own. Practically speaking, there was nothing the Admiralty or the Empire could do to assist it.

In the tropics, crews were decimated by dysentery, yellow fever, malaria, and a host of other deadly diseases. Fever killed so many men on the Great African Survey, its charts were said to "have been drawn and coloured with drops of blood." Ships were splintered on uncharted reefs, swallowed up by hurricanes and white squalls, or literally chewed to pulpwood by legions of ravenous *teredo* worms. Aboard hermetically sealed vessels on polar voyages, men perished from contagious airborne diseases like influenza and pneumonia or were killed wholesale by "the curse of the Arctic regions," scurvy. Ships were holed by icebergs, crushed by pack ice or, perhaps more terrible, permanently entombed and carried off. If a man was fortunate enough to survive a tour of "Discovery Service," he quite likely bore the scars—in the form of recurrent malaria, or amputated fingers and toes from frostbite—for the rest of his life.

Money was the only real incentive to get men to undertake such duty and the navy offered it. In fact, comparatively speaking, it offered a lot. At the time, an admiral in the Royal Navy was paid some 1,825 pounds a year or about U.S. $123,000 in present value, while middle-class merchants and skilled tradesmen earned about 300 pounds a year (roughly U.S. $20,690 today). At the bottom—and most of Victorian England existed at the bottom—the annual wage of cotton weavers was 26 pounds ($1,747), laborers 18 pounds ($1,210), and housemaids but 14 pounds ($940).

In comparison, "Discovery Service" pay was enough, as the Admiralty intended, to make a man forget he could well be dead before he earned it. The expedition's warrant officers—engineer, carpenter, boatswain—got annual salaries of 84 pounds ($5,644), 75 pounds ($5,040), and 70 pounds ($4,704) respectively. Even able-bodied seamen got 60 pounds ($4,032) a year—more than three times what a laborer could make ashore. That kind of money was not easily found anyplace else in Victorian England.

But it was the advance pay that attracted most men to sign on. Officers (as befitting gentlemen, their pay was not grossly recorded in the muster books for all to see) drew a hefty five month's advance. Everybody else got a two month's advance, plus what was called river pay while the expedition was fitting out. For an able-bodied seaman, this amounted to 23 pounds or about U.S. $1,545 in present-day value. This may not seem much, but for the time, it was a godsend for a man with a family. A working-class family could live for a year on that. A pound of fresh beef, mutton, or veal cost 10 pence, so one gold sovereign could buy 24 pounds of it. A week's worth of fresh produce cost but 12 pence (about U.S. $0.28 today). A puncheon of strong ale (about 70 gallons) ran about 4 pounds

($268). Lodgings could be rented for 60 pence a week or 12 pounds a year.

Not surprisingly, officers and men rushed to enlist. Also not surprisingly, the overwhelming majority had never seen any "Discovery Service" or made a polar voyage before. Of the 134 officers and men finally entered in the expedition's muster books, only 8 experienced polar hands could be induced to reenlist. No amount of money could convince the rest.

Probably by design, the final ships' companies were overwhelmingly English. Seeing as he paid rapt attention to every other detail of the voyage, this was undoubtedly Barrow's doing. The expedition that found the Passage would properly consist almost exclusively of Englishmen.

With the exception of the Irishman Crozier and two Scotsmen (an ice master and an assistant surgeon), the expedition's other twenty-one officers were *all* English. Of the 110 crewmen carried on the muster books, 99 were English, 7 were Scots, 3 were Welsh, and 1 was Canadian (from Nova Scotia).

Barrow seems to have intervened personally to keep things that way. On April 25, less than a month before the expedition was to sail, he was shocked to discover Crozier had enlisted ten Scots for *Terror,* all experienced sailors, the day before. That would simply not do. Barrow discharged them to shore at Woolwich for passage aboard HMS *Perseus* back to Dundee in Scotland, presumably where he thought they belonged. They were replaced, to a man, by Englishmen. These fellows not only lacked "Discovery Service" experience, but most were *first entry* men, newly recruited in the Royal Navy. Crozier registered no complaint; if it was Englishmen Barrow wanted, it was Englishmen Barrow would have. Before the voyage was out, he would make Jack Tars, naval seamen, out of them.

Meantime, he scrambled to enlist every old polar hand he could find who was willing to sign on for another tour. He snapped up Thomas Jopson, the steward who'd served with him in the Antarctic, dismissing a steward he'd enlisted only a day before to make room for him. Likewise, he signed on Thomas Johnson, *Terror*'s old boatswain's mate, and somehow stole the *Erebus*'s cook, John Diggle, right out from under Commander Fitzjames's aristocratic nose.

He was glad to get all three. As captain's steward, Jopson not only tended to the officer's mess, but was also responsible for managing the whole ship's provisioning. Boatswain's Mate Johnson, who'd kept *Terror* sound, dry, and in one piece for five years during the Antarctic voyage, was equally invaluable. Among his other duties, a bosun's mate acted as a captain's "instrument of discipline," administering floggings. Just as vital were the services of Diggle, the cook, who was skilled at making endlessly monotonous victuals varied and short rations last. This job was so important to morale in the Arctic, in fact, that Diggle was paid more than the boatswain's mate.

Somehow, Crozier also convinced three able-bodied seamen who'd served aboard *Terror* in the Antarctic to reenlist. This was a testament to the regard that his sailors accorded his seamanship and leadership. These men, dismissed by most as simple, illiterate sailors, were anything but simple or stupid. The skills required to work a square-rigged ship were both extensive and complex and took far longer to master than many of today's computer programming languages. They knew all too well the brutal hardships and dangers of voyaging in the ice; to volunteer for it again, so soon, was a measure of their confidence in Crozier.

Not a single officer with previous polar experience, north or south, volunteered for the expedition. In Crozier's case, this may have been because he was harder on his officers than on the men. More likely, no officer who had endured the witches' brew of claustrophobic confinement, stultifying boredom, and stark terror of Arctic voyaging wanted to repeat the experience if he could possibly avoid it. It was, as one remembered, "quite like being buried alive and forgotten." Surviving it once was quite enough.

The officers who did volunteer were splendidly qualified in all aspects, save a total ignorance of what they were getting themselves into. Crozier's engineer, for example, was Warrant Officer James Thompson, engineer first class, from the navy's new, advanced steam factory at Woolwich, which had opened in 1836 to overhaul marine engines and train seagoing engineers. But *Terror* wasn't a steam

*Royal Navy Seamen* Taken in 1854, when the search for Franklin was at its height, these three sailors are typical of those who accompanied him. Left to right: a coxswain, a boatswain, and a leading seaman. (Wilkinson-Latham Collection, London, England)

factory; her engine was a bastardized railroad locomotive, not a purpose-built marine model, and there were no engineers to train. Caring for this unfamiliar, jerry-built machinery, with its experimental driveshaft and propeller, in an alien environment thousands of miles from his Woolwich shops, would be Thompson's job alone. It was almost certainly more than he bargained for.

Crozier's other officers were similarly the best the Royal Navy could offer, but similarly mismatched to the task at hand. Second Lieutenant George Hodgson, Third Lieutenant John Irving, and First

Mate Fredrick Hornby came from the navy's elite gunnery training vessel HMS *Excellent.* The fact that *Terror* carried no guns but small arms and *Excellent* was an old three-decker without masts, permanently moored in Portsmouth and that hadn't seen the sea in fifteen years, didn't rule them out. They were a cut above the rest, had enthusiastically volunteered to be "frozen in," and would do their duty like Englishmen, even if they had no earthly idea of the duties involved.

Likewise Dr. John Peddie, Crozier's chief surgeon, and John Lane, his boatswain, had seen long service together aboard HMS *Mary,* but that service had been in the Mediterranean and neither had laid eyes on an iceberg. But no matter, they would do. Second Master Giles MacBean and Second Mate Robert Thomas, who volunteered from HMS *Mastiff,* had also never voyaged beyond the middle latitudes.

For *Terror*'s all-important first lieutenant (the ship's executive officer), Crozier picked Edward Little, a skilled officer, like himself on half pay, but like the rest totally lacking any Arctic experience. As assistant surgeon, he enlisted a Scotsman, Dr. Alexander McDonald, who was similarly inexperienced in the ice.

Of the twenty-one petty officers Crozier enlisted—the noncommissioned officers who truly run armies and navies—he was fortunate indeed; fifteen were Royal Navy veterans. But six specialists critical to a voyage in the nineteenth century—his sailmaker, caulker, blacksmith, armorer, and two quartermasters—were first entry men, new to the navy. Unlike the officers, however, many of these petty officers and seamen, new to the navy or not, had probably experienced an Arctic voyage. Beginning in 1820, British regulations mandated that whalers and vessels fishing Arctic waters had to carry at least five seamen with no previous experience in the ice. This measure, intended to create a pool of men familiar with the rigorous duty, gave the expedition's crews a decided advantage over its officers. Many of them, in the vernacular of the day, had already "taken the ice."

Still, with so many new hands aboard, Crozier took special care to recruit a very tough, seasoned contingent of marines to ensure discipline. On average, they were five years older than the rest of the ship's company and all of them were regulars. The most-junior private had been a Royal Marine for seven years; the rest had seen from twelve to seventeen years service and were a hard-boiled lot, indeed. They needed no encouragement keeping first entry men in line or separating sailors from their advance money in games of chance. Compared to the 60 pounds the navy paid able-bodied seamen to crew its "Discovery Service" ships, a marine sergeant received but 24 pounds ($1,612 U.S. today), a corporal 16 (U.S. $1,075), and a private only 10 pounds (U.S. $672). What's more, they received none of it in advance. It's no wonder marines had no love for sailors. Only midshipmen, given a pittance of 8 pounds ($537 today) a year, earned less.

At ages nineteen and eighteen respectively, Robert Golding and Thomas Evans, though properly midshipmen, were still listed as *boys*. Golding was going to sea for the first time; but Evans had already served part of his six-year's apprenticeship aboard HMS *Lynx*. Crozier, under pressure of special interests, enlisted a third—William Eaton, eighteen, from Hackney, but he was discharged after only three weeks "By order of Commander Collier, K.C.B." This was the same officer who'd abruptly discharged his Scottish seamen. As captain, Crozier clearly outranked Commander Collier, but Collier, a knight, was Barrow's hatchet man and Crozier knew it. Midshipman Eaton went home to his obviously concerned family, no doubt earning the gratitude of another of Barrow's interests.

When *Terror* sailed, Crozier had mustered the best officers and men he could find, but over 30 percent of his crew were newcomers to the service. As flagship, Fitzjames's all-English–officered *Erebus* came off much better. Only 16 percent of its complement were first entry men.

But—as Barrow intended—the expedition was composed of Englishmen.

# CHAPTER 9

# Outward Bound

*The Lords Commissioners of the Admiralty have, in every respect, provided most liberally for the comforts of the officers and men of an expedition which may, with the facilities of the screw-propellor, and other advantages of modern science, be attended with great results.*

—*The Times,* May 12, 1845

For weeks the newspapers had been talking about little else but the Northwest Passage and the expedition to the "frozen regions." Sir John was lionized in the *London Daily Chronicle* and his Arctic exploits floridly recounted in the *London Telegraph.* Reporters from the *Illustrated London News* gave readers a pictorial tour of the waiting ships. Sir John and Lady Franklin were feted by London society at countless balls and receptions—so many, in fact, that Sir John grew exhausted and came down with the flu.

The expedition's officers were lavishly entertained and the crews treated to drinks at every dockside pub they entered.

Normally staid, even *The Times* waxed euphoric: "There appears to be but one wish amongst the whole of the inhabitants of this country . . . that the enterprise in which the officers and crew are about to be engaged may be attended with success." On the eve of the voyage, public enthusiasm was so charged that another observer marveled that "one would fancy England celebrating Franklin's return rather than his departure."

The expedition's sailing instructions, which Barrow had written himself, were formally handed to Franklin on May 5, 1845. They were—like everything else Barrow did—detailed, precise, and unequivocal.

Issuing sailing instructions for a voyage into a vast, unknown region, where instructions were necessarily groundless and essentially meaningless, may seem odd and downright pretentious. But in the spirit of the times, they were nothing of the kind. England's cumulative achievements between 1815 and 1845 had made the world subject to her science, wealth, and power. The Arctic would yield as well. It was only necessary to issue Englishmen the proper instructions.

This belief was not unfounded, by any means. The pace of England's technological development seemed to have already brought nature to heel. In less than twenty-five years, the blast furnace (1828) and locomotive engine (1829) harnessed iron and steam; the electric motor (1822) and electromagnet (1824) tapped a new power source; iron-hulled ships (1821) and flanged railroad rails (1831) revolutionized transportation; the steam hammer (1839) and Portland cement (1845) transformed production and construction. This pace of fundamental, world-altering technological development would not be equaled again until the computer revolution. *All* these inventions, it need be said, were English.

As leader, indeed maker, of the Industrial Revolution, England's mines and factories boasted an output greater than the rest of the world combined. England's merchant fleet brought global wealth—coal, iron, cotton—into its modern factories to produce even greater wealth. The world's oceans had largely been plumbed, charted, and made into English lakes by its 500-ship navy. The world's secrets—from the evolution of the species to the source of the Nile—were being laid bare by England's explorers and naturalists.

By the spring of 1845, it was strikingly evident that England could do pretty much whatever it intended to do. At a time when, as a contemporary observer noted, "Coal commands the age," the Royal Navy's adoption of steam permitted—for the first time in history—the issuance of sailing instructions with a fair degree of confidence that they could be carried out despite wind, weather, and tide. This confidence was very much shared by Barrow and quite nearly everybody else.

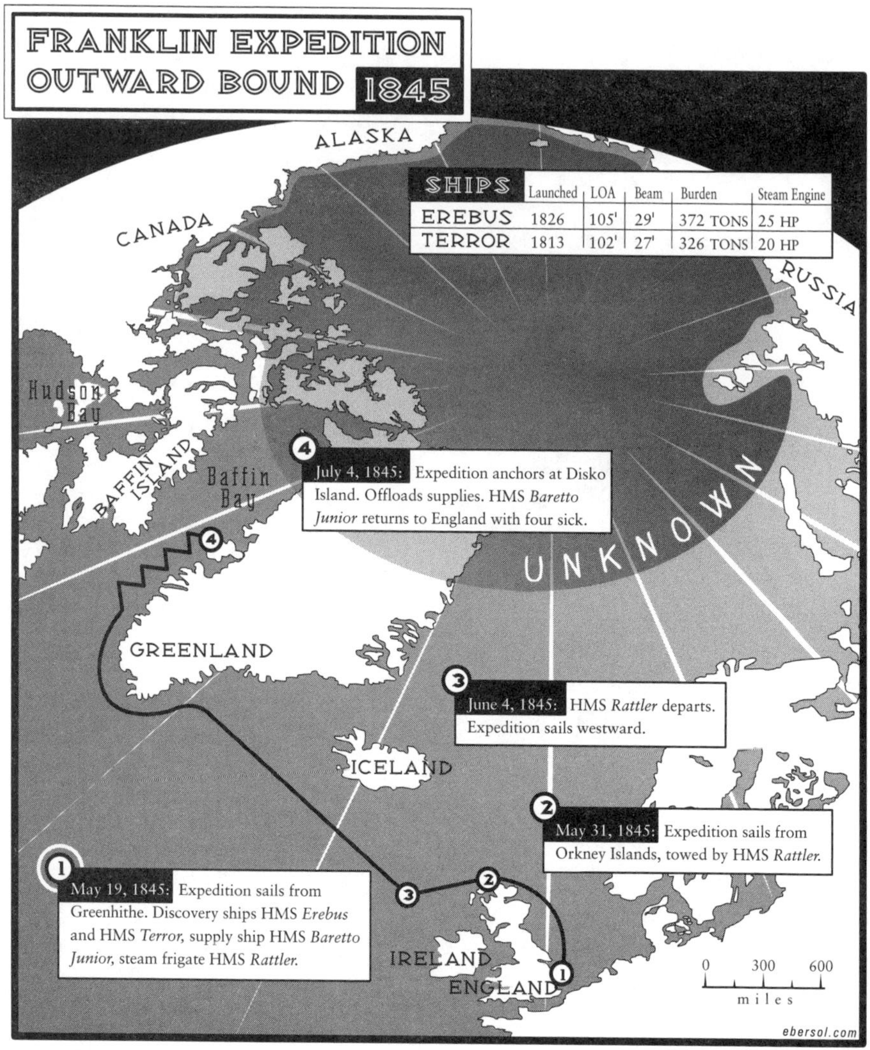

(Map by Rob Ebersol)

Franklin's expedition was simply to follow the instructions and sail through the Passage—as surely as if it were marked on the charts. Barrow ordered the expedition to proceed to Greenland, accompanied by the transport ship *Baretto Junior,* which carried additional coal and supplies. As soon as these were off-loaded, it was to cross Baffin Bay and proceed some 900 miles west through Lancaster Sound to Barrow Strait. At Cape Walker, near the Strait's westernmost end, it was to steer south into the unknown, following any open seaway, until reaching the North American mainland. Once this 500-mile blank spot on the charts had been traversed—the Passage surely—it was to proceed west along the coastline mapped by Dease and Simpson, and Franklin himself, to the Bering Strait and enter the Pacific beyond.

It was an optimistic plan, reflecting the unbridled optimism of the age. It assumed Baffin Bay, whose icy waters once confounded Parry for four months, could be negotiated in one. Likewise, it assumed Lancaster Sound would be largely ice-free and passable in the summer months. In large part, these assumptions were based on belief in the expedition's state-of-the-art technology.

Viewed through these technological glasses, the blank spot on the charts, the missing piece of the Passage puzzle, looked tantalizing. It appeared to be, after all, only about 500 miles or so. Powered by steam engines, with retractable propellers impervious to damage—even picking through floe ice at a marginal speed of 2 knots—the ships could negotiate that distance within a few weeks. Back on the charts, it would be a straightforward business to reach the Bering Strait.

These misconceptions were extreme. While it looked to be only 500 miles, among the myriad unexplored islands of the Arctic Archipelago it could just as well prove to be 1,000. The waters—if there were indeed open waters—were wholly uncharted and unplumbed. Too shallow and the ships might go aground and be unable to get off. That misfortune had claimed Parry's *Fury* in 1824 and Ross's paddlewheeler *Victory* in 1829. Worse yet, the whole area might be solid land—or solid ice. All the navy's previous voyages had demonstrated but one thing positively. The Arctic was a madman's maze of islands, shallows, serrated coasts, dead-end inlets, and pack ice which capriciously yawned open and snapped shut. There was no other place on Earth so tailor-made for becoming hopelessly and forever lost and—once lost—no place so hell-like to escape.

But in the frenzy of Passage fever, in part whipped up by Barrow himself, these obstacles weren't rightly considered obstacles. They were problematical, but they would surrender to English initiative, scientific process, and rational thought. Franklin's expedition, equipped with every resource and invention at the empire's command, was the man-and-machine algorithm painstakingly devised to solve the problem. Every conceivable variable and contingency had been taken into account. All that remained was to put the algorithm to work.

On May 8, 1845, Franklin and his officers were entertained at a formal Admiralty reception. They turned out in full-dress uniform: white collars and black silk cravats; royal blue, double-breasted swallowtail coats with sixteen gold buttons; and royal blue, gold-striped trousers. Facings and cuffs were scarlet. Rank was distinguishable by gold-fringed epaulettes on their shoulders. Captain Sir John Franklin, Captain Crozier, and Commander Fitzjames wore fancy ones embossed with crown and anchor emblems. The expedition's lieutenants wore plain ones, and mates a single epaulette on the right shoulder. Completing these outfits were gold-embroidered swordbelts, scimitarlike Mameluke swords, and (anachronistically for such an up-to-date expedition) "fore-and-aft" cocked hats of the kind Lord Nelson wore.

Officers of the civil branch—the expedition's ice masters, surgeons, paymaster, and pursers—were dressed more plainly. They wore single-breasted blue coats with ten gold buttons and simple, unfringed shoulder plates. In a receiving line, they were first presented to Viscount Melville, the First Lord of the Admiralty and Barrow's sponsor. Then, in quick succession, there followed introductions to the Lords Commissioners of the Admiralty; Sir John Barrow; Admiral Sir Thomas Martin, Controller of the Navy; as well as the presidents of both the Royal and Geographical Societies. This assortment of high-ranking septuagenarians was probably intimidating enough for the junior officers, but also awaiting them in line was the navy's so-called Arctic Council.

These officers had all "seen the elephant"—confronted the unknown—they were so soon to meet. They were living legends. All of them had voyaged in search of the Passage; all of them had been roundly defeated, and most had been lucky to escape with their lives.

There was little warmth in their reception, rather a manifest sympathy. They were polite and offered words of encouragement, but their eyes were oddly impassive and their thoughts seemed fixed somewhere thousands of miles to the north.

One had but to look at them to see ghosts. There was tall, patrician, white-haired Sir William Parry—four failed attempts to find the Passage at the cost of two men dead and *Fury* sunk. There was the coarse, leathery Scotsman, Sir John Ross—two failed voyages, *Victory* crushed like paper in the ice, one man dead and the rest marooned for four nightmarish years in the Arctic. There was the still youthful, handsome Sir George Back—two failed assaults on the Passage, which cost three men their lives and left *Terror* a wallowing, half-sunk wreck. Finally, there was the quiet Dr. John Richardson, who'd accompanied Sir John on the disastrous 1819 expedition, forever haunted by the nine men they'd left to freeze to death in the "barren lands."

Still, the only doubts recorded that evening were voiced by elderly Sir John Ross, whose 1818 voyage had sparked the navy's renewed interest in the Passage in the first place. His 1829–1833 voyage and miraculous escape from the maw of the Arctic gave him license. Near seventy, he was as fit and fulminating as a man half his age. He questioned everything without a blink.

He wondered why in the world Franklin was taking 134 men (8 of whom were stewards whose sole duty was to serve the officers). His shipwrecked crew on the *Victory* had numbered but twenty-three and even that had proven a devilish number to feed and care for. He thought the ships, at 326 to 372 tons, were too big and drew too much water. *Victory* had been only 165 tons and it had grounded. Finally he questioned Franklin himself about his contingency plan. He was shocked to learn that, beyond the ships' boats embarked to carry off the crews, there really was none. Nor did Franklin plan to leave food caches in his wake should he have to retreat the way he'd come. The expedition would not fail. If it had not been heard from after three years, the Admiralty would go looking for it. That was all. Aghast, Ross promised Franklin he'd go looking for it himself if it had not returned by 1848.

The next day, final inspection of the ships took place. Freshly painted black and yellow, bright work varnished and gleaming, their refitting was judged complete. Everywhere else pandemonium raged. Only one-tenth (about 800 cans) of the expedition's all-important supply of canned provisions had been delivered. But mountains of biscuit (18,000 cans), flour (360 hogsheads), oatmeal and barley (300 casks), salt meat (150 casks), sugar and peas (220 casks), 1,200 kegs of lemon juice as well as hundreds more kegs of pickled cranberries, cabbage, and onions were piled dockside. However, most of it could not be stowed until the canned provisions arrived. In modern parlance, the ships had to be *"combat loaded";* intricately and systematically packed so every item could be accessed in the order needed. This mountain of supplies grew daily as rum (916 jugs), chocolate (914 cases), and tea (230 cases) and practically all other provisions, except the canned ones, arrived.

Nonetheless, seamen worked around the clock. Over 180 tons of coal, in sacks, was passed from man to man up the gangways and down into the coal bunkers. The ships' wardrobe of sails—each suit consisting of thirty or more sails, the whole weighing more than 2 tons—were hauled to the Sail Room. Each ship carried a spare suit plus several tons more of storm sails, light weather sails, and spare heavy canvas. Extra masts, yards, booms, and gaffs were carried aboard and stowed in specially built cribs ringing the upper deck. Tons of spare planking and timber were manhandled into overhead racks between beams on the lower deck. Miles of tarred hawser, rope, and chain were painstakingly coiled and hauled into lockers; spare engine parts were abundant and flowed into the hold.

But other vital stores—medical supplies, light canvas (for topsails and royals), cordage—were nowhere in evidence. And while most of the crews labored nonstop, some remained absent and a number of officers had yet to report.

Couriers raced all over London to inquire about overdue shipments. The head of the Victualling Yard at Deptford sent ever more frantic messages to the food contractor, begging delivery of the canned provisions. Pursers and clerks found some medical supplies in crates marked "Surgeon's Stores"; others were marked "Medical

Purveying Depot," while others bore no markings at all. Marines scoured the Woolwich and Deptford dockyards for wayward men; brother officers were sent after their fellows.

This confused state of affairs was made worse aboard *Terror.* Franklin, with Lady Jane, took up residence in the great cabin aboard *Erebus* in the days before sailing. Though Franklin was still recovering from the flu, things there were at least tempered by a semblance of family life and the unflagging optimism of Commander Fitzjames. Dignitaries and officials flocked to visit them. On May 11, 1845, alone they received the Earl of Haddington (First Lord of the Admiralty), Vice-Admiral William Gage, the Marquis of Northampton, Sir Edward Parry, and, according to *The Times*, "a number of [other] ladies and gentlemen."

Aboard *Terror,* by contrast, Crozier was altogether pessimistic, depressed, and disinterested in everything going on around him. He morbidly told a fellow officer he didn't expect to return. His heart still ached over Sophia Cracroft and his pride still hurt at being passed over a third time for command. Fitting out for a seventh voyage into oblivion held no attraction whatever. Even amidst the dockside crowds, the accolades of London society and the press, he remained very much isolated and alone.

He left almost all details to Mr. E. J. Helpman, his clerk, and apparently took to the bottle. This was not uncommon among officers of long service. By and large, they were not drunkards, for the instant the wind shifted or the sea changed, they were on deck as sober and grim as judges. Rather it was the tedium and routine that corroded them like acid and they guzzled strong drink to stop it.

Crozier was the same, only more so. Twelve years of "Discovery Service" and ten pitch-black winters in the ice were enough to bring any man to his breaking point. He was, in fact, suffering a kind of polar combat fatigue. It was plainly apparent to his officers, one of whom wrote: "Look at the state our commander's ship is in, everything in confusion." As Mr. Helpman worked dawn to dusk to sort things out, Crozier sought to piece himself back together.

On May 17, 1845, two days before the expedition sailed, the canned provisions finally arrived. For the next forty-eight hours, no one got any rest as the food was frantically loaded. On May 18, 1845, Franklin held Divine Services for his crews, and, as Franklin was a pious man, these lasted a long time. On May 19, a crowd, estimated at more than 10,000, mobbed the docks at Greenhithe to see the expedition off. The ships' companies mustered on deck in new blue cloth jackets and black silk handkerchiefs. Officers, properly making no public display of affection, discreetly bid farewell to their wives and sweethearts. There were speeches, blaring bands, and resounding cheers, which turned deafening when the ships cast off.

Franklin waved a brightly colored handkerchief so that Lady Franklin and daughter Eleanor might see him. It's almost certain that Franklin's niece, Sophia Cracroft, was in the crowd; whether she saw Crozier or he saw her is not recorded.

Drawn by steam-powered tugs, HMS *Erebus* and HMS *Terror,* accompanied by the navy's newest steam frigate, HMS *Rattler,* and the hired transport ship *Baretto Junior,* dropped down the Thames and out to sea.

The ships stopped briefly at Stromness Harbor in the Orkneys, where they enjoyed a tumultuous reception. It seemed every pleasure craft and fishing boat in the islands had come to see them off, flying handmade Union Jacks. They departed on May 31, 1845. The *Rattler,* equipped with a very powerful 220-horsepower steam engine, towed the vessels westward from Cape Wrath, the northwesternmost tip of Scotland. On June 4, it dropped its cables and watched Franklin's ships vanish over the horizon.

The passage across the North Atlantic to Greenland took thirty days. The bluff-bowed, nearly flat-bottomed bomb vessels were never built for speed. Heavily loaded, according to *The Times,* "with every species of provisions for three years . . . stores of every description for the same time and fuel in abundance," their sealed gunports were only 4½ feet out of the water. In the open ocean, they were dreadfully slow. One previous skipper of *Terror,* before she was weighted down with steam engines, doubled hull, and iron plate, rated her a dismal sailer: "5 knots close-hauled. Just over 9 knots with the wind large or aft and the ship equally leewardly. She does not lie to well . . . and cannot carry sail at all." Neither the wind nor weather on the Greenland passage was good. The wind was out of the west, the seas rough, and Crozier wrote, "Our passage across was very boisterous." Fitzjames was more blunt, calling the weather "anything but favorable." Wallowing westward at a speed of about 5 knots, the ships were further slowed by dense fog banks and icebergs.

Morale on the outward journey, however slow, was sky-high. Commander Fitzjames aboard *Erebus* was delighted with Franklin: "We are very happy and very fond of Sir John Franklin, who improves very much the more we come to know of him." Commenting about perceptions on Franklin's age and timidity, he noted: "He is anything but nervous or fidgety: in fact I should say remarkable for energetic decision in sudden emergencies." He won the confidence of *Erebus*'s junior officers, too. James Fairholme, the ship's most junior lieutenant, wrote happily: "I never felt the Captain was so much my companion with anyone I have sailed with before."

Franklin himself was practically walking on air. He was living his dream. He had a flotilla of three ships, he wrote his wife, "amply provided with every requisite for my passage." His enthusiasm was infectious, almost gushing. "Oh, how I wish I could write to each of them [their relatives]," he wrote Lady Jane, "to assure them of the happiness I feel in my officers, my crew, and my ship!"

The wording speaks volumes: *my* passage, *my* officers, *my* crew, *my* ship. Everything he had ever wanted was finally, miraculously, his. He entertained no possibility but his own success; it was as much an article of faith as his belief in the Almighty. If he feared anything, it was probably the knowledge that this was his final voyage. It would certainly cap his career, his life; but at sixty, it would just as surely be the last he would make. An old man would not get another chance at such a thing. Every emotion, every sensation was redoubled as he fixed them in his memory.

The expedition rounded ominously named Cape Farewell, at the southernmost tip of Greenland, in early July. For most of the men, this was their first real glimpse of the polar world, and it was chilling. Ten times the size of all England, the ice-buried island filled the horizon from edge to edge and seemed to dam the ocean itself.

Before it, the ships seemed Lilliputian and the men microscopic. But it was the sheer, vaulting scale of the icecap—one mile high, the unmelted remnants of 10,000 winters—that was staggering. The largest permanent ice pack in the northern hemisphere, it blocked out the sky and ceaselessly sent a heavy, frigid wind roaring out to sea. If this was but an indication of what lay ahead, the men reckoned the cape well named. As they beat upwind into Davis Strait, the towering icecap glowed green in the twilight, then gray, like a living thing passing into death.

On July 4, 1845, at the red and black storehouses of a Danish whaling station at Disko Bay on the west coast, the expedition stopped to offload supplies. Ten live oxen from the *Baretto Junior* (two had died during the passage) were slaughtered, and the crews feasted on fresh meat. Tons of coal were moved from the transport, the dust blackening everything and everybody. So much food was hauled aboard that Crozier was at a loss as to where to stow it all, writing: "I am still in *hopes* we shall be able to stuff into her three years provisions." Dried fish obtained from the Danes was hung in the rigging. The quarterly June muster books, final dispatches, and personal letters were put aboard the supply ship.

Four men, reckoned unfit by the surgeons, were invalided home. Two—able-bodied seaman John Brown and Private William Aitken of the marines, both from *Terror*—would not be much missed. Two others—James Elliott, *Terror*'s sailmaker, and Thomas Burt, *Erebus*'s armorer—would be. With their departure the expedition, still largely dependent on sail, was left with only one sailmaker. Only one armorer remained to repair its muskets and fowling pieces. But Crozier noted that, even with the reduction, the crew "is quite enough too many still," especially since "now we have more officers . . . and less working men."

On July 12, 1845, to three hearty cheers from the *Baretto Junior*, the expedition set sail across the ice-dotted waters of Baffin Bay. The ships were last seen by two Arctic whalers—the *Prince of Wales* and the *Enterprise*—on July 26. They were moored to an iceberg, atop which they had built a temporary observatory, ostensibly for taking meteorological sightings (more probably, it was for scouting out the

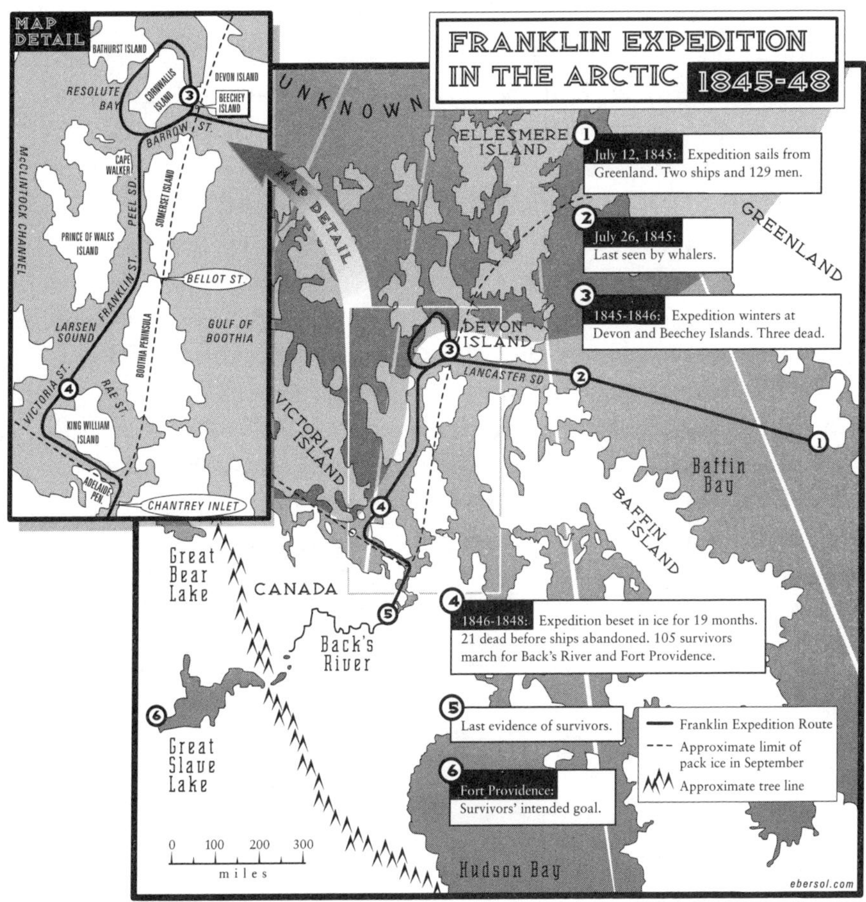


(Map by Rob Ebersol)

fastest, most direct course through the ice). The crews were shooting auks (diving seabirds) by the hundreds and salting them down in barrels. Captain Dannert of the *Prince of Wales* reported "Both ships' crews are all well, and in remarkable spirits, expecting to finish the operation in good time." Yet oddly, Franklin told Captain Robert Martin of the *Enterprise* that he had provisions for five years and, if necessary, could "make them spin out seven years." These were hardly the comments of a man expecting to finish the voyage "in good time," but rather of a man flintily determined to finish it however long it might take.

Early in August, Franklin pushed west as hard and fast as he could go. His progress, as later determined, was phenomenal. He crossed Baffin Bay in less than a month. The temperatures and ice that summer were among the mildest ever recorded in the Arctic. The winds were apparently favorable or the steam engines propelled him along merrily when they were not. He ripped up Lancaster Sound and—stopped by ice in Barrow Strait, which prevented his going west—audaciously steered north searching for a way through. At the upper reaches of Wellington Channel, he was again stopped by ice. Undismayed, he circumnavigated Cornwallis Island. In September, when the sea began to freeze, he found a safe harbor in the lee of Beechey and Devon Islands and went into winter quarters.

It was the first of three terrifying winters the expedition was to suffer.

# CHAPTER 10
# Beechey Island

*. . . amid the sterile uniformity of snow and slate, were the headboards of three graves . . .*

—Dr. Elisha Kent Kane,
Surgeon, USS *Advance,* on reaching Beechey Island in 1850 in search of Franklin

The expedition would spend the next ten months locked in ice at Beechey Island, almost 600 miles north of the Arctic Circle. Plunged into polar dark, pummeled by blizzards and cyclonic gales, its good fortune almost immediately turned bad.

As the sea ice began to freeze, the ships anchored between Beechey and Devon Islands, a musket shot from shore. The islands, brooding slate and granite monoliths towering hundreds of feet above the sea, were connected by a gravel bar, almost awash at high tide. This formed a stout anchorage, with a good holding bottom, largely protected from the elements on three sides. Crozier, sorely familiar with what lay ahead, most likely took charge of preparing the ships' winter defenses. The expedition's officers and crew quickly learned that duty in the ice was duty doubled.

The ships' upperworks had to be entirely dismantled. All yards and running rigging were struck down and carried ashore. The topgallant masts and topmasts were likewise struck down, leaving only the stumps of the lower masts exposed. It was critical to strip the upperworks; otherwise, weighted with tons of ice, they could easily dismast or capsize the ships. All shrouds and standing rigging remaining were loosened to bear any accumulation of ice and snow.

The upper decks were cleared of all disposable gear and the ships' boats were secured on the sea ice. The upper decks were then covered with a foot or more of hard-packed snow for insulation, which was, in turn, covered with sand for secure footing. Finally, the spars on the lower masts were turned fore-and-aft to make a ridgepole and the upper decks roofed with rafter and canvas, so the crews could take exercise even in the worst weather.

Caulkers sealed all drafts with oakum and pitch and the men shoveled snow even with ships' bulwarks to insulate them from the deepening cold. Stoves and warming apparatus were put to work. Rows of posts were sunk in the ice to show the road from ship to ship in polar darkness and storm. Fire holes, six feet square, were sawed in the ice so a ready supply of water was at hand to fight any conflagration.

On the shore of Beechey, Crozier had a storehouse built and offloaded great quantities of provisions and stores, relieving the cramped conditions aboard. A small shop for the carpenters and a blacksmith's forge were also raised.

In October, the long polar night commenced. Little by little, the sun vanished. It would not reappear on the horizon until the end of January. The ships were soon buried in snow drifts as well as darkness. For most aboard who had never experienced it, the feeling of being entombed was pronounced. The lower decks were lit like a catacombs with flickering candle lanterns and sooty oil lamps. Outside, the isolation was absolute. Commander Robert McClure, who wintered nearby in 1850, remembered it in his journal: "No pen can tell of the unredeemed loneliness of an October evening in this polar world; the monotonous, rounded outline of the adjacent hills and the flat, meandering valleys were deadly white with snow."

On New Year's Day 1846, less than three months after arriving at Beechey, the first man died. Twenty-year-old John Torrington, lead stoker aboard *Terror*, died of tuberculosis. It was not unexpected; he'd been sick since the onset of winter and under the care of *Terror*'s two surgeons. Other than feeding him rice and white Tenerife wine, there was nothing they could do. A first entry man from Manchester, he undoubtedly had contracted the disease long before sailing. In fact, he may have been urged to enlist by a doctor back home. Ocean voyages were often prescribed as a specific against consumption, or tuberculosis, and the quickest way a poor man could get to sea was to join the navy.

But as a stoker, on an Arctic voyage, Torrington found himself in about the worst place a tubercular victim could be. Shoveling coal in the unventilated hold, inhaling lungs full of coal dust, would've been enough to give a healthy man anthracosis (black lung). For Torrington, it was a death sentence. His hardening, bacteria-riddled lungs filled with dust like vacuum cleaner bags until he could barely draw a breath. The condition left him vulnerable to any kind of airborne infection floating miasmalike in the hermetically sealed ship. One of these supervening diseases, most likely pneumonia, quickly sealed his fate. (An autopsy of Torrington's frozen corpse conducted by Dr. Owen Beattie in 1984 confirmed both pre-existing tuberculosis and fluid in the lungs, suggestive of supervening pneumonia.)

He was buried ashore, by lamplight, in Stygian darkness and cold. Sir John himself superintended the burial service.

Death revisited the expedition just three days later. Able-bodied seaman John Hartnell, twenty-five, of the *Erebus,* died suddenly and without warning. So soon after Torrington's death, it came as a complete shock. Unlike Torrington, he was neither visibly consumptive or new to the navy. He'd been discharged from the frigate *Volage* (28 guns) on February 1, 1845, having seen action during the Opium Wars and service on the China Station. He signed on with the expedition less than two months after returning home, apparently in good health. Whatever killed him was devilishly quick.

*Erebus*'s surgeons conducted an immediate autopsy seeking the cause (the quick and cursory nature of the procedure was discovered by Beattie when he exhumed and reautopsied the corpse in 1986). Hartnell's trachea, heart, and lungs were vigorously dissected, tubercular lesions discovered, and the corpse quickly buried alongside Torrington. Death was most likely attributed to consumption; nineteenth-century surgeons would have entertained no other possibility. But they also knew tuberculosis was a relatively slow-moving disease (untreated, about half those with active tuberculosis die within two years) and Hartnell's death had been anything but slow. Given the suddenness and virulence of his death, it was more likely caused by something else—viral or bacterial pneumonia perhaps.

Within ninety days, death struck yet again. Private William Braine, thirty-three, a marine from *Erebus,* died, apparently while away from the ships on a sledging expedition. His corpse was dragged back to the burial ground on Beechey Island. The surgeons didn't attempt to autopsy the body. It had begun to decompose and its lesioned mouth and emaciated condition bore all the classic signs of scurvy. Later examination of Braine's frozen corpse (Beattie, 1986) revealed he too had suffered from tuberculosis and pneumonia, though the actual cause of death could not be determined.

Three deaths, so early in the voyage and so close together, were both threatening and perplexing. No previous Royal Navy Arctic expedition, so abundantly supplied and well sheltered, had suffered so many casualties so soon. The surgeons could probably make no sense or pattern out of it. Torrington's tuberculosis had been abundantly evident and, they may have guessed, plainly infectious; but no one else aboard *Terror* contracted the disease. If they were right, Hartnell perished from the same affliction; but Hartnell, aboard *Erebus,* could scarcely have gotten it from Torrington. What's more, his death was a matter of seventy-two hours, not weeks, after Torrington's, and despite the close quarters, no sailor on *Erebus* had suffered the same fate. There was no way Private Braine should have died of scurvy. The expedition had quit Greenland only eight months earlier and he had received the same allowance of lemon juice, canned meat, and vegetables as everybody else. No one else died of scurvy. Something, somewhere—they had no idea what—was terribly wrong.

When the ice released Franklin in the summer of 1846, he left Beechey Island like a man fleeing a nightmare.

# CHAPTER 11
# The Last Summer

*No vessel could have gone south through Peel Sound. All I could see for fifty miles was an unbroken sheet of ice.*

—Captain Sir James Clark Ross,
reporting his abortive 1848 search for Franklin
in Peel Sound, the route Franklin had taken

The expedition's health improved with the sun above, the wind behind, and decks moving beneath its feet again. The graveyard at Beechey, the dreariness and monotony of winter captivity were soon forgotten. Once again, there was purpose and progress.

The ever-lengthening hours of Arctic sunlight revealed a sweeping palette of sheer, startling color—and it was color, during a winter of deadly white snow and inky blackness, that the men missed most. The sea flashed bottle green, aquamarine, teal, and cobalt. Though still dotted with floes, the waters teemed with seals, walrus, and whales enough to lamp the world. The islands lining Lancaster Sound lacked any trees, to be sure, but were instead ablaze with purple saxifrage, low-bush cranberry, delicate blue harebell, and acres of dog lichen and moss as green as any English garden. Even the icebergs, kissed by the sun, melted into meringue—blushed ruby red, lavender, and buttermilk. Tough old Captain John Ross, who'd witnessed the same spectacle many times and was anything but poetic, never forgot its grandeur: "It is hardly possible to imagine anything more exquisite . . . by night as well as by day, they (icebergs) glitter with a vividness of colour beyond the power of art to represent." It was the beginning of one of the warmest summers ever recorded in the Arctic. Franklin, captivated or not by the spectacle, meant to make the most of it and meant to make the dead at Beechey the last he would leave behind.

He raced west down Lancaster Sound with determination and energy. At Cape Walker, the last headland marked positively on his charts, he discovered a mysterious channel (today's Peel Sound) threading almost due south amongst the islands. The previous season it had been invisible, walled over and impassable with ice. Now, providentially, it beckoned like an open door, largely ice-free and leading precisely in the direction he was ordered to go. He plunged into it, apparently stopping neither to lay caches or leave messages (none were ever found); the outstanding weather was too good to waste. For nearly 250 miles, he steamed south.

The expedition's ice masters—James Reid on *Erebus* and Thomas Blanky on *Terror*—successfully piloted the ships through these unknown waters as much by sound as by sight. When the ships encountered so-called *sludge ice,* it made a kind of glug-glug-glug noise, indicating the way was open and no cause for worry. When the bows made a rasping noise, like cutting through fine sugar, it indicated *pancake ice,* first sign of a freeze, but this usually was heard only during the brief hours of darkness and melted during the day. More worrisome, as the channel constricted, was *young ice* reaching out from shore. Formed by the coagulation of pancake ice, it was up to a foot thick, but the iron-plated ships, under steam, bulled through it easily. Behind it was *fast ice* or *coast ice,* 3 feet thick or more, pinned in place by the vagaries of shoreline, tide, and current and no danger, so long as it remained in place.

It was loose, moving ice encountered in today's Franklin Strait, that probably first caused the ice masters concern. There was plenty of *brash ice,* the lowest denomination of the summer break-up, and larger slabs of *drift ice,* 1 to 2 feet thick. These could thump the thick-hulled ships, but do them no harm. *Bergy bits,* icebergs as big as houses, calved from larger bergs, were easily avoided and given a wide berth.

But floating toward them, some white and some as blue as sea water and virtually impossible to detect until they were on top of

*HMS* Endurance *in the Ice* This is Ernest Shackleton's ship, shown attempting to escape the Antarctic pack ice under steam in 1915. Franklin's ships employed the same tactic in the Arctic and suffered the same defeat seventy years earlier. (National Maritime Museum, Greenwich, England)

them, were hundreds of *growlers.* Most of these were the size of cottages and, as their name implied, complained noisily against the hulls as the ships churned ahead. Among them, however, were numerous, ominously snow-backed chunks of ice called *hummocky floes.* It wasn't their size that alarmed the ice masters; it was their sheer number and meaning. The deep snow on them and the tide marks on their sides signified *old pack* or *screwed pack* and a monstrous lot of ice somewhere ahead.

The news was certainly reported to Franklin. But by that time, lookouts in the mastheads spied the dim outline of King William Island, explored 16 years earlier, lying immediately to the south. This was a revelation: from King William Island to the North American mainland was an estimated distance of but 200 miles! The expedition stood at the very portal of the Passage. Also visible from the mastheads, however, was a massive ice field to the southwest, precisely what the ice masters most feared.

The ships most probably hove to while Franklin called his officers together. With the weather near perfect, the steam engines apparently functioning flawlessly, and two years' provisions, Franklin was confident. The pack ice ahead was still melting and veined with open leads. In a week, perhaps two, they could push through.

Crozier and the ice masters may have argued to the contrary. It was nearly the end of August, the end of summer in those latitudes, and the weather could change at any time. Like every Arctic whaleship captain, Crozier and the ice masters knew there were but six to twelve weeks to plumb those forbidding waters. If they overestimated the season, by a week or even a day, they could expect to spend the next ten months locked in a white wasteland of moving pack ice, where temperatures often dropped to 50 degrees below zero. In the kind of pack ice they saw ahead, the ships could just as easily be crushed in twenty-four hours. Perhaps it would be safer to use the weather that was left to find a safe anchorage, winter over, and renew the attempt next season.

The decision, of course, was Franklin's alone; no doubt attended by prayer. The memory of graveside services at Beechey may have influenced him. The "man who wouldn't hurt a fly" had seen three of his men die already; another winter could mean more. God had guided him this far, a scant few hundred miles from their goal. It was still summer and there were open leads ahead. The crews were eager and the ships sound; their chances would never be better. As he had written to Lady Franklin from Greenland, he felt "comforted with every hope of God's merciful guidance and protection." That faith had not diminished a particle. He ordered steam laid on. The crews sent up three cheers. Crozier and the ice masters may have winced. In line ahead, the ships entered the pack.

# CHAPTER 12

# Beset

*Then DeHaven came down to tell me the worst: the ice had got us, we were frozen in for the winter, 'glued up' . . .*

—Dr. Elisha Kent Kane

One of the most stunning features of an Arctic summer is its shortness and almost unimaginably abrupt end. Sometime in early September, it apparently ended overnight. The temperatures plunged and the loose brash ice turned the consistency of wet cement, gluing up the leads ahead and behind the ships. Franklin's *Erebus,* probably in the lead by virtue of her larger engine, bulled through this without too much difficulty at first. But as the thermometer fell, the ice thickened and the ship was soon forced to repeatedly back its engine and proceed full ahead to break a path. At the same time, young ice grew outward from the surrounding pack, choking the narrowing channels with oncoming slabs of drift ice and floes that the helm could no longer avoid. This loose ice suddenly posed a genuine danger to the ships' delicate propellers and rudders. Without adequate seaway to use sail, the ships were almost totally dependent on steam.

If progress was to be maintained, the vulnerable propellers and rudders could not be retracted out of harm's way, as intended. They may, in fact, very well have been damaged during this time. That fate befell American Robert E. Peary's *Roosevelt* in the Arctic around Cape Sheridan in the summer of 1905. As the ship worked through channels in the pack, ice sheared the propeller clean off, ripping away the rudder and entire sternpost at the same time. At once, the *Roosevelt* began taking on so much water that it almost overmastered the ship's pumps and Peary prepared to abandon ship.

Jury-rigged repairs to the hull barely kept it afloat, but it was all but helpless. Fortunately, the current carried the pack ice, and *Roosevelt* along with it, south for a month and a half, until the ship could be beached for repairs. Even if Franklin's vessels had been spared a similar ordeal, their experience among the congealing floes must have demonstrated other, equally dangerous, weaknesses in the ships' technology.

As engineers John Gregory on *Erebus* and James Thompson on *Terror* quickly discovered, the railway locomotives, while capable of driving the ships through open water, were woefully underpowered for bulldozing through the rapidly accumulating ice. At 25- and 20-horsepower respectively, even with full steam laid on, they could not propel the ships faster than a pensioner's walk. The strain of pushing 370-ton vessels through thousands of tons of ice overworked them terribly, and almost certainly resulted in frequent mechanical failure.

The unreliability of ships' engines during the period was manifest. The USS *Merrimack,* a steam and screw-driven frigate built ten years after Franklin sailed, with engines far more powerful and advanced, was notorious. Her engineer reported that "During a cruise of two years whilst I was attached to this ship, they [the engines] were constantly breaking down, at times when least expected, and the ship had to be sailed under canvas during the great part of the cruise." The single-expansion steam engines on Franklin's ships operated only at the extremely low pressures of which the technology of the day was capable—about 25 pounds per square inch. It wasn't until the development of more efficient designs (double- and triple-expansion engines), using stronger steel boilers rather than iron, that higher, more powerful pressures were achieved.

These feeble pressures were crippled by other inefficiencies. Up to 25 percent of the locomotives' indicated horsepower was expended simply overcoming internal friction and transmission losses. Engaged in a brute shoving match with the pack ice, it quickly became apparent to Gregory, Thompson, and the expedition's five stokers that coal was being consumed at a frightful rate.

The USS *Savannah* (350 tons), the first auxiliary steam-powered vessel to cross the Atlantic, carried single-cylinder engines similar to those on Franklin's ships. It made the eastward or so-called *downhill passage* (boosted by prevailing winds and currents) in 29½ days, during which the engine was used only 3½ days (85 hours). In that time, the ship's entire supply of 75 tons of coal and 25 cords of wood was consumed. HMS *Sirius* (700 tons), in 1838, the first ship to cross the Atlantic in the opposite direction, from England to America, entirely under steam, had a very powerful 320-horsepower engine. The passage took 18 days and 10 hours, during which all the ship's coal was exhausted and the crew had to burn cabin furniture, spare yards, and even the mast en route to keep steam up in the boiler. Franklin's ships, which left Greenland with 90 tons of coal apiece thirteen months before, were equally fuel-inefficient.

Each vessel burned over a half ton of coal a day just to keep steam in the boilers. Underway at 3 to 4 knots—about their optimum cruising speed—each vessel gobbled from 2 to 3 tons of coal a day. Following the serpentine leads of the pack, repeatedly backing and steaming ahead at full power, coal consumption was even greater. How much coal had already been expended powering the ships in the summer of 1845 and heating them at Beechey during the winter of 1845–1846 is, of course, unknown. But in 1915, beset in the Antarctic pack, Sir Ernest Shackleton calculated it took 125 to 150 pounds of coal a day just to heat his ship, the *Endurance,* which was about the same size as *Erebus* and *Terror.* If as much as 75 percent of the coal aboard Franklin's ships remained (an optimistic estimate), this represented less than 14 days' steaming under normal conditions. If the expedition had managed to push through Peel Sound and Franklin Strait in only two or three days, which is all but inconceivable under sail and barely conceivable under steam, it would have entered the pack with a very thin margin for error, and the conditions it confronted in the close-packed ice were scarcely normal. By any calculation, in late summer 1846, the remaining fuel supplies must have been alarmingly low.

The engineers would have certainly reported the rapidly dwindling coal reserves, leaving Sir John and Crozier—standing quite literally at the point of no return—with only two options. They could continue the assault on the ice, expending fuel at a prodigious rate, in an all-out gamble to follow the ever-narrowing leads and force a passage to the mainland before they closed completely. Or they could turn back at once, get out of the ice (if it was not too late), find any kind of anchorage, and conserve enough coal to heat the ships through the winter with enough left over to power them through next summer as soon as the ice broke up. In one of the greatest ironies of the Franklin Expedition, its dependence on steam power and coal did not, as Barrow had intended, set it free. It had propelled it to a place where its destiny was utterly dependent upon the one man Barrow had hesitated entrusting it to in the first place.

The situation probably came as a complete shock to Franklin, who knew nothing about boilers, cylinders, pistons, and condensers. The ice masters, if they were worth their salt (and as evidenced in getting the vessels so far so fast, they certainly were) probably argued to put about. They had probably not been keen about entering the pack at all so late in the season; to go farther looked like suicide. Commander Fitzjames, who'd experienced only two seasons of unprecedented good weather and had unbridled faith in steam, may have argued to go on. Forcing the passage had always been a race, after all, and to quit it halfway run was clearly not the way to win it. From the mastheads, open leads were still visible to the southwest, precisely the direction they wished to go.

With contrary opinions flying and little time to make a decision, the opinion Franklin probably most heeded was that of the expedition's most experienced Arctic officer—the melancholy, hard-drinking Irishman, Captain Crozier. It's hard to say what course of action Crozier counseled. Knowing the peril and shortness of the season, it may have been the most shocking course of all. He may very well have suggested abandoning one ship, loading all the coal on the other, and pressing forward at all speed. This would have been very much in character with his no-nonsense, practical nature—not to win the race for the Passage, as Fitzjames would argue, but to win the race against winter, to escape the pack as quickly as possible and reach the mainland at all cost. The ice might not break up next summer or even the summer thereafter. Then the question of coal would be moot in any case; best to use it to advantage so long as it lasted. The nearer the mainland, the better the chance of survival. It may have come down to that.

The whole of this came crashing down on Franklin's head. He had gambled against the onset of winter before, on the 1819 Coppermine expedition, and lost. He had practiced patience and perseverance on the 1825 Mackenzie expedition and won. Patience and perseverance had, in fact, preserved him for the twenty years since and brought him to the brink of a breathtaking success. It could be his before winter, if he gambled everything. But one more winter, husbanding the coal, would insure it. More than likely, Franklin chose the latter course. The boiler fires were drawn and the steam let down.

Every stratagem was then employed to desperately move the ships out of the rapidly closing trap into whatever protected anchorage could still be reached. This had worked for Franklin before, in 1818, warping the *Dorothea* through the pack ice, and the same methods were doubtless employed now. Fatigue parties with 12-foot-long ice saws, picks, axes, ice chisels, and black powder labored around the clock to keep the lead open. The ice masters shifted ballast, backed sail, and set kedge anchors in the fast ice and winched the vessels forward or backward a ship's length at a time. The ships may have progressed in this manner for perhaps a week, maybe less. But on September 15, 1846, some 25 miles off the northwest shore of King William Island, Franklin's luck ran out.

During the night the ice closed firmly and heavily around the ships. At first light, in every direction as far as the eye could reach from the mastheads, stretched an unbroken field of ice. The vessels were trapped.

Crozier, who knew full well what the early onset of winter meant, must have been horrified. This was no secure anchorage like Beechey. They were beset in moving pack ice, on a lee shore, with no protection whatever from wind or weather. None aboard who had been beset, neither Crozier or the ice masters, had ever seen ice of such thickness, ferocity, or extent. They were, in fact, caught in the maw of the Beaufort ice stream, which pours off the polar cap from the northwest with almost glacial power. When the sun vanished, it would grow even more monstrous, expanding with each hour of darkness, and the pressure against the hulls would build incalculably. The effects could be swift and catastrophic.

Sir Ernest Shackleton, whose ship *Endurance* was trapped in similarly close-packed ice in the Antarctic in 1915–1916, suffered three violent attacks from the ice in just ten days. As Shackleton wrote: "the ship was subjected to a series of tremendously heavy strains. In the engine room, the weakest point, loud groans, crashes and hammering sounds were heard. The iron plates on the floor buckled up. . . . Meanwhile the floes were grinding off each other's projecting points and throwing up pressure ridges." The following day, these pressure ridges fractured in a resounding explosion: ". . . huge pieces of ice shot up from under the port bilge. Within seconds the ship heeled over until she had a list of thirty degrees to port. . . . Everything moveable on deck and below fell to the lee side, and for a few minutes it looked as if the *Endurance* would be thrown on her beam ends." The end came just six days later. "The onslaught (of the ice) was all but irresistible. The *Endurance* groaned and quivered as her starboard quarter was forced against the floe, twisting the sternpost and starting the heads and ends of planking . . . the ship was twisted and actually bent by the stresses. She began to leak dangerously at once . . . moving laterally across the stern (the ice), split the rudder and tore out the rudder-post and stern-post. The decks were breaking upwards and the water was pouring in below. It was a sickening sensation to feel the decks breaking up under one's feet, the great beams bending and then snapping with a noise like heavy gunfire. The water was overmastering the pumps. . . ." Shackleton and twenty-eight men abandoned her as the ship was "crushed concertina fashion."

Crozier realized full well the same thing could happen to *Erebus* and *Terror* at any time during the coming winter. While seemingly fast-frozen and immovable, the ships were, in fact, perched atop a kind of icy San Andreas Fault. Pressure caused by millions of tons of opposing ice all around them—the equivalent of tectonic plates

*HMS* Endurance *Beset* Shackleton's ship being crushed, constrictorlike, by ice in the Weddell Sea off Antarctica. Franklin's ships looked much the same, but survived their ordeal far longer. The *Endurance* was sunk after nine months; *Erebus* and *Terror* survived nineteen months before being abandoned intact. (National Maritime Museum, Greenwich, England)

grinding against one another—would eventually reach a breaking point. When it did, the pack would shake with tremors, then fracture in a lethal cataclysm of frozen earthquakes and icy eruptions. By similar dynamic, towering pressure ridges, propelled by part of the pack driving over or under another part, could close upon the ships as fast as a man could walk—sometimes as fast as a man could run. Any of these events could crush the vessels like paper.

Further darkening Crozier's outlook was likely the relentless but mystifying current. Depending on how it eddied and flowed, it might slowly swing them in circles all winter or carry them swiftly into the serrated shallows of King William Island. There was no way of knowing. The only certainty was that they were beset in a maelstrom of ice in the heart of the Arctic archipelago and there was absolutely nothing to be done about it.

It's doubtful this news was shared with the crews. But the peril of their predicament must have been chillingly obvious. As bleak and dismal as Beechey had been, this looked far worse. There, at least, they'd been out of moving pack ice, and there'd been stout islands about and shelter from gales. A fellow could wander the shore, visit the smithy and carpenter's shop. There, at least, the decks had been cleared and life aboard made "fair tolerable."

Here everything was different. Everybody must have known it and everybody must have been scared. In part, it was because a man could see so far, even if he tried not to. In every direction, all the way to the horizon, stretched a jumbled, windswept desert of lifeless ice. The ships seemed like flecks in it. Just staring at it was enough to strike a man with vertigo. They must have felt like the only people on earth. The nothingness went on forever.

# CHAPTER 13

# Imprisoned

*The winter of the arctic regions had now come on us, in its character of darkness, gale, cold and snow . . . some disagreements were taking place in the different messes as individuals suffered more or less from the cold. Plethoric ones exclaimed against the heat, the lethargic of cold drafts, the testy bemoaned the impure ventilation.*

—Commander Robert McClure,
HMS *Investigator,* searching for Franklin in 1850

The only real, habitable world that now remained was belowdecks in the ships. It was a troglodytic world Crozier knew only too well and had come to dread.

Its dimensions, claustrophobic to begin with, were made worse by the fact that the expedition dared not offload anything onto the sea ice. Sealed off from the outside—crammed with men, provisions, and stores—it was suffocating.

A single hatch (the fore hatch had been sealed) led down an almost vertical 7-foot ladderway to the lower deck. This was the only heated deck and the sole berthing place for everyone aboard: sixty-five to sixty-seven men in a space measuring 96 feet long and 28 feet wide, with but 7 feet of headroom. But for the headroom, this is roughly the size of a contemporary suburban home, comfortably accommodating a family of four or five. For over sixty men, however, it resembled purgatory.

On both vessels, the layout was almost identical. Aft of the ladderway, down a tunnel-like companionway little more than 2 feet wide, were the officers' quarters. On *Terror,* housed in sixteen tiny cabins, lived Crozier, three lieutenants, two masters, two mates, two surgeons, the ships' clerk, three warrant officers, and four stewards. All but the warrant officers, who berthed together, got a cabin to themselves.

Each cabin, even Crozier's, was but 5 feet wide and just under 6 feet long, about half the size of a cell in London's notorious Pentonville prison. Half this space was filled by a built-in, cradle-sided bunk, topped by a horsehair mattress. One shelf overhead and four drawers beneath the bunk provided the only storage. The other half consisted of a sliding door to the companionway, flanked by a drop-leaf writing table on one side (the officer had to sit on his bunk to use it) and a triangular washstand with basin on the other. Out of his bunk, there was barely enough space for a man to stand and dress.

Overhead a "Preston Patent Illuminator," a circular glass skylight 6 inches in diameter, was supposed to admit daylight. But in polar dark, with the upper deck covered in canvas and buried by snow, it winked black all winter long. A single whale oil lamp affixed to the bulkhead provided the only light. Since lamp oil, like candles, was strictly rationed, this light lasted but a few hours a day.

The thin sliding doors afforded the illusion of privacy but no quiet. The lower deck was a cacophony of slamming hatchways, thudding scuttles, mumbling, wooden stumblings, and cursing, aggravated by the constant coughing, sneezing, snoring, belching, and flatulence of over sixty men. This racket was punctuated by the rattle of crockery, clattering plate, and clinking tinware.

But there were far more haunting, frightening sounds. The wind outside seldom abated, rising from a near constant moan to a shivering howl that actually shook the ship. Against the hull, a foot from a man's head, the ice creaked and scraped incessantly like claws on a blackboard. Farther out, the shifting pack ice sometimes sounded like crashing surf, but when it buckled and broke the report was "like a 32-pound gun." The rest of the time, as the American polar explorer Elisha Kent Kane described it, "the uproar of the surging pack rang . . . almost as if the ice were alive, issuing animal-like shrieks and plaintive cries, like those of a nighthawk."

On the unheated decks below, the subzero temperatures made themselves unmistakably heard. "The ship echoed the sufferings of

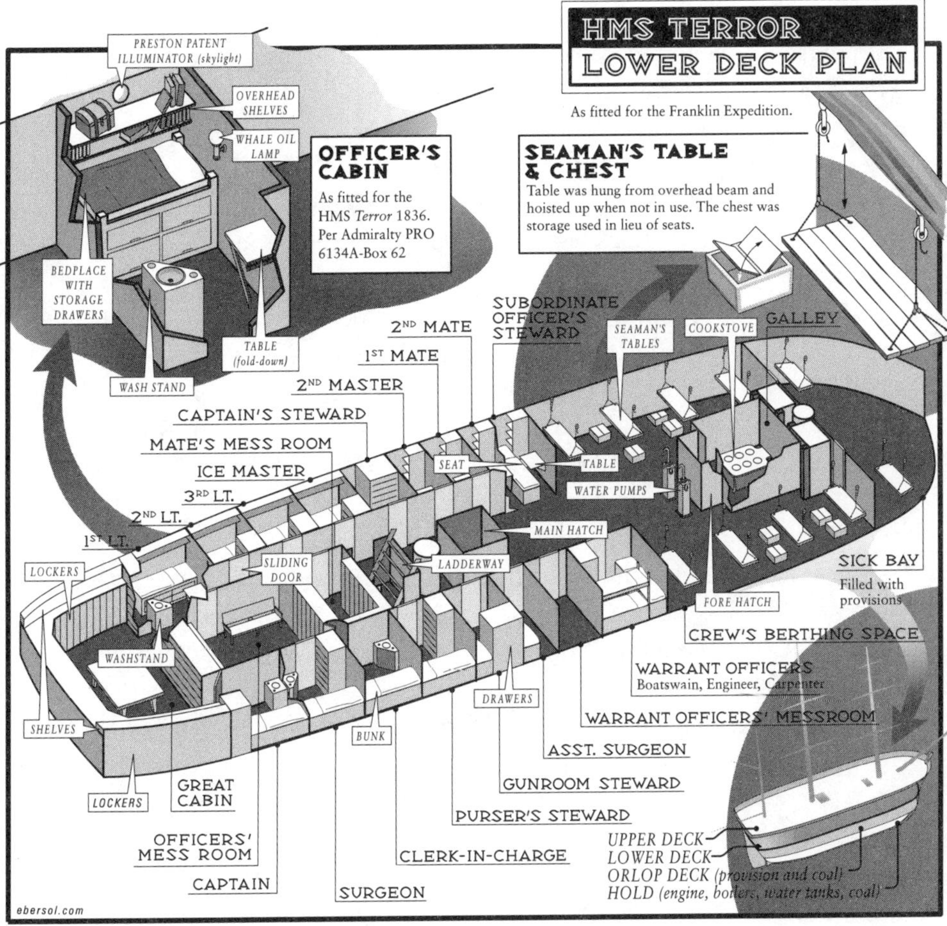


Erebus *and* Terror, *Lower Deck* Up to sixty-seven men inhabited this space—96 feet long, 28 feet wide, with 7 feet of headroom—for over three years. It was the only heated deck. Officers occupied sixteen tiny cabins, the men berthed forward in hammocks. There were mess rooms aft for officers, mates, and warrant officers; the men ate from swing-down mess tables forward. Each seaman was allowed one hinged chest (upper right) for his personal possessions; it doubled as a seat at mess. At the stern was the Great Cabin, filled with a library of some 1,200 volumes. Though the plan is remarkably open, every square inch was crammed with provisions and stores. (Illustration by Rob Ebersol)

the men," recounted Captain Robert McClure, whose vessel was similarly trapped in pack ice, "The bolts and fastenings cracked in the −60F cold" and sounded "like pistol shots" as they gave way. In another of the ironies of the long polar night, sleep was made almost impossible.

In the middle of "officer's country"—windowless, its skylight covered over and black—was the officers' mess room, or what would be called the wardroom today. It was 12 feet long and 10 feet wide, with a built-in, horsehair-backed-and-bottomed couch on one side and a sideboard with cupboards on the other. A stout mess table and wooden bench filled the center of the room.

At mealtimes, Crozier, 1st Lt. Little, 2nd Lt. Hodgson, 3rd Lt. Irving, Chief Surgeon Peddie, and Helpman, the clerk-in-charge, crowded together in this mess room. Thomas Jopson, the captain's steward, assisted by Edward Genge, the paymaster's steward, served them—eight men in a dimly lit space but 120 feet square. The subordinate officers (the two masters, two mates, and assistant surgeon) had a smaller mess room next door and were served by their own steward. The warrant officers (engineer, boatswain, and carpenter) had a still smaller mess room to themselves, and were served by the gunroom steward. One head at the stern on the upper deck, labeled a *water closet* on the Admiralty's refit plans, accommodated all eighteen officers, regardless of rank.

Aft of the officers' mess room, occupying the stern of the ship, was the great cabin, the only truly capacious place aboard. It was 12 feet long by 24 feet wide, with lockers on three sides and bookshelves, holding 1,200 volumes, on the fourth. A large table, 6 feet by 5 feet, sat in the center of the cabin. The selection of books was extensive. There were narratives of Ross's and Parry's expeditions, geographical journals, works on navigation, astronomy, natural history, philosophy, medicine, and religion. For the less serious, there were novels, including *The Vicar of Wakefield* and *Ivanhoe,* and bound copies of *Punch.* A hand organ, supplied with fifty punched metal disks, could crank out as many tunes. For amusement, there were chess sets, playing cards, and draughts (checkers). This was the officers' primary refuge throughout the winter, the only place where a man could forget, for a time, the freezing menace lurking outside.

As confining as the officers' quarters were, the men's were positively cagelike. The entire crew, forty-two men and two midshipmen, ate, slept, and spent their off-duty hours penned in the forward third of the lower deck. This space, just 36 feet long and 28 feet wide, was horrendously overcrowded. Dr. Elie-Jean Leguillou, a ship's surgeon in D'Urville's 1840 Antarctic expedition, reported such overcrowding "conducive to the spread of contagious diseases . . . if it was raining, snowing, the ship hemmed in by ice, there would be forty to sixty individuals in the orlop deck, spitting, drinking, eating, while all openings were tightly shut . . . The smells from the hold, from the storeroom, the smoke, steam and smells from the kitchen, the exhalation from the lungs and skin were not dispersed by the faintest breath of fresh air; daylight hardly entered . . ."

The 7-foot headroom in this area was reduced to less than 6 feet, since spare planking, timbers, and sail rig, along with hammocks and mess tables, were stowed overhead. Each man was allotted a space only 14 inches wide for his hammock; about the width of a coach class airline seat today. When slung from hooks in the deck beams, each man's hammock touched his neighbor's, packing the deck as closely as sardines in a tin. The only way fore and aft through this hanging maze was an aisle on either side of the ship, each but 18 inches wide. When not in use, the hammocks were lashed up, with the blankets inside them, by nine turns of a rope.

There was no mess room for the men. They ate from eight mess tables (6 feet long by 2½ feet wide) suspended from the deck beams like the hammocks. Their small hinged sea chests served as seats. Two *seats of ease,* or heads, located on either side of the bow on the frigid upper deck, served all forty-four men. Most nights however, buckets were used, to spare the men the cold; the contents could be used to fight fire until they were dumped over the side in the morning.

As crowded as it was, the men did not have the berthing deck to themselves. Smack in the center stood the ship's cast-iron *Frazer's Patent Stove,* upon which everything aboard was cooked. It was a monstrous device with an oven, six burners, built-in desalinator, and a hand-powered pump nearby to draw water (if it had not frozen) from iron tanks in the hold. It kept the crew's quarters quite warm, but it also ceaselessly billowed clouds of steam. This condensed into frost throughout the berthing deck. As fast as it melted into black drip water, it was replaced by a fresh frosting, so the crew's quarters were perpetually damp. Since Mr. Diggle, the ship's cook, was up most of the night preparing the next day's meals, the galley stove was also a positive disturbance. At first the grating of coal, slamming stove doors, clanging pots, thudding scuttles (through which provisions were brought up from the hold), and Diggle's cursing were unbearable. But the warmth and smell of the near-continuous operation counterbalanced the cold and the stink of the men's sweat, soggy clothes, and damp blankets. The fact that the cook was at work, even as they tried to sleep, was evidence the ship's heart still beat.

Forward of the galley, the bulwark having been removed, stood the cook's cupboards and shelves—off limits to all. In the ship's forepeak was "sick bay," but this was a misnomer. Its entire area, from deck to overhead beams, was stacked high with provisions. The sick—and the struggle to escape the pack had doubtless resulted in cases of frostbite and hernia—were daily mustered by Mr. Diggle's stove, examined and, if found unfit, sent to their hammocks.

Beneath the lower deck, down a 6-foot ladderway, lay the primordially dark, unheated orlop deck. Work parties, carrying lanterns and bundled in their warmest clothes, descended to this level to fetch the ship's "consumables"—food, stores, tools, and spares. In the bow on the starboard side was the carpenter's storeroom, packed with hammers, mallets, saws, planes, files, gouges, and nails. On the port side was the boatswain's storeroom, equally crammed with tools meticulously stowed in lockers and drawers.

Aft of these was the all-important Bread Room. It was filled to every cavity with flour, ship's biscuit, oatmeal, barley, rice, peas, pickled cabbage, parsnips, walnuts, cranberries, dates, dried apples, and canned carrots. On either side, constricting the ship's 28-foot width even more, were built-in sleeves housing what remained of the coal.

Just aft of the Bread Room, the entire midship portion of the orlop deck was stacked to the beams with crates of canned provisions; hogsheads of ale; casks of salt meat, peas, sugar, and vinegar; kegs of lemon juice; and cases of chocolate and tea.

Behind this was the most protected part of the ship—the padlocked Spirit Room. It was filled with perhaps one-and-a-half years' worth of the expedition's remaining rum, plus brandy and wine. It also contained 200 muskets and sword bayonets in side-mounted arms stands. Cutlasses hung in racks overhead. The Spirit Room had scuttles (hatchways) directly up into the officer's mess room and the Great Cabin; insurance against mutiny.

On either side of the Spirit Room were other critical storerooms. Two chain cable lockers, the mate's storeroom, and the Sail Room with all the ship's sails, spare canvas, grommets, gaskets, sheets, heavy needles, and leather-palmed sailmaker's gloves. The Slop Room, administered by the ship's clerk, contained all the crew's heavy clothes—felt-soled boots, sou'westers, Welsh wigs (watch caps), mittens, and socks.

Further aft were the magazines and Gunner's Storeroom, with the powder, shot, and cartridges to render any weapon aboard effective. Unless the men forced the Spirit Room's locked and guarded door to gain access to the muskets and ammunition (to which the officers had immediate access through the scuttles), insurrection or mutiny would have been unlikely, if not impossible, which is why the Royal Navy planned and fitted the ships that way.

In the sternmost part of the ship, not without similar forethought, lay the Captain's Storeroom. This was perhaps his finest perquisite of rank. It contained select viands like beef tongues, calves heads, jugged hares (whole rabbits pickled in brine), cured hams, and cheeses. Most important—at least in the case of Crozier's ship, for Franklin was a teetotaler—it contained spirits.

A final, dark ladderway led down to the hold. Few men ventured here unless they had to. Below the frozen waterline, it was unbearably cold, ankle-deep in meltwater, and reeked of sewage, coal dust, and fumes. It held not only twenty-one square iron water tanks containing 38 tons of fresh water, but more provisions, stores, an immense amount of coal, and the ship's wheezing boiler. In guttering lamplight, around the clock, the engineer and three stokers shoveled coal to heat the lower deck. Heavy sacks of coal had to be hauled to the boiler from all parts of the ship. It was tended constantly, in shadow made dimmer by polar night and ascamper with legions of scuttling rats.

The routine aboard this self-contained, frozen prison was prescribed and never-ending. Officers and men were rousted at 6 A.M.—officers from their horsehair-mattressed bunks, the men from their canvas hammocks. Officers were brought hot water by the stewards, but shaved and washed themselves. The men slung their hammocks, blankets, and comforters. They consulted their small, hinged sea chests for any items they might need during the day. Then they lowered the mess tables from the overhead beams.

At 7 o'clock breakfast was served. The men filed past the galley stove and were given ship's biscuit with some jam, hot cocoa or tea, and oatmeal or Scotch barley mush with sugar. In the officer's mess room, the fare was somewhat better; stewards served them bread, butter, bacon, tea, and coffee.

At 7:30 A.M. there was an inspection of the men and all parts of the ship. Men feeling unwell reported to sickbay in the forepeak to see the surgeons. The rest were dismissed to *holystone* the deck. This was not just make-work. It helped to combat disease. Hot water and sand were poured on the deck and the men scoured it with square blocks of sandstone. Smaller stones, called "bibles," were used to get into the corners. The deck was then washed down and swabbed dry until "a lady in a long white dress could stroll the ship without fear of getting her dress soiled."

At noon, the grog was issued. This was certainly the high point of the crew's day. They mustered around the scuttlebutt, a butt or cask that had been "scuttled" by sawing a square piece out of the widest part of its curved side, so that no more than half a cask of water (63 gallons) was available for the crew daily. This was done to conserve water (which, in the winter, required melting prodigious quantities of ice, since the water in the ship's iron tanks was fast-frozen). As he came forward with his cup, each man was first given his issue of lemon juice and sugar to prevent scurvy. Even sweetened, this sour dose was not well liked. But it was immediately followed by a carefully measured gill (1/4 pint) of concentrated West Indian rum. The proof of this—from 130 to 140—was stunning, so it was just as quickly diluted with 3/4 pint of water into "grog" (if a man was being punished, the water was doubled). The effect of this liquor happily carried the men to 1 P.M., when dinner was lashed up.

The winter allowance varied from the usual issue. Extra items, called "luxuries" by the Victualling Department, were added (or more properly substituted) to boost variety and keep up morale. With this winter allowance, if the men were lucky they got canned roast beef, barley mush, and hot bread with an ounce of butter. If they were not, they got "Poor John"—salted codfish, boiled, with rock-hard ship's biscuit. They also received hot tea, sugar, and 1 ounce of tobacco a day.

After a pipe or a chew, they resumed their duties. Work parties bundled up in heavy clothes and went topside. There—for hours in polar darkness, screeching wind, and brutal cold—they shoveled snow and struck ice from the ship. This was vitally necessary, for the ice buildup could weigh tons and prevent the ship from rising as the pack squeezed it. It was also back-breaking, punishing labor. Every inch of ice had to be sledgehammered or chopped away and moved by hand. With pickaxes and crosscut saws, other parties continually cleared holes in the ice so a ready supply of water would be at hand to douse any fires.

Those fortunate enough to remain in the relative warmth and comfort of the lower deck were employed in "make-and-mend." Sails were repaired, gaskets made, worn rope laid up anew, and old rope feazed (picked apart) into oakum (loose hemp) for the caulkers to seal the ship's seams. Some moved victuals up from the Bread Room or Spirit Room to the lower deck. Others hauled coal through the scuttles and carried it below. Stokers shoveled it in a black, choking dust to fuel the boiler firing the ship's heating apparatus. Carpenters, caulkers, and blacksmiths fashioned sledges, filled seams, and mended fittings. Stewards scoured plate, cleaned lamp globes, and polished silver. The cook—endlessly—cooked.

At 4 P.M. hot tea, well sugared, and biscuit were served and dispatched without formality.

At 6 P.M. the day's labor in the darkness ceased. The mess tables were lowered again and supper was served. For the men this might be salt beef, salt pork, or canned mutton or veal, canned vegetables, pickled cabbage, or parsnips—and, with the winter allowance of "luxuries," an ounce of cheese and a half pint of Burton's ale or porter. On so-called "flour days," the cook made up a flour pudding with raisins. Occasionally, when ordered by the captain, they might also get a little pickled herring or salmon. All this (which wasn't much considering the subzero temperatures and the amount of work) was accompanied by salt, pepper, mustard, and vinegar.

For the officer's mess, the stewards labored to prepare and serve supper in "proper" courses. Starting perhaps with canned oxtail soup, followed by Findon haddock, then canned mutton, canned potatoes, pickled onions, hot bread, and butter. This was followed by cheese (double Gloucestershire or cheddar), with pickled gooseberries or Normandy pippins. Dessert would have been pudding or *hardbake* (walnuts baked in molasses into a kind of sticky brittle) or currants accompanied by madeira, followed by tea sweetened with canned milk and sugar—and a spot of brandy.

At 7 P.M. the men could attend carefully planned classes in reading, writing, mathematics, geography, navigation, and astronomy. School books, spelling primers, pencils, and paper were listed in the ship's manifests. Occasionally there were amateur theatricals—anything to keep the men occupied. Officers adjourned to the Great Cabin to use its library, play chess, cards, or draughts, and enjoy a pipe or cigar.

At 9 P.M. the men unslung their hammocks, cocooned in their four blankets, and fitfully slept, tormented by the never-ending wind and shrieking ice outside. Officers returned to their tiny cabins, perhaps to read or write a little before dropping off to sleep.

If sleep could be found, a man might slumber an hour or two before waking, shivering with cold, wide-eyed to the explosions of the rupturing pack ice, or bitten by rats crawling under his blankets. Promptly at 6 A.M. the following day the eternal routine would resume.

# CHAPTER 14

# The Curse

*Nearly all men die of their remedies, and not their illnesses.*

—Molière

It could not have been long that autumn before the surgeons began seeing evidence of scurvy again: men calling sick with ulcerated gums, blood-blotched limbs, and pain and swelling in the joints. For reasons the surgeons did not understand, the daily issue of lemon juice—one ounce per man per day—was ineffective. They could not have known why: an ounce of fresh-squeezed lemon juice contains about 40 mg. of vitamin C, less than half the 90 to 100 mg. per day now considered minimum. What they did know was that the juice, stored in 5-gallon wooden kegs, lost its potency over time. The decline in strength was a common complaint. After only eighteen months in the Arctic in 1830, Sir John Ross reported the lemon juice "[v]ery weak, scarce half the strength approved." The surgeons knew that much (even today's pharmaceutically processed and well-packaged multivitamins have a maximum shelf life of only two years). They also knew that, unless something was done quickly, half the crews could be dead before spring.

They may have consulted Dr. Lind's *Treatise of the Scurvy* and *Essay on the Most Effectual Means of Preserving the Health of Seamen,* or Sir Gilbert Blane's *Observations on the Diseases of Seamen;* the books were among the 2,900 volumes aboard *Erebus* and *Terror.* Their first defense would have been to increase the daily dosage. But even doubling the dosage, weak as it had become, did nothing to stop the disease. However, one of the surgeons—either chief surgeons Stephen Stanley and John Peddie, or assistant surgeons Harry Goodsir and Alexander MacDonald—noticed that *something* in the crews' winter allowance did.

During the summer, the men were fed an unendingly monotonous diet of one pound of bread and 1¼ pounds of salt meat (either beef or pork) a day. With the exception of the lemon juice, each man got only one pint of peas and ¾ pound of barley a week. These were the sole antiscorbutics but for "Potatoes, Fresh, occasionally in place of barley" and "Vegetables, Fresh, as required for the soup," both of which were long since gone by the fall of 1846. In retrospect, it's fortunate that Arctic summers were so short (eight to twelve weeks); on this ration, most of the crew was certainly suffering from scurvy before winter.

But to conserve fuel in the darkest, coldest months, the Admiralty abruptly varied its victualling plan. As soon as the ships went into winter quarters, the flour ration was reduced by 25 percent to save the fuel necessary to bake bread. The rum ration was halved to prevent drunkenness (the men receiving ½ pint of ale or porter instead). The weekly issue of salt meat, a favorite of the crew, was cut by a fifth to save the fuel required to melt fresh water to soak it in and fry it. The issue of peas was halved, since it took an awful lot of cooking and fuel to make them palatable.

To make up for these sore-missed items, each man received 2 pounds of canned meat, 2¼ pounds of canned vegetables, and ¾ pound of canned vegetable soup a week. In addition, every day each man got 1 ounce of pickles (pickled cucumbers, cabbage, onions, or cranberries), 1 ounce of butter, and 2 ounces of cheese. Twice a week, on so-called flour days, every man also got 1 ounce of raisins or gooseberries in his flour pudding. Pickled salmon or herring was also issued at the captain's discretion.

Vitamin-wise, this made a day-and-night difference. Suddenly, the scurvy ceased to spread.

It was probably this that convinced the surgeons to treat canned meat, vegetables and soup, and pickled cabbages, onions, and cranberries as medicine rather than food. They went down easier and with less complaint than the bitter lemon juice. The men ate them greedily and, miraculously, began to get well almost at once.

Intuitively, without training, they had hit on something quite remarkable: the canned food, as well as the pickled vegetables and berries, were proof against scurvy. They somehow parsed this seemingly simple but confoundingly complex solution out themselves; despite the fact they were simple ships' surgeons and not doctors. In the nineteenth century, the distinction between the two was vast. Surgeons, who learned their trade by apprenticeship, were considered medical mechanics. They sawed off limbs, splinted broken bones, and bound up wounds—things more highly educated doctors did *not* do. Doctors administered drugs, lots of drugs, and were generally addressed as *doctor.* Surgeons, whatever their station, were dismissed as *mister.* The difference was plain.

Yet following the three deaths at Beechey Island, these simple surgeons suffered no more fatalities or serious disease for fourteen months; even locked in the pack ice with no resource beyond their own ingenuity. In an age long before preventive medicine was known, they appear to have practiced it exceedingly well. There is no other explanation for Commander Gore's "All well" message in the spring of 1847.

The men and ships had been kept scrupulously clean and free of lice, preventing typhus, commonly called "ship's fever." Though there must have been colds in plenty, not a man died of pneumonia or influenza. Amputations for frostbite may have been common, but no one died of gangrene. Besides scurvy, they somehow also managed to keep a Pandora's box of other deficiency diseases in check. These included nightblindness and xerophthalmia (due to lack of vitamin A), osteomalacia (softening of the bones, caused by lack of vitamin D and sunlight), pernicious anemia (lack of folic acid and vitamin $B_{12}$), abnormally long blood clotting (deficiency of vitamin K), and various degenerative nervous, digestive, and coronary diseases.

Miraculously in June of 1847, after ten months trapped in the pack ice, everyone was alive and well. During the summer of 1847 however, the surgeon's brilliantly improvised cure, for reasons beyond their or anyone else's understanding, became the expedition's curse.

# CHAPTER 15
# The Culprit

*In submitting this their Lordships will be pleased to observe that I foresaw . . . that delay would arise on the part of this contractor in making his deliveries.*

—Captain Superintendent, Deptford Victualling Yard

Like most evil men, Stephan Goldner would have passed unnoticed in a crowd. His frock coat, cravat, collar, and stovepipe hat disguised a void. Outwardly, he looked and played the part of a proper merchant. Behind the scenes, he pursued profit without conscience or qualm, with no regard for life. His manufactory was located on Houndsditch Road in London and the street name suggested something about the character of the man who operated it. No one remembers his fate. He simply vanished from Admiralty correspondence in 1852, seven years before anyone found evidence of his grotesque handiwork.

Goldner was one of dozens of victualling contractors vying for the business of provisioning Franklin's ships in 1845. The competition was particularly cutthroat. With no wars to fight or blockades to maintain and much of the Royal Navy demobilized, demand and prices had plummeted. In the scramble for the remaining business, the navy's "Discovery Service" contracts were golden and the richest of these, by far, were for polar voyages.

Most victualling contracts involved provisioning ships for four to six months. Arctic contracts involved provisioning ships for up to three years. Typical Admiralty tenders called for little more than salt meat (the navy yards baked their own biscuit), pickles (vegetables and fruits pickled in malt vinegar and brine), rum, and various sundries. Ships were expected to reprovision with fresh food at ports of call. Arctic expeditions, on the other hand, were expected to be completely self-sufficient for the full duration of their voyage, requiring a far greater variety of victuals in huge quantities. Arctic contracts called for not only more provisions, but a great many specially prepared, premium-priced ones.

Goldner competed brutally to win these contracts. He dealt in newly invented canned goods—meats, vegetables, soups, gravy, and milk. This was where profits were highest and, not incoincidentally, Admiralty oversight and knowledge of canning technology were negligible. He purveyed lower-profit bulk items, too, like salt meat, preserved apples, pickled cabbages, parsnips, and onions. But his specialty was his own line of patented, specially processed canned goods. "These provisions are free from the objectionable gaseous flavour so much complained of in those preserved by the old process," read his handbill, "and the very moderate prices at which they are sold, renders them advantageous for Home Consumption as well as Sea Stores."

He offered an astonishing variety. His handbill listed seven kinds of canned vegetables and fifteen different soups. In canned meats, he listed fourteen preparations of veal, thirteen kinds of beef, seven types of mutton, and four varieties of lamb. Also advertised were canned turkeys, geese, ducks, capons, and pigeons. The selection of game included guinea fowl, venison (haunch or hash), whole jugged hare, partridge, pheasant, grouse, ptarmigan, and rabbit (curried or in onion sauce). In seafood, he offered canned lobsters (in the shell), stewed eels, salmon steaks, cod, "real West Indian turtle," herring, and Yarmouth bloaters (mackerel, lightly salted and smoked).

The extravagant selections didn't end there. He carried a premium line of forty-five canned "French Dishes," ranging from beef a la Flamande and calf's tongue sauce piquant to truffled pheasant and teal en salmi. For condiments, he offered lobster, oyster, mushroom, and shrimp sauces.

To a nineteenth-century palate, this mouth-watering menu of delicacies, already prepared and warranted to keep indefinitely, must

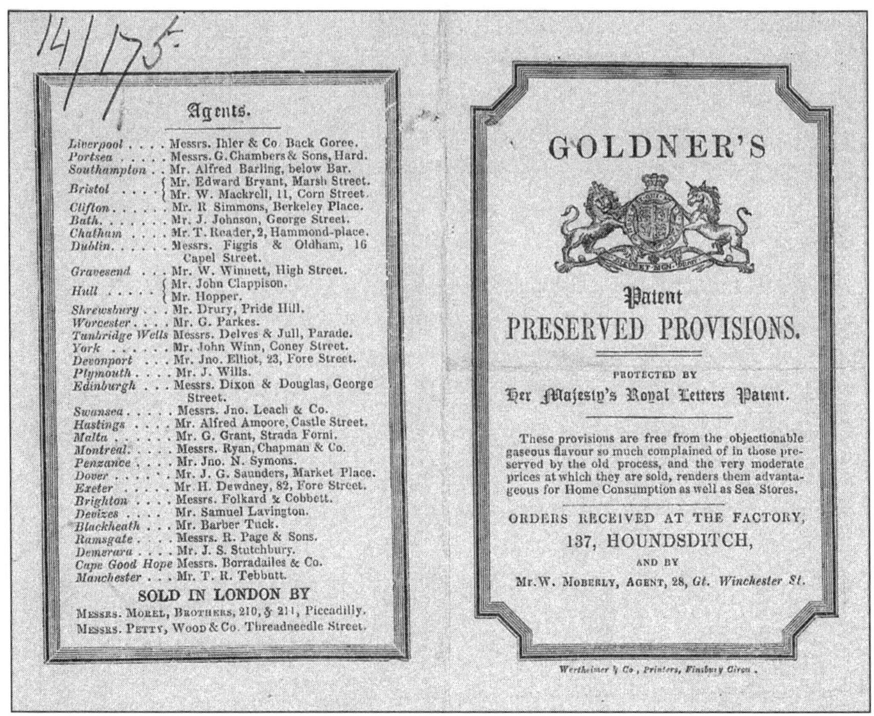

14/175

Agents.

Liverpool . . . . Messrs. Ihler & Co Back Goree.
Portsea . . . . . Messrs. G. Chambers & Sons, Hard.
Southampton . . Mr. Alfred Barling, below Bar.
Bristol . . . . Mr. Edward Bryant, Marsh Street. / Mr. W. Mackrell, 11, Corn Street.
Clifton . . . . . . Mr. R Simmons, Berkeley Place.
Bath. . . . . . . . Mr. J. Johnson, George Street.
Chatham . . . . Mr. T. Reader, 2, Hammond-place.
Dublin. . . . . . Messrs. Figgis & Oldham, 16 Capel Street.
Gravesend . . . Mr. W. Winnett, High Street.
Hull . . . . . Mr. John Clappison. / Mr. Hopper.
Shrewsbury . . . Mr. Drury, Pride Hill.
Worcester . . . . Mr. G. Parkes.
Tunbridge Wells Messrs. Delves & Jull, Parade.
York . . . . . . . Mr. John Winn, Coney Street.
Devonport . . . Mr. Jno. Elliot, 23, Fore Street.
Plymouth . . . . Mr. J. Wills.
Edinburgh . . . Messrs. Dixon & Douglas, George Street.
Swansea . . . . . Messrs. Jno. Leach & Co.
Hastings . . . . Mr. Alfred Amoore, Castle Street.
Malta . . . . . . . Mr. G. Grant, Strada Forni.
Montreal. . . . . Messrs. Ryan, Chapman & Co.
Penzance . . . . Mr. Jno. N. Symons.
Dover . . . . . . Mr. J. G. Saunders, Market Place.
Exeter . . . . . Mr. H. Dewdney, 82, Fore Street.
Brighton . . . . Messrs. Folkard & Cobbett.
Devizes . . . . Mr. Samuel Lavington.
Blackheath . . . Mr. Barber Tuck.
Ramsgate . . . . Messrs. R. Page & Sons.
Demerara . . . . Mr. J. S. Stutchbury.
Cape Good Hope Messrs. Borradailes & Co.
Manchester . . . Mr. T. R. Tebbutt.

SOLD IN LONDON BY

Messrs. Morel, Brothers, 210, & 211, Piccadilly.
Messrs. Petty, Wood & Co. Threadneedle Street.

GOLDNER'S

Patent

PRESERVED PROVISIONS.

PROTECTED BY

Her Majesty's Royal Letters Patent.

These provisions are free from the objectionable gaseous flavour so much complained of in those preserved by the old process, and the very moderate prices at which they are sold, renders them advantageous for Home Consumption as well as Sea Stores.

ORDERS RECEIVED AT THE FACTORY,
137, HOUNDSDITCH,
AND BY
Mr. W. Moberly, Agent, 28, *Gt. Winchester St.*

*Wertheimer & Co., Printers, Finsbury Circu.*

*The Culprit's Card* Stephan Goldner's business card, the one which won him the lucrative Admiralty contract to supply the Franklin expedition. On paper his operation—thirty-six sales agents and thirty-two locations stretching from Canada to England, to Malta and the Cape of Good Hope—appeared beyond reproach. His patented provisions were anything but. (Public Records Office, London, England)

have appeared fantastic. That, indeed, was Goldner's whole purpose in promoting it. Who could resist a 1-pound can of "Ox Cheeks & Vegetables" for 12 pence? Or hearty "Irish Stew" for 10 pence? Or a pound of carrots in a shiny can for just 6 pence? To casual buyers, this was all innocuous stuff; to crews in the Arctic, however, it literally meant the difference between life and death.

Like almost all victualling contractors of the time, Goldner practiced a shadowy, yet well-calculated, art of deceit. It was part and parcel of the business. Given that the Admiralty almost always chose

LIST OF PRICES OF GOLDNER'S PATENT PRESERVED PROVISIONS.

|  | s. | d. |
|---|---|---|
| **MILK.** | | |
| Milk . . . . per quart | 1 | 3 |
| Ditto . . . . per pint | 0 | 9 |
| Ditto . . . . per ½ pint | 0 | 6 |
| **SOUPS.** | | |
| Real Turtle . . per quart | 10 | 6 |
| Mock Turtle . . . . ,, | 2 | 2 |
| Ox Tail . . . . . ,, | 2 | 2 |
| Ox Cheek . . . . . ,, | 2 | 2 |
| Giblet . . . . . ,, | 2 | 2 |
| Hare . . . . . ,, | 2 | 6 |
| Vegetable ✗ . . . . ,, | 2 | 6 |
| Carrot ✗ . . . . ,, | 2 | 2 |
| Mulligatawny . . . ,, | 2 | 6 |
| Concentrated Gravy . ,, | 3 | 4 |
| Chicken Broth . . . ,, | 3 | 0 |
| Veal Broth . . . . ,, | 2 | 6 |
| Mutton Broth . . . ,, | 1 | 8 |
| Hotch Potch . . . . ,, | 2 | 0 |
| Soup and Bouilli . pr. lb. | 0 | 8 |
| Ditto from 6 lbs. upwds. ,, | 0 | 6 |
| **VEGETABLES.** | | |
| Green Peas . . . pr. lb. | 1 | 0 |
| Onions ✗ . . . . . ,, | 0 | 10 |
| Carrots and Gravy . . ,, | 0 | 10 |
| Carrots, plain . . . ,, | 0 | 6 |
| Turnips . . . . . ,, | 0 | 10 |
| Beet Root ✗ . . . . ,, | 0 | 6 |
| Parsnips . . . . . ,, | 0 | 7 |
| **BEEF.** | | |
| Roast Beef . . . pr. lb. | 1 | 0 |
| Spiced Beef . . . . ,, | 1 | 0 |
| Boiled Beef . . . . ,, | 0 | 10 |
| Boiled Round do. . . ,, | 1 | 0 |
| Stewed Beef . . . . ,, | 0 | 9 |
| Ditto from 6 to 16 lbs. ,, | 0 | 7½ |
| Ditto from 16 lbs. upwds. ,, | 0 | 7 |
| Rump Steaks Stewed . ,, | 1 | 2 |
| Stewed Brisket of Beef ,, | 0 | 10 |
| Beef Alamode . . . ,, | 0 | 10 |
| Gulyas Beef . . . . ,, | 1 | 0 |
| Ox Tongue . . . . each | 6 | 6 |
| Tripe and Onions pr. lb. | 1 | 0 |
| Ox cheek and vegetables ,, | 1 | 0 |
| Russian Tongues . each | 4 | 0 |
| **MUTTON.** | | |
| Roast Mutton . . pr. lb | 1 | 0 |
| Roast Leg of Mutton . ,, | 1 | 0 |

|  | s. | d. |
|---|---|---|
| Boiled Mutton per. lb. | 0 | 10 |
| Boiled Leg of Mutton ,, | 1 | 0 |
| Hashed Mutton . ,, | 0 | 10 |
| Haricot Mutton . ,, | 1 | 0 |
| Irish Stew . . ,, | 0 | 10 |
| **LAMB.** | | |
| Roast Lamb per lb. | 1 | 6 |
| Roast Leg of Lamb ,, | 1 | 6 |
| Stewed Lamb and Vegetables. . ,, | 1 | 3 |
| Lamb and Green Peas | 1 | 4 |
| **VEAL.** | | |
| Roast Veal . pr. lb. | 1 | 2 |
| Roast Fillet of Veal ,, | 1 | 6 |
| Knuckle of Veal ,, | 1 | 2 |
| Stewed Veal and Vegetables . . ,, | 1 | 2 |
| Veal and Green Peas | 1 | 4 |
| Veal Cutlets . . ,, | 1 | 6 |
| Minced Veal . . ,, | 1 | 6 |
| Veal Collops . . ,, | 1 | 6 |
| Calf's Head . . ,, | 1 | 0 |
| Ditto and Bacon . ,, | 1 | 6 |
| Ditto Hashed, with Bacon and Brains ,, | 1 | 6 |
| Calf's Brains . . ,, | 1 | 6 |
| Calf's Feet and Jelly ,, | 1 | 0 |
| Curried Veal . ,, | 1 | 4 |
| **PORK.** | | |
| Pork Cutlets pr. lb. | 1 | 6 |
| Sucking Pig . 12s. to | 15 | 0 |
| Hams . . . pr. lb. | 1 | 2 |
| **POULTRY.** | | |
| Turkeys, Roasted or Boiled each 7s. to | 15 | 0 |
| Geese, Roasted | 9 | 0 |
| Ducks, Roast. ea. 4s. to | 4 | 6 |
| Do. and Green Peas | 5 | 0 |
| Fowls, Roasted or Boiled ea. 3s. 6d. ,, | 5 | 6 |
| Dorking Capons each | 6 | 6 |
| Pigeons, Roasted, per couple | 2 | 0 |
| Ditto and Green Peas ,, | 3 | 0 |
| Pigeons, Steak & Giblets for Pies . per case. | 3 | 0 |

|  | s. | d. |
|---|---|---|
| **MADE DISHES.** | | |
| Ragout of Goose, pr. lb. | 1 | 6 |
| Ditto of Turkey ,, | 1 | 6 |
| Ditto of Fowl . ,, | 2 | 0 |
| Ditto of Mutton ,, | 1 | 2 |
| Ditto of Veal . ,, | 1 | 4 |
| Ditto of Lamb . ,, | 1 | 4 |
| Ditto of Giblets ,, | 1 | 6 |
| Curried Fowls, each | 7 | 6 |
| **GAME.** | | |
| Guinea Fowls each | 6 | 0 |
| Venison, Haunch 3l. to 5l. | | |
| Venison, Hashed pr. lb. | 2 | 0 |
| Hare, Roasted, each | 6 | 0 |
| Hare, Jugged, pr. lb. | 2 | 0 |
| Partridges, Roasted ea. | 2 | 6 |
| Pheasant, Roasted ,, | 6 | 0 |
| Grouse, Roasted ,, | 3 | 6 |
| Ptarmigan, do . ,, | 3 | 0 |
| Black Game, do. ,, | 6 | 0 |
| Wild Duck, do. ,, | 3 | 0 |
| Rabbit, Curried pr. lb | 1 | 6 |
| Rabbits with Onion Sauce . . . ,, | 1 | 6 |
| **FISH.** | | |
| Real W.I. Turtle, Calipash and Calipee ,, | 10 | 6 |
| Ditto Steaks . . ,, | 5 | 0 |
| Salmon . . . ,, | 1 | 3 |
| Cod Fish . . . ,, | 1 | 6 |
| Stewed Eels . . ,, | 2 | 0 |
| Lobsters in Shell ,, | 3 | 6 |
| Fresh Herrings . ,, | 1 | 6 |
| Yarmouth Bloaters ,, | 1 | 6 |
| Cod Sounds . . ,, | 1 | 6 |
| **SAUCE.** | | |
| Lobsters for Sauce pr. pt | 2 | 6 |
| Ditto . per ½ pint | 1 | 6 |
| Oysters . . per pint | 2 | 0 |
| Ditto . per ½ pint | 1 | 3 |
| Mushrooms . per pint | 2 | 6 |
| Shrimps . . . . ,, | 2 | 0 |
| **FRENCH DISHES.** | | |
| Beef, à la Flamande pr. lb | 2 | 0 |
| Beef a la Royal . ,, | 2 | 6 |
| Ox Palate . . . ,, | 3 | 0 |
| Ditto Italian . . ,, | 3 | 3 |
| Ditto with Peas . ,, | 3 | 0 |
| Tendrons of Veal . ,, | 3 | 0 |

|  | s. | d. |
|---|---|---|
| Ragout of Veal . . pr lb. | 2 | 0 |
| Veal Cutlets Jardinière ,, | 2 | 0 |
| Ditto with Peas . ,, | 2 | 6 |
| Ditto Tomata . ,, | 2 | 6 |
| Ditto Italian . ,, | 2 | 0 |
| Sweetbread . . per case | 6 | 0 |
| Minced Veal . . . pr. lb. | 2 | 6 |
| Noix de Veau . . . . ,, | 2 | 0 |
| Fricandeau . . . . . ,, | 3 | 0 |
| Calf's Tongue Sauce Piquante | 3 | 0 |
| Calf's Tongue with Peas . ,, | 3 | 0 |
| Ditto Smoked . . . . ,, | 3 | 0 |
| Mutton Cutlets, Tomata . ,, | 2 | 6 |
| Ditto Italian . ,, | 2 | 0 |
| Ditto Jardinière ,, | 2 | 0 |
| Ditto with Peas ,, | 2 | 6 |
| Ragout of Mutton . . . ,, | 2 | 0 |
| Lamb Cutlets, Jardinière ,, | 2 | 6 |
| Ditto Italian . . ,, | 2 | 6 |
| Ditto Tomata . . ,, | 2 | 6 |
| Ditto with Peas . ,, | 2 | 6 |
| Leg & Shldr. of Lamb braised ,, | 2 | 0 |
| Ragout of Lamb . . . ,, | 2 | 0 |
| Kidney Sauté . . . . ,, | 2 | 6 |
| Pheasant . . . . . each | 8 | 0 |
| Ditto Truffled . . . ,, | 15 | 0 |
| Partridge . . . . . ,, | 3 | 0 |
| Suprème of Fowl per case | 12 | 0 |
| Fricaseed Fowls . . pr. lb. | 2 | 6 |
| Duck and Peas . . each | 6 | 6 |
| Teal en Salmi . per case | 6 | 0 |
| Grouse en Salmi . . ,, | 6 | 0 |
| Partridge en Salmi . ,, | 6 | 0 |
| Pheasant en Salmi . . ,, | 8 | 0 |
| Green Peas . . . . ,, | 2 | 0 |
| *2d. extra charged for 1lb cases on French Dishes.* | | |
| Grouse Soup . . per quart | 3 | 6 |
| Superior Turtle Soup . ,, | 15 | 0 |
| Clear ditto . . . . ,, | 21 | 0 |
| Julienne . . . . . ,, | 3 | 0 |
| **POTTED MEATS.** | | |
| Potted Beef . . . pr. lb. | 3 | 0 |
| Do Veal . . . ,, | 3 | 0 |
| Do Giblets . . . ,, | 3 | 0 |
| Do Tongues . . ,, | 3 | 0 |
| Do Ham . . . ,, | 3 | 0 |
| Do Shrimps . . ,, | 4 | 0 |
| Do Lobsters . . ,, | 4 | 0 |

*The above can be had in Canisters containing from 1lb to 500lbs. each.* One penny extra charged for 1lb. cases.

*Recipe for Disaster* The flip side of Goldner's card touted the variety and low cost of his canned goods. In fact, the variety was an invention and the quality a cruel illusion. Men would eventually be poisoned and starve as a result of his reckless profiteering. (Public Records Office, London, England)

the low bidder, the only way to win contracts and still pocket a profit was to cut corners. Horseflesh was often substituted for beef, which is why, in seaman's slang, it was called *salt horse* and the barrel it came from a *harness cask*. Sawdust was added to flour and sugar was cut with sand. Cheese was mixed with saltpeter for bulk; sometimes it was colored orange with hemlock (a bit served as dye, too much was deadly). Salt pork contained everything but the squeal: "the cheeks, ears, feet and other offal of the hog were thrown in as part of the men's allowance," complained one navy captain, "bones, crag-ends, souse and hog's feet." Rotten produce was frequently packed into the bottom of barrels with fresh packed on top; pickled in vinegar, after a few months at sea, no one could tell the difference. Spices—salt, pepper, curry—were replaced by gunpowder, which answered for all three. Coffee and cocoa, if not specified to be furnished in the whole bean, could easily be adulterated with iron filings or dirt to add weight. There were hundreds of ways to cut corners; and a clever fellow, practiced in the victualler's trade, could do it with little risk, blame spoilage on other factors, and get away with it.

Goldner was more clever than most and canned goods provided the perfect subterfuge. Once sealed, his patented canned provisions—except for the samples forwarded to the navy—were impervious to inspection. In the days before food labeling, Goldner could put whatever he wanted into his cans, call it anything he liked, and sell it for as much as the market would bear. Consequently, his "Veal Cutlets Tomata," which sold for 30 pence a pound, could've been identical to his "Veal Cutlets Italian," which sold for 24. Likewise, his "Real Turtle Soup," for which he charged an amazing 126 pence per quart, could easily be sold as his "Superior Clear Turtle Soup," which earned him twice as much. His high-priced "French Dishes" were, in all likelihood, identical to his lower-priced beef, veal, and lamb dishes, except for the label.

Goldner played the same name game with his more pedestrian canned goods too—the ones in which the navy was primarily interested. "Stewed Beef," for which he charged 9 pence per pound, could be relabeled "Stewed Rump Steaks" and sold for 14 pence per pound. Cans labeled "Roast Veal" brought him 14 pence per pound; called "Roast Fillet of Veal," it earned him 20. His canned "Beef Alamode" (sic) retailed for 10 pence per pound; labeled "Roast Beef" or "Spiced Beef" it commanded 12 pence per pound. No one knew the difference. It was the perfect scam.

This deceit, while seemingly a matter of pennies, increased Goldner's gross on many items from 50 to as much as 200 percent. These were his golden eggs. His golden goose was minimizing costs by any and every nefarious means he could devise. Since almost everything sold to the Admiralty was priced by the pound, cans were weighted with bone, gristle, even gravel, and charged off as meat. Soups could be made largely of water and thickened with alum. The contents could be undercooked, or not cooked at all, saving money on fuel and labor. Seams on the cans themselves could be half-soldered, cutting time and expense. The angles were virtually endless and Goldner played them all.

He was scrupulous about only one thing: maintaining what was as clearly recognized in the nineteenth century as in the twentieth—credible deniability. All his Admiralty correspondence was couched in carefully worded generalities. Quantities of deliverables were seldom specified; phrases like "the greater part of the order" or "a portion" were used instead. Delivery dates were kept suitably vague ("within a week") and all commitments carefully modified ("I will engage to deliver a part by the 13th."). All correspondence was meticulously scrubbed of culpability. Everything, even his personal letters, was carefully dictated to his personal secretary, Mister Richie, and everything bore Richie's signature, not his own.

Goldner was an almost completely unknown supplier to the Admiralty. He'd emigrated to England in 1839, noting upon his application for naturalization that he was a subject of the Hungarian Empire, from the outermost realm of the empire, near modern-day Presov, Slovakia, deep in the Carpathian Mountains. Like many other newly arrived eastern European immigrants, he took up residence in the Whitechapel slums. He gave his occupation as "preserved meat merchant." This was a pedestrian, rather vile occupation: buying animals "on the hoof," slaughtering them, rendering them into pieces, impregnating the meat with salt to retard spoilage, putting it up in casks, and selling the product quickly. It was not a business calculated to make a man rich.

But in 1841, Goldner, alive to the greater profits to be made in canned foods, applied for and was granted Patent No. 8873 for "a period of 14 years . . . in all Her Majesty's Dominions." His was a new, untried method for canning food. "Animal and vegetable matter," read the patent, "are to be preserved by burning off the atmospherics in water boiling at 212 degrees . . . [with a] solution of nitrate of soda . . . to raise the temperature to 250 degs F." By chemically boosting the cooking temperature, cooking time was reduced—accelerating production and, not incoincidentally, lowering cost. Unlike previous methods, Goldner's canned foods were not cooked in stoves directly over wood or coal fires. The cans were placed in shallow troughs of chemically treated water heated by steam pipes. Goldner's promotion of this process caught the Admiralty's attention. His primary competitor—the firm of Donkin, Hall & Gamble, which first patented the tin plate can—had comfortably been supplying the Admiralty small quantities of canned provisions since 1830. But Goldner's provisions were markedly cheaper than Donkin, Hall & Gamble's, his patented process seemed more advanced, and his ability to deliver large quantities within very short timeframes was impressive.

On paper, he ran a large organization. In addition to his factory in Houndsditch, he also operated a cannery in Galatz, Moldavia—far from the prying eyes of Admiralty inspectors. From these two factories, he swiftly built a steady trade with the Admiralty. He employed thirty-six sales agents, all on commission, at every major port in England, Scotland, and Wales. He also had agents working for him in Dublin, Montreal, British Guyana, Malta, Capetown in South Africa, and Devonport in modern-day Tasmania. These, his low prices, and the high quality of his product, he advertised heavily. His factories and his patented technique for processing, canning, and preserving food, were kept very much a secret— with very good reason.

To win contracts, he routinely underbid, over-promised, and then covered over the discrepancy. To win the canned food contract for the Franklin Expedition, he outdid himself. The tender was massive; one of the largest the Admiralty had made up to that time for preserved provisions. It requested bids on 9,500 cans of meat and vegetables in rigorously specified 1-, 2-, 4-, 6-, and 8-pound cans and more than 20,000 cans of soup in 1-pound containers. The deadline was just as stunning. At a time when "producing 60 'hole and cap' cans a day was considered good output" for the most accomplished tinsmith, the Admiralty wanted *everything* delivered in less than sixty days.

This alone caused a number of victuallers to drop out of the bidding altogether. Of the four firms who made offers—Cooper & Aves, Gamble, Hogarth, and Goldner—Goldner was, by far, the lowest, most voracious bidder. In fact, on most items his bid was *half* that of his competitors. What's more, while his competitors quoted delivery times of two to four weeks, incredible as that seemed, Goldner promised "immediate" delivery. Not two days, not one, but immediate delivery. He threw in crating and drayage for free.

It was too good a deal for the navy to resist. In fact, it was too good a deal to be true. Ironically, Goldner was awarded the contract for canned provisions on April 1, 1845—April's Fool Day—barely a month and a half before the expedition was scheduled to sail. Altogether it was valued at over 3,800 pounds (U.S. $255,000 by today's values), a huge sum for its time and more than enough to turn Goldner a very rich profit.

In the rush to get to sea, no one at the Admiralty examined any of the particulars of Goldner's bid, only his bottom line quote. If they'd market-priced the foodstuffs, they would have seen at once they amounted to more than 26 percent of his bid. If they'd been familiar with the materials and labor involved in canning at the time, they would have been shocked to discover they amounted to almost 80 percent of Goldner's bid. Digging further, they would have found that coal for cooking fires, laborers to tend them, and cooks to supervise the process, accounted for about 14 percent more. Goldner's other costs—rent, transport of goods to and from the factory, production equipment, tools—were not considered, nor were his motives.

It should have been evident that it was a money-losing proposition from the start and, equally evident, begged the question why Goldner proposed it in the first place. The only person who expressed any suspicion was Commander Fitzjames, who wondered why the Admiralty awarded the contract to an unknown supplier simply because he'd quoted the lowest price. How Goldner planned to turn any profit on the transaction was never asked. That was his business, or misfortune. The Victualling Department had got all it asked for.

# CHAPTER 16

# Houndsditch

*On opening some [of the tins], the meat was found to be bad, cannisters defective, the meat effervescing and a great nuisance.*

—Deptford Victualling Yard
Returns Report, HMS *Lady Franklin* and HMS *Sophia*

Goldner's factory was located at 137 Houndsditch Road in Whitechapel: the blackest slum in London's East End. Whitechapel was notorious for its appalling squalor and wretched overcrowding. Its twisted streets were lined with tall, narrow "rookeries," dilapidated tenements housing two or three families to a room, and fetid rooming houses where filthy straw-filled ticks could be rented by the night—or, by prostitutes, by the hour. In the rabbit warren of its dingy alleys, there were an astounding number of beer houses and gin mills and an astonishing number of drunks. By day, the manure and garbage-heaped cobblestone streets teemed with the foulest characters of Dickensian England—rag gatherers, bone-grubbers, rat catchers, and pure finders (who eked out a miserable living scouring the streets for alkaline-rich dog droppings to sell to tanneries). At night, the back alleys and dark entrances were haunted by prostitutes grown so haggard and hideous they could find trade nowhere else. In turn, they and their customers were terrorized by swarms of pickpockets, muggers, and thieves.

It was no accident Goldner set up shop in Whitechapel; both the location and its poverty were perfect for his purpose. The dockyards were nearby, keeping delivery costs of his goods to a bare minimum.

Rent for the abandoned brick warehouse he grandly called a manufactory was next to nothing. The poor provided an abundant source of labor willing to work under the worst conditions, for any wage, without complaint. Just as important, Whitechapel wasn't the sort of neighborhood where the Admiralty's officers and gentlemen were likely to call, and Houndsditch wasn't easy to find. To the contrary, Goldner never voluntarily opened it to inspection. Unvisited and undisturbed, he was free to go about the serious business at hand—defrauding the navy on virtually every term of his contract.

Short of financial ruin and professional suicide, there was no other course for him to take, which troubled him not a particle. The contract was, quite obviously, impossible to meet any other way; not at the prices and delivery times he'd quoted. Those, as Goldner designed, had merely been bait dangled to hook the order. Getting the Admiralty to bite had been ridiculously simple. Keeping the fish hooked and bringing it into the boat were where his real artifice came into play. It had to be done so skillfully that the fish would never know it had been caught. And no one in the shadowy victualler's trade, none of the swindlers or confidence men in Whitechapel, played a mark more coolly or more audaciously than Stephan Goldner. He was both daring and cunning.

His first gambit was to totally ignore the one thing that won him the contract in the first place: *immediate* delivery. He delivered *nothing* whatsoever for a month. Defaulting on the contract, before the ink on it dried, was as dangerous as it was risky. Goldner bet everything that the navy wouldn't call his hand, at least for a few critical weeks. If it did, he was finished, for he had nothing to deliver. If it did not, without time or possibility of finding another supplier to take his place on similar terms before the expedition sailed, he rightly guessed there was nothing the navy could do about it. He played the game with perfect sangfroid. But he wasted not a minute in the interim. Unscrupulously, he went about defrauding the navy on a scale as massive as the contract itself—beginning with the cans.

Canning was then in its relative infancy. The first English canning factory had opened in Bermondsey, London, about thirty years earlier (operated by Donkin & Gamble), but the technology and

*The Expedition's Curse* One of Goldner's cans, brought back from the Arctic. Over 3,000 of these were found on Beechey Island, where the expedition spent its first winter. At that time, with coal abundant, the toxins within them were boiled away. (National Maritime Museum, Greenwich, England)

process were by no means well understood, perfected, or systematic. There was no machinery for fabricating tin plate cans, no automation whatever. Each can was made by hand. To do it right was very much a craft, which required skilled tinsmiths (called plumbers), forges, forms, specialized tools, and copious quantities of sheet iron, lead, tin, arsenic, borax, and coal—expenses which were surely anathema to Goldner. To make each can involved an exacting, sixteen-step process and considerable time, of which Goldner had none to spare. Fabricating 29,500 cans, in five custom sizes in less than forty-nine days, which was what he'd contracted to do, would have been almost impossible.

There were only two conceivable ways for him to do this. The first, for a man like Goldner, was completely out of the question. He could hire an army of tinsmiths and work them around the clock. This, of course, would have cost him too dear. Skilled plumbers, who could cut and bend tin to exacting specifications, accurately mix and melt solder for proper wetting and hardening, and properly solder seams, didn't come cheap. They were paid a half crown a day (about U.S. $8.50 in present-day terms) and Goldner would have needed more than a hundred of them.

There was another way, eminently practical, if altogether unethical, which was much more to his liking. Less skilled (in some cases unskilled) workers could be used. They could be got for one shilling a day (roughly U.S. $3.40 today), and there were hordes of them, eager for any work they could get. The product wouldn't be anywhere near equal to that made by real plumbers, but there'd be more of it, gotten up faster, at a fraction of the cost—and nothing in Goldner's contract specified using plumbers in the first place.

Production could further be speeded up by changing some details of his canning process. As Goldner correctly calculated, the Admiralty, fully occupied with other matters, never studied or closely examined it. Consequently, the process could be adapted however he saw fit; nothing serious or outwardly obvious, of course, just little things. The critical joining surfaces—where the sides, tops, and bottoms of the tins came together—did not necessarily have to be cleaned and coated with borax to make a bond before they were soldered together. More arsenic could be added to the lead solder; it hardened faster that way, even if it made the weld somewhat spotty. One did not necessarily have to wait for one seam of solder to cool before applying the next. In fact, the seams themselves did not really need to be sealed on both the inside and the outside of the can; just the visible, outside seam was sufficient. Neither was it imperative they be sealed their full length: the flanged tops and bottoms of the cans would hide any unsoldered areas and, once the cans had been painted, no one would be the wiser.

Each of these shortcuts meant profit for Goldner, but had potentially disastrous consequences for the expedition. If the bonds didn't hold the solder, if they were not given time to set, or if all seams weren't fully sealed, the cans were very likely to rupture. This was, in fact, a common fault of tin plate cans at the time. It plagued the French explorer Jules D'Urville on his 1837–1840 Antarctic expedition. Of over 300 meat tins embarked, 213 were found "putrid" and "foul-smelling" because "the drums exploded; the gas having escaped through the seams, they finally burst." The stuff was thrown overboard and the crews were reduced to a scurvy diet that incapacitated half of them and killed a quarter. Mixing too much arsenic with the solder speeded production but added another lethal toxin to the already dangerously high lead content (up to 90 percent) in the solder itself. Either of these, contaminating the food, was potentially fatal.

But all these mechanical shortcuts—and Goldner appeared to have used them all—still didn't come close to producing the number of cans required; especially the small, hard-to-make, 1-pound cans that constituted almost 70 percent of the order. The only practical way to do that was to reduce the number of cans altogether. Goldner did this very cagily, coolly waiting until the Admiralty got almost frantic about its overdue shipments, then begging its permission to deliver "a portion" of the order in cans larger than the contract called for to "ensure greater dispatch."

This was classic bait-and-switch. The Admiralty tender strictly specified over 20,000 1-pound cans. Bigger cans, of course, meant far fewer were needed. What's more, the bigger ones were faster, easier, and cheaper to make. Goldner very specifically avoided mention of what "portion" of the order he planned to deliver in larger cans or how much larger they would be. It was only learned later that virtually *none* of the order consisted of 1-pound cans. Goldner substituted much larger and cheaper 9-pound and in some cases 12-pound cans in their stead. Just as specifically, he never offered the Admiralty a refund on the original number contracted for. He merely held out the carrot of delivery "with greater dispatch." He knew precisely which of his customer's buttons to push: "Immediate delivery" helped win him the contract initially and the same carrot worked again. The Admiralty agreed.

For Goldner, it was another bet won. He had smugly violated almost every term of his contract regarding the cans. He had not provided the number of cans agreed upon, he had not provided them in the sizes specified, and he had not provided immediate delivery. He had wormed his way clear of accountability for those three aspects of his contract, yet he still held the Admiralty to the price.

But fabricating the cans was only the first dilemma Goldner faced. He had contracted to provide "fresh" beef, mutton, veal, and ox cheeks plus potatoes, carrots, parsnips, cucumbers, cabbage, onions, mixed vegetables, and cranberries. Simply procuring the raw materials—over 90 tons of it (prior to processing)—in less than a month would have been difficult. Most livestock at the time was typically slaughtered in the autumn, after it fattened in summer pastures and when cooler temperatures helped prevent spoilage of the meat. It brought higher prices then and spared the owners the expense of feed throughout the winter. All that was left for Goldner to purchase that spring was the gleanings of the fall kill; none of it was prime or fresh, but meat already half a year old, salted and decomposing. Any live animals slaughtered that spring, after a winter on lean forage, were likely thin, undernourished, and tough. This fit Goldner right down to his boots: it could all be got at bargain prices.

Considering the season (early April), fresh vegetables, in the quantities Goldner needed, would have been virtually impossible to come by. Most fields were still fast-frozen and covered with snow melt. Cold-cellar stores—sprouting potatoes, limp carrots, half-frozen parsnips, cabbages and onions—were the best he could hope to get.

Quickly transporting such quantities from all over England, or from the continent, posed another cost and a logistical nightmare. Produce and animals would have necessarily come from dozens of sources and, whatever Goldner's agents purchased at the source, its value diminished with every day on the road. Winter-weakened animals, driven on the hoof, lost more weight. Winter-worn vegetables, packed in wagons, likely rotted more on the way to Goldner's factory. Everything moved only as fast as horses could drag it. Little of it arrived at Houndsditch in time and none of it all at once, necessitating storage and further spoilage, until it did.

Considering the immense deadline pressure, it's doubtful Goldner even tried to source food properly. There was obviously little time for that, but there were ways around it. Any meat he could procure cheaply and quickly enough—horses and mules included, it did not matter—was bought locally. When live animals and whole produce couldn't be found at Goldner's price, there was no shortage of alternative sources in Whitechapel. Meat could be scrounged from *secondhand* meat shops, which resold the scraps, offal, and garbage of the wealthy to the poor. Leavings from slaughterhouses and tanneries, putrefying and rotten, could be had for a pittance. Word could be put out to night armies of bone grubbers to fetch loads of bone and gristle to Houndsditch. Legions of costermongers (fruit and vegetable peddlers) could be alerted to bring in whatever produce they couldn't sell and any remnants—peelings, tops, and roots—they could find.

Goldner's problems did not end there. Preparing such enormous quantities of food, in so little time, precluded much preparation at all, none of it careful, sanitary, or systematic. Everything was bedlam. Bawling livestock (cattle, pigs, sheep) was packed shoulder-to-shoulder in pens, foul with manure and urine. Wagons dumped heaps of vegetables, meat scraps, and bones anywhere convenient, at all hours of the day and night. All of it sat untended, unrefrigerated, exposed to flies, rats, roaches, pigeons, and coal dust, until common laborers, as filthy as Whitechapel, could haul it inside. Behind the brick walls of 137 Houndsditch, it was frantically made ready.

Processing food on an industrial scale, even today, is an exceptionally messy, bloody, dirty business. Safety regulations are lax, compliance mostly voluntary, and inspections frighteningly few and infrequent (it's estimated less than 10 percent of the U.S. food supply undergoes federal inspection). Even with today's understanding of dangerous foodborne bacteria, sanitary measures to prevent their spread, and monitoring by the USDA's Food Safety and Inspection Service, every one second someone in the United States gets sick from eating contaminated food.[1] According to the Council for Agricultural Science and Technology, as many as 33 million Americans suffer from poisoning from foodborne pathogens every year. The U.S. Centers for Disease Control and Prevention puts the number at up to 80 million. Globally, the World Health Organization estimates that foodborne diseases may be 300 to 350 times more frequent than the reported number of cases tend to indicate—sickening up to 10 percent of the world's population. Although foodborne illness most often results from improper food handling, many of the pathogens that are its cause are present at the processing stage.

In 1845, food processing was in the Dark Ages. And Goldner, in pinching pennies and cutting corners, created conditions that, even by nineteenth-century standards, were appalling. To be fair, no one at the time had any inkling of the biohazards involved in food processing. But he certainly knew stinking meat from fresh, whole vegetables from peelings, and bone, animal hair, mold, and rat droppings when he saw them. Even if he did not venture out of his tiny paper-filled office, he could hardly have avoided smelling them. But, to Goldner, it looked and smelled like money. What he couldn't see or smell was the fact that Houndsditch was a bacterial and viral Chernobyl approaching meltdown.

Inevitably, food processing on an industrial scale produces bacteria on an industrial scale. In hacking apart animals and produce teeming with bacteria, either benign or pathogenic, that bacteria is released. Its sole object is to go on living. With a billion years' more survival experience than humans have, bacteria is exceedingly hard, if not sometimes nearly impossible, to kill.

Its first course is to reproduce itself on a massive basis. Massive is an understatement. Under favorable conditions, a single-celled microorganism can divide once every thirty minutes. After fifteen hours—about the length of a laborer's shift in Goldner's factory—it can produce roughly *one billion* offspring, more than enough to

[1] Council for Agricultural Science and Technology, 1998.

guarantee its survival. If conditions are unfavorable for reproduction, it builds itself a spore—a shell-like hull remarkably resistant to temperature, moisture, and the passage of time. In the 1986 autopsy conducted by Dr. Owen Beattie on one of the three Franklin crewmen buried in the permafrost at Beechey Island, *Clostridium* spores were found in the intestines. These spores—after 140 years—were cultured and brought back to life. Although not *Clostridium botulinum,* the finding demonstrated that this type of bacteria had survived quite comfortably all that time, dormant in its hosts.

There was a galaxy of pathogenic and potentially toxic bacteria in the penned livestock and mountains of rotting vegetable matter awaiting processing at Goldner's factory. Indeed, as the food was processed in unrefrigerated, unsanitary conditions, it represented what microbiologists would now term an almost ideal biological-growth medium—a bacterial banquet for some very unwelcome guests. Undoubtedly there was *salmonella* present in the intestines and feces of livestock; almost 2,000 serotypes of it cause food poisoning in humans. Goldner's unwashed workers almost certainly contaminated food with *shigellosis,* which causes bloody dysentery. Everything likely teemed with *Staphylococcus aureus,* another virulent bacterium that thrives in unrefrigerated foods and produces hundreds and thousands of food poisoning cases in the United States each year. In vegetables and animals alike, there were also undoubtedly present various species of *Clostridium* bacterium, whose deadliest form causes botulism poisoning.

All that this bacterial tidal wave was waiting for was a way out. Stephan Goldner's unskilled laborers not only provided it, they added to it in rivers. By twentieth-century definition, Goldner's workers would be considered slave laborers. Dirty, sickly, vermin-infested and malnourished, they were as rich a biological-growth medium for pathogens as were the sloppily slaughtered livestock and rotting vegetables, perhaps more so. The typical laborers Goldner hired to handle food had but two characteristics: they were desperate for work at any wage and desperately filthy. Like thousands of England's poor in the Industrial Revolution, they had flocked to London looking for whatever work they could get, only to find there was no work. To the illiterate, unskilled, and starving, a laborer's place at Mister Goldner's manufactory beckoned like salvation.

For fourpence a night, a laborer took lodgings in a rooming house within walking distance of the factory, where a flea-filled mattress in an unlit, unheated room was shared with up to twelve other strangers. At night, the stuffy, windowless room echoed with snoring, sneezing, and coughing men spreading an infectious blanket of tuberculosis, influenza, and pneumonia. But he didn't know that, he only knew he was out of the rain, with a job to go to in the morning. He had long since grown used to lice and fleas. He had no idea they carried bacteria that caused typhus and plague; they were merely companions of poverty. He scratched the bites and fungal rashes on his skin with his dirt-encrusted fingernails until they scabbed over. He never thought of bathing; there was no soap or facilities for that.

There was a single, communal privy in the back alley, so his hands and unwashed clothing were contaminated not only with his own fecal matter but everyone else's, too. More than likely, bacteria in this fecal matter gave him diarrhea. If he was fastidious, he rinsed his hands and face at the public water pump. But the untreated water was crawling with *Vibrio cholerae* (cholera) and other pathogenic bacteria that wouldn't be identified for another hundred years.

In the predawn darkness, he trudged to work. The hours Goldner demanded—5 A.M. to 7 P.M.—were long, but longer hours meant more pay and, at a food manufactory, the chance to pocket a cragend of meat or turnip top to quiet his growling stomach. On a cold spring morning in 1845, he entered 137 Houndsditch Road, his thin-soled shoes gummy with bacteria-laden horse manure. Along with other laborers, he stood in the factory yard, cap in hand, while a foreman assigned tasks. He was told nothing of Mister Goldner's patented process or much of anything else. Wiping his dripping nose on his sleeve, he was detailed to chop up quarters of fresh-slaughtered beef.

He was handed a greasy cleaver and put behind a wood-planked table. Almost at once, a quarter of bloody, still quivering beef was dropped in front of him. It smelled bad—the rusty, ironlike smell of congealing blood mixed with the overpowering and unmistakable stench of excrement. In fact, it had been slaughtered so quickly and sloppily, excrement from its intestines and excrement-covered hairs from its hide were all over it. A few whacks of the cleaver showed it was dull, but Goldner provided few tools and no time to sharpen it. Knowing nothing about butchering, he chopped; driving hundreds of thousands of pathogenic bacteria spores into the meat. The pieces were tossed into an uncovered holding barrel of cold brine, supposedly to preserve it until it could be cooked. The weak salty water, in fact, quickly formed a fecal stew, spreading contaminants to every piece of meat in the barrel.

Before he was halfway finished, another quarter of meat was dropped on the blood-covered table. By that time, the slimy, raw wooden surface was itself a massive bacterial colony. The work went on nonstop, with pathogenic bacteria of a dozen different types cross-contaminating the table, until the factory dinner bell rang at noon.

He was given half an hour. Outside the factory gates, there was an oyster vendor. They were abundant and cheap—"Oysters and poverty go together," Dickens wrote—and he bought a dozen raw ones for a penny. Taken from the sewage-fouled Thames, they were likely tainted with hepatitis. He wolfed them down, visited the factory privy, dirtying his hands again, and went back to work.

At 7 P.M., drenched in sweat and spattered with blood, he collected his wages—1 silver shilling, the equivalent of 12 copper pennies. For him, it was good money. It bought another night's lodging, with 8 pence left over. This bought him a couple of glasses of gin at a penny apiece. "Drunk for a penny," went a popular saying at the time, "dead drunk for twopence." Sore-tired, he likely went the two-penny route or further. Hurrying back to the rooming house to assure himself a bed, he bought some stale bread and cheese made from raw milk, the latter tainted with *Campylobacter* bacteria, another cause of foodborne disease that would not be identified for over a hundred years. Full drunk and half-fed, he was asleep by 8 P.M.

In his first day's work, he had perhaps rendered twenty quarters of beef into pieces for Mr. Goldner's patented provisions. Unknowingly, he likely also contaminated them with hepatitis A, and *Salmonella, Shigella, Staphylococcus aureus,* and *Clostridium perfringens* bacteria, as well as spores of *Clostridium botulinum.*

As he slept, Goldner's second shift of laborers stuffed the uncooked meat into unsterilized cans using dirty hands and utensils. The cans were lowered into vats of boiling water. Part of Goldner's patented process included adding a liberal dose of nitrate of soda (calcium chloride) to the water, considerably increasing the processing temperature once the bath came to a boil. This speeded production and saved money. The concept was sound and advanced for its time, but the process was completely new and by no means perfected. To kill disease-causing bacteria and the heat-resistant spores they inhabit in low-acid foods (such as red meat and vegetables) requires cooking them as long as seven to eleven hours at 250 degrees F in the kind of boiling-water canners Goldner used—far longer than Goldner's process allowed.

It was at this critical stage—the last and only defense against the bacterial spores—that everything was sacrificed for speed. In his rush to fulfill the contract, Goldner, confident in his patented calcium chloride process, almost certainly failed to cook the food adequately. Boiling food long enough (30 to 75 minutes) and hot enough (a constant 212 degrees F) usually destroys the toxins produced by bacteria. The spores they inhabit, however, are not nearly so easily eliminated. In fact, they are extremely difficult (sometimes seemingly impossible) to kill. According to *The New York Times,* in the spring of 1988 Russian germ scientists attempted to kill hundreds of tons of anthrax spores from their bacteriological weapons inventory. The anthrax was soaked in a caustic, killing bleach at least twice, packed in 66-gallon stainless-steel containers, and sunk in eleven burial pits on a remote island in the heart of the inland Aral Sea. More than a decade later, samples from six of the eleven pits revealed that the spores were still very much alive and as deadly as ever.

Goldner's method relied solely on heat to rid food of bacteria. But food is a notoriously poor conductor of heat. Without adequate

*Canned Poison* As Goldner rushed to meet his contract, many of the over 29,000 cans of food he agreed to provide to the Franklin expedition were shoddily made. Some ruptured, spoiling the contents, others remained intact, containing botulism toxin. Either meant doom for the expedition. (National Maritime Museum, Greenwich, England)

cooking time, even if the water temperature never falls below 250 degrees F, heat doesn't penetrate the food in the center of the can. This leaves a so-called, uncooked "cold spot." Within this refuge, huge quantities of spores remain alive. Once they begin to germinate and reproduce, they secrete toxic waste. Some toxins produced by foodborne microorganisms cause severe food poisoning. Others, particularly *Clostridium botulinum*—one-celled, spore-forming, anaerobic (non-air-breathing) bacterium—are stunningly deadly.

*Clostridium* is commonly found in compost and soil. In fact, it's one of the principal bacterial eating machines that relentlessly reduces plant matter into soil in the first place. In turn, however, it's commonly absorbed by growing plants and reproduces in fodder and vegetables and moves on to any animals feeding on them. Some symbiotic forms continue their digestive work in animal and human intestines. Other forms—given the proper conditions—are so virulent, so massively reproductive and toxic that they are among the most lethal bacteria on earth. Introduced in wounds, they're the cause of deadly tetanus and gangrene.

But the most malevolent and toxic of all is *Clostridium botulinum,* the cause of botulism, which flourishes in improperly processed canned foods. If it is exposed to air, the bacterium dies quickly. If not, its genetic programming takes over and it reproduces, secreting its toxic waste—the most potent poison known to man. *Botulinum* neurotoxin is roughly 6,000,000 times more toxic than rattlesnake venom. It is 15,000 to 100,000 times more toxic than sarin, the organophosphate nerve gas used in the terrorist attack on the Tokyo subway system by the Aum Shinrikyo cult in 1995.[2] Even in minute quantities, its lethality is mind-boggling. Following the Persian Gulf War, Iraq revealed it had loaded 11,200 liters of *botulinum* toxin into specially designed SCUD missile warheads. It was estimated that as little as 1 gram of this aerosolized botulism toxin had the capacity to kill at least 1.5 million people.[3] In all, Iraq's stockpile of botulism weapons was calculated to be sufficient to kill every vertebrate on earth.

Soldered shut in Goldner's sealed cans, the non-air-breathing *botulinum* spores, which had not been killed during cooking, happily began to reproduce. Crated and stacked in Goldner's factory, the expedition's nightmare sat in the darkness awaiting delivery to the ships.

[2] *Annals of Internal Medicine;* 8/01/98; Vol. 129, No. 3.

[3] *JAMA;* 8/06/97; Vol. 278; No. 5.

# CHAPTER 17
# Schedules

*Only one-tenth of the Preserved Meats ordered appears to have been delivered by the contractor.*

—Captain Superintendent, Deptford Victualling Yard

On May 5, 1845, two weeks before the expedition was to sail, Goldner had still delivered virtually nothing. The Admiralty was near panic. The canned provisions constituted nearly one-third of the expedition's food supply and a large part of the antiscorbutics necessary to combat scurvy. A letter was sent to Goldner that day begging "to be informed when the preserved meats ordered on the 31st of March for the Erebus and Terror can be delivered."

He waited three days before favoring the navy with a response. His brief reply was a masterpiece of obfuscation. It appeared to answer the Admiralty's question, but did nothing of the kind. There is an attorney's artifice in it—a clear stamp of the slippery character behind it.

"In addition to those already forwarded," he wrote, "the greater part will be delivered within this week and the whole may be received at HM Victualling Yard on or before Monday next, the 12th instant." The provisions he'd already forwarded amounted to somewhat less than the one-tenth the Admiralty had generously credited him for. The quantities of the "greater part" of the order he intended to deliver weren't specified. The time frame, "within this week," was suitably vague. His pledge that "the whole may be received" by May 12 was wholly equivocal. What's more, he failed to mention anything about the greatest part of the overdue shipment—the more than 20,000 cans of soup; the Admiralty had not asked about them.

The deadline came and went. On May 12, the head of the victualling yard wrote the Admiralty that "the preserved meats for Her Majesty's Ships Erebus and Terror have yet to arrive for them." The next day, frantic to find out exactly what was overdue from Goldner, he wrote the navy yard storekeeper: "The Preserved Meat Contractor not having sent in any supplies since 5 May . . . instructs the Storekeeper to report exact quantities of what may be due from him for the Arctic ships." Goldner, who'd promised immediate delivery, was then forty-three days late. Franklin was scheduled to sail in but six days. Only 800 meat cans of the 9,579 contracted for had been delivered; none of the more than 20,000 cans of soup had arrived.

On May 13, the storekeeper reported the canned meats had finally arrived ". . . but none of the soups have yet been received from the contractor." Of all the canned foods, the egregiously overdue shipment of the soups should have been most suspect. On a unit basis, they were two to three times more expensive than any other items in Goldner's contract and constituted over two-thirds of the cans he had promised to deliver. If he was to make money any place on the deal, it necessarily had to be made on the soups, the largest and most lucrative part of the order. He promised to deliver 10,000 cans on May 13, but never did. This can only mean he had not even a portion of the order ready to deliver—or did not want to.

The question, of course, is why not? He delivered 10 percent of the canned meats as soon as he could to keep the Admiralty off his back. With Deptford frantically clamoring about the soups, why wouldn't he have sent whatever soups he had? Clearly, he wanted to wait until the last possible moment, when there would be no time or opportunity to examine them.

He had already wheedled the agreement to pack them in larger cans to cut his costs. It's quite probable he took further steps to cut costs drastically. Most likely, the soups were largely water, weighted with bone, thickened with alum. They were either undercooked or—given the fact that the highly publicized expedition was so soon to sail—not cooked at all. Goldner could have easily rationalized not cooking them; as a matter of course the expedition's cooks would do that by reheating them.

The soups, literally processed at the last minute, in all probability contained the highest concentration of *Clostridium botulinum* spores of anything Goldner canned. The level of *Clostridium* species contamination in vegetables, particularly those harvested directly from the soil, is generally higher than that found in meats and may in part explain why preserved vegetables are more frequently implicated [in outbreaks of botulism poisoning].[1] The three kinds of soups Goldner provided the expedition—beef and vegetable, vegetable, and "soup & boulli"—contained potatoes, carrots, and parsnips, all root vegetables harvested directly from the soil and especially subject to *Clostridium* contamination. What's more, some of them were likely prepared with *Clostridium* contaminated beef and beef bouillon.

Prepared in Goldner's much larger 9- and 12-pound cans, the soups would have necessarily required more cooking time at a temperature to kill the *Clostridium* spores in them than if they'd been cooked in the original 1-pound cans the Admiralty had originally ordered. Because of the rush to deliver the soups, in all likelihood they were not cooked long enough or hot enough. This, in fact, made matters far worse than not cooking them at all. According to botulism experts from the U.S. Centers for Disease Control and Prevention, a nonkilling heat shock may actually enhance germination and toxin production by *Clostridium botulinum* spores. Thus, the soups provided the spores with an almost ideal environment, in which all the requisites for their germination were assured. They were in a largely water, low-acid, lightless and airless environment and the heat shock of Goldner's cursory cooking jump-started them to reproduce.

[1] *JAMA;* 4/14/99, Vol. 281, No. 14.

There was little likelihood anyone would discover any short-cuts Goldner had taken in preparing the soups. The longer he delayed delivery, the less likely it became. Once the cans were soldered shut, painted, and crated, the soups would have been impossible to examine in detail before they were loaded onto the ships. A handful, struck open, would have revealed little to the eye but soggy "mixed vegetables," which, as Goldner intended all along, could be any vegetables he could lay hands on. Looking at them, no one could tell whether they were cooked or not. To the palate, they would have tasted of salt. Unseen and unknown, their fluid, airless environment would have been a tailor-made breeding ground for *Clostridium botulinum.*

On May 15, three days past his already expired delivery date, Goldner requested yet another extension. "I beg to inform you," he wrote the victualling superintendent, "that I shall be able by tomorrow to deliver the whole of the soups for the Polar Expedition."

Nothing arrived on that date. Finally, on May 17, less than forty-eight hours before the expedition sailed, the canned soups were dumped dockside. Furiously, without examination, the deadly stuff was trundled aboard and stowed below.

Nobody but Goldner and his personal secretary, Mr. Richie, gleefully tallying their profit, were aware of the facts. The samples given the navy were to specification and of good quality; the remaining 90 percent of the contract was not. Most of the cans were shoddily made and improperly sealed. The meat and vegetables in them were neither first quality or fresh. The soups were not processed or prepared "With the utmost care," as Goldner promised, but with little care whatever.

Before the expedition even sailed, the *Clostridium* in them began to reproduce.

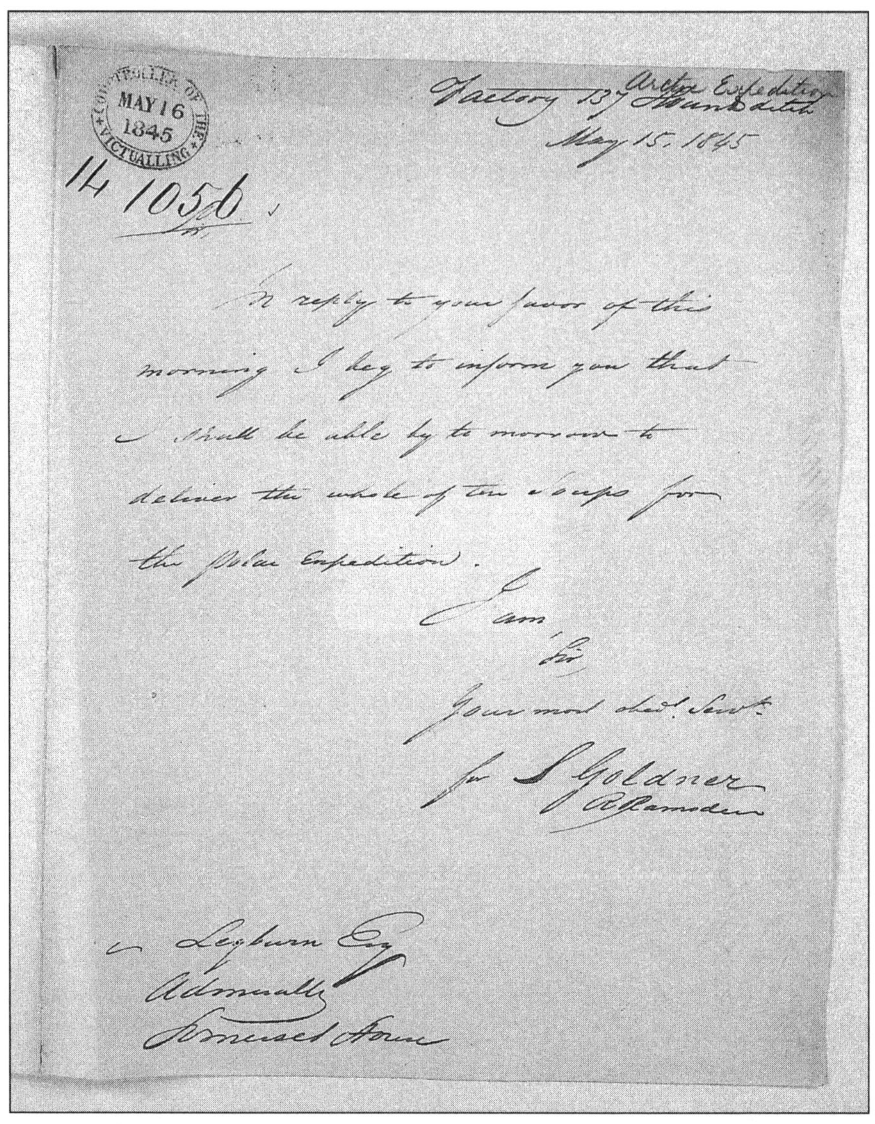

Comptroller of the Victualling
May 16
1845

Arctic Expedition
Factory 137 Houndsditch
May 15, 1845

14 1056

In reply to your favor of this morning I beg to inform you that I shall be able by to morrow to deliver the whole of the Soups for the Polar Expedition.

I am
Sir
Your most obedt. Servt.
for S Goldner
R Ramsden

Leyburn Esq
Admiralty
Somerset House

*Goldner's Dodge* Already forty-three days late after promising "*immediate delivery*," Goldner was still stalling for time. This note, written four days before the expedition sailed, again promised delivery of his entire order. It did not arrive until less than forty-eight hours before Franklin's departure—too late, as Goldner intended, to allow its inspection. (Public Records Office, London, England)

# CHAPTER 18
# The Dying Time

*. . . the total loss by deaths in the Expedition has been to this date 9 officers and 15 men.*

—James Fitzjames, Captain, HMS *Erebus*
—F. R. M. Crozier, Captain and Senior Officer

By late May in the lower Arctic, the thaw is usually well under way. Abundant pack ice remains, but the so-called close pack has sloughed into discrete pans, loose floes, and brash ice. Blue water leads open in the ice. Beluga, bowhead, and right whales surface in them to breathe, feeding on schools of herring. Ringed and harp seals sun themselves on the floes; deep-diving walrus, which use their tusks to dig oysters and clams out of the bottom, do likewise. Clouds of migrating birds—guillemot, little auk, eiderduck, teal, petrel, puffin—return to nest. But none of that happened in the late spring of 1847. Spring didn't come.

*Erebus* and *Terror* remained locked in the iron mask of the pack, almost exactly where it had trapped them nine months before. The ships were, doubtless, worse for the ordeal: hulls gouged by ice, metal plates sheared off, planking sprung, leaks everywhere—but afloat. By a miracle—for which Franklin, no doubt, thanked the Almighty—both vessels, beset in the maw of the Beaufort Ice Stream, survived intact. They had withstood the glacierlike pack of ice pouring down from the Pole, unprotected, for an entire winter without serious damage or loss of a man. But as spring edged toward summer, the lookouts in the mastheads could detect no change in the ice field around them.

This was cause for serious concern. By the end of May 1847, on full allowance, the expedition had but eleven months of food left. A good part of the already slim supply of coal had been consumed to heat the ships through the winter. Each day that passed without sign of the ice breaking up was a day less to escape when it did. If it didn't break up by midsummer, scarce six weeks away, it was unlikely to break up at all. If it didn't, the expedition faced, not another winter's trial by the ice, but a full year at least. At the end of that time, nearly every consumable aboard—food, coal, medicine, rum, lamp oil, and candles—would be gone. It was imperative to find a way out of the pack at once.

On May 24, 1847, Franklin sent a sledge party over the horizon, beyond where lookouts in the mastheads could see, to search for any sign of a breakup, any open leads the ships might reach. He may have sent parties out in all directions, but the one that left the ships on May 24 made a telling beeline southeast, straight for King William Island. This was the shortest, quickest route out of the pack. If a way, however convoluted, could be found to an ice-free bay or inlet there, the expedition might still find safety before the onset of another winter.

The importance Franklin attached to this reconnaissance is reflected by the fact that he put in charge 1st Lt. Graham Gore, the flagship's most senior officer after Commander Fitzjames. More significantly, Gore was ordered to cache a message ashore in the one place Franklin was almost certain it would be found: "a cairn of stones six feet high" built by James Clark Ross at the western-most point of his explorations seventeen years earlier, in which he had enclosed "a canister containing a brief account of the proceedings of the expedition since its departure from England." Ross had named the place Victory Point and the surrounding headlands, prophetically, Cape Jane Franklin and Franklin Point. The positions of all these features were as clearly marked on the Admiralty's charts as on Franklin's. Since they lay precisely on the course he had been ordered to take, beyond which everybody's charts were blank, it would appear to be the obvious first place to look for him. Unfortunately, it would prove to be the last place the Admiralty would look.

The message Gore was instructed to leave indicated nothing wrong. The ships were not reported beset, as they most certainly had been and remained, but merely that they had "wintered in the ice." The expectation was still that the coming summer would release them and that they would soon be on their way. The message included a record of the expedition's route and progress to date, plus a fix of its precise position ("Lat. 70-05′N, Long. 98-23′W") and situation ("Sir John Franklin commanding the expedition. All well.").

But the clear indication of this message is that Franklin suspected the situation might not remain well for long. It was the first and only time he felt compelled to leave any kind of message at all or to go to such lengths to deliver one (though the expedition was supplied with 200 airtight brass cylinders, expressly embarked for leaving messages). In this instance, however, he somehow felt it critical to leave word of the expedition's whereabouts: still in the ice, still fixed at Lat. 70-05′ North and Long. 98-23′ West.

Accompanied by Second Mate Charles DesVoeux of *Erebus* and six seamen, Lt. Gore set out across the pack for King William Island on May 24. Traveling parties took every precaution for this perilous duty. The ship's purser, Charles Osmer, issued the men the warmest slop clothing aboard—flannel underwear, woolen drawers, blue cloth trousers, red wool shirts, blue knitted wool jackets, and heavy outer frock coats of strong twilled wool. Every man also got several pair of woolen mittens, a 5-foot-long comforter (scarf), a Welsh wig (woolen watch cap) and a pair of wire-mesh snow goggles to prevent snow blindness. For footwear, Osmer issued them an abundance of worsted wool socks, along with stout shoes cleated for ice work and high-topped waterproof canvas fisherman's boots.

Aboard their sled was packed a small, brown Holland tent, eight wolfskin blanket-robes (6 feet long by 5 feet wide) and up to twenty-four Hudson's Bay Company blankets, pinned or sewn together into sleeping bags. They took a specially made cook kit, nested in wicker baskets, containing a kettle, frying pan, spirit stove, cotton-wicked spirit lamp, and a large number of pint-sized bottles of pyroligneous ether for fuel. Extra towing lines, an axe, and two shotguns with powder and shot completed the equipment. On top of this was piled one week's worth of provisions—250 pounds in all. Half of it consisted of Goldner's canned food.

It took the party five days to cover the twenty-three miles to landfall. The dismal progress reflected the still monstrous condition of the ice field. The route remained walled by towering pressure ridges. Nearer to shore was a higher, mountainlike range of icebergs that had grounded in the shallows. But for pools of meltwater, from which Gore's men drank greedily, the pack underfoot remained fast-frozen and up to 7 feet thick.

Gore located Ross's cairn and cached his message sometime on May 28. Some four miles to the south, he saw that today's Collinson Inlet, like the pack he'd just crossed, was still solid ice and impassable for ships. He crossed the mouth of the inlet, cached a nearly identical message in a cairn he built there and made for the ships. Around June 1—half-frozen, half-soaked, and fully exhausted—he returned to the *Erebus* with the worst possible news. There were no open leads nor sign of any. There was no way out.

Shortly afterward, Franklin likely mustered the crews and told them the news. There was to be no release that summer, no voyaging, no crack at the Passage. All that would have to wait another year. They were still beset, as fixed in the ice as insects in amber. The news came as a crushing blow. The summer not yet begun, and the men, expecting parole, were suddenly re-sentenced to another year in the ice. By the grace of God, they had survived one horrendous winter. How they could survive another was a question no one probably asked. But that was not the only bad news.

Rations, per regulation, were most probably reduced to a four-upon-six allowance. This was standard operating procedure in the Royal Navy when voyages were prolonged and food looked likely to run short. Six men were issued the allowance for four, in effect cutting each man's ration by one-third. Usually this was no great hardship; sailors, in fact, received extra pay equal to the value of the provisions denied. Men simply tightened their belts and took consolation in the few pence a day it earned them until the thing was over. But it was crystal clear to the crews now that the thing was not going to be over any time soon, and food they could eat meant far more than money they couldn't spend. After two years in the Arctic, a man knew quite comprehensively that food made the difference between being warm or cold, staying sound or sick, and having a strong hand rather than a shaking one.

But food, as Franklin no doubt made clear, was not the only concern. Far more worrisome was the fuel situation. Compared to the expedition's store of provisions, coal reserves in 1847 must have been critically low. Estimating conservatively, each ship may have had as little as 20 tons remaining.[1] There was simply not enough to heat the lower deck, cook three hot meals a day, melt sufficient drinking water for 126 officers and men and still have enough left to power the ships out of the pack in 1848. To do so required a Draconian reduction in the coal allowance. The lower deck likely could be heated only during the coldest hours of the coming winter. Meals, save for one a day, would have to be eaten cold. Water would be doled out sparingly.[2]

Like everyone else aboard, able-bodied seaman William Orren almost certainly listened to this litany of bad news. Sir John tried to put a good face on it. To hear him tell it, they would just over-winter and be on their way next season, straight through to China. By rationing the food and coal, there'd be enough to tide them over and the extra pay would put a jingle in their pockets once they got there. In the meantime, the rum and tobacco issue would continue at full allowance. That was the good news.

---

[1] Indeed, this is probably an overly generous estimate. Best case, each vessel consumed about 3 tons of coal a day for each day's steaming time. Assuming the ships voyaged under steam alone for only twenty days between leaving Greenland in July 1845 and being beset in September 1846—about 10 percent of the time they were actually underway—each vessel would've burned 60 tons of coal. Heating and cooking during the same period, again estimating conservatively, would have consumed an additional 20 tons and 4 tons, respectively, per vessel. By June 1847, each ship may, in fact, have had as little as 6 tons of coal left, a frightening prospect with yet another winter ahead.

[2] In winter, the water in the ship's iron holding tanks likely froze solid. Melting ice and snow for drinking water required yet more coal.

But Orren had been in the navy long enough to smell trouble and the smell of things wasn't right. They were still fast in the ice on a lee shore. The four-upon-six allowance was always a sign of worse to come. If the ships had been underway, bound for someplace to reprovision, it wouldn't have bothered him much. A fellow could do on what was called "short commons" for a few months. A year was something else. What made it worse was that the two-thirds ration a man got was bound to get more stale, sour, or stinking with every passing day. It was also sore plain that the infernal cold would be no easier to bear with the boiler fired only a few hours a day. Dismissed with the others and sent forward where "they belonged," he may have thought no more about it. It was, after all, "officers' business," not his. There was no occasion for worry yet. They might go bloody hungry and bleeding cold for a time, but Sir John would bring them through.

Ten days later, Sir John Franklin died. It probably struck every man aboard dumb. For the officers, it must have been incomprehensible. In thirty years of Arctic voyaging, no Royal Navy officer had ever died—no captain, commander, or lieutenant, certainly not an expedition leader. If Franklin—the expedition's light, soul, spiritual shepherd—could die, they all could.

Whatever killed him was relatively quick. He was apparently fine when Lt. Gore left the ship on May 24. He was stone dead on June 11. It could not have been due to starvation or scurvy. At two-thirds allowance, food was not yet in short supply and Franklin enjoyed not only the greater issue and more varied fare of the officer's mess, but a privately stocked storeroom of his own. He may have been stricken with pneumonia, influenza, typhus, tuberculosis, cholera, or half a hundred other infectious diseases. But Franklin was less exposed to that risk than any man aboard. He was largely segregated from everybody but *Erebus*'s senior-most officers. He had his own sleeping cabin and messed with but five or six officers who were similarly segregated from any kind of infection. His clothes, quarters, and eating utensils were kept scrupulously clean by two stewards. He had plenty of hot water and soap. He was spared hard labor or any exposure to polar cold and wet. At the first sign of a sniffle or cough, he was attended by two surgeons. Arguably, he was the last man in the expedition one would expect to fall victim to bacterial or viral infection.

But something happened during those seventeen days that killed him first of all. It may have been a sudden heart attack or stroke. Franklin, after all, was the oldest man in the expedition. During his lifetime, he'd been wounded, shipwrecked, starved, riddled with scurvy, and almost certainly exposed to malaria and tuberculosis (his first wife had died of the disease)—all of which would have chipped away at his immune system. He had just turned sixty-one that spring and was overweight; after two winters in the ice, his heart may have simply worn out. The bitter disappointment of Gore's news, the almost certain realization of his own failure, may indeed have triggered it. In many ways, that would make Franklin's death the easiest to explain—he was a broken old man dying with his dream.

Lt. Gore's death shatters that explanation. Only two of nine officers who died before the ships were deserted were identified in Crozier's last message: Franklin and Gore, both from the *Erebus*. Gore, a much younger, fitter man, died not long after Franklin, apparently shortly after returning to the ships from King William Island. His death cannot be as easily explained as Franklin's. He was leading sledge parties over the pack in June, work only the fittest, heartiest men could perform. He would hardly have been assigned, nor could he have successfully carried out, this duty if he had showed any signs of sickness.

Yet within a stunningly short time both men—the elderly Franklin, warm, safe, and well-tended aboard ship, and the young, robust Gore, hauling sleds in abominable conditions far from the vessels—shared exactly the same fate. Their circumstances could not have been more different if Franklin had been on the earth and Gore on the moon. Yet they had one startling thing in common which in retrospect appears obvious but at the time was anything but. Officers messing aboard ship and sledging parties away from them got more of Stephan Goldner's canned provisions than anyone else.

Aboard ship, the stewards would have routinely served the officers a proper gentleman's meal. For supper, even in the Arctic and especially for Sir John (who as Governor Simpson noted, "must have three meals per diem"), this would normally have consisted of four courses—perhaps one of Goldner's canned soups, pickled fish, Goldner's canned meats, and sweets (raisins, nuts, or pudding).

Away from the ship, Gore's sledgers gorged on every ounce of Goldner's more portable, easily prepared soups and meats that they could scrape out of a can. In a way, they thought they were lucky. On sledging trips, as physically punishing as they were, a fellow at least got his full ration of rum while those left aboard got half. He also got his full allowance of shipboard "luxuries"—pickled vegetables and fruit, raisins, butter, cheese, and tobacco. Even better, while a man aboard ship got 5 pounds of canned provisions a week, on sledging trips, he got almost 15 pounds. Not only was a fellow free of the stinking confinement of the ships and the everlasting holystoning of the deck—he ate better, drank his fair share and, but for the misery of hauling a sled in the bleeding cold ("pully-hauly," the men called it)—he had no worries.

The result, however, was the same. Both groups ingested *Clostridium botulinum* spores. Aboard ship, however, the neurotoxins produced by the bacteria were boiled away. Away from the ships, among the sledging parties, the poison may have been boiled away; more likely it was not.

The completely unexpected deaths surely shocked chief surgeons Stephen Stanley and John Peddie. They were at a loss. Then, as now, determining an exact cause of death is largely a matter of educated guesswork and they had almost nothing to go on. Even today, with full knowledge of microbes and infectious diseases, and batteries of sophisticated clinical tests, it remains problematical. With none of this knowledge, Franklin's surgeons were clueless and helpless.

About all the surgeons knew was that two of the expedition's most senior officers were suddenly, inexplicably dead. Perhaps one of them may at least have been familiar with the name of the disease they faced. In the late eighteenth century, European physicians had first recorded a disease they'd never seen before. Its onset was remarkably swift and its outcome, in 60 to 80 percent of cases, fatal.

The symptoms had been documented. But it's doubtful the expedition's surgeons were familiar with them. One day patients complained of stomach cramps. The following day, the muscles in their faces went flaccid, followed by the muscles in the neck, shoulders, arms, and legs in drastically quick, descending progression. By the third day, patients were more or less paralyzed and the disease, moving relentlessly, had already attacked the respiratory muscles. As these failed, the patients lost all ability to breathe and, quickly, though coherent and alert, suffocated. The disease took just three days to kill. There was no explanation for it, no treatment, no cure.

The only thing generally, if inexactly, known by the nineteenth century was that the source of the disease was linked to eating sausage that had, in some way no one could fathom, become contaminated. All the early physicians could do was give the disease a name. After the Latin word for sausage, *botulus,* they christened the killer *botulism.*

Both Franklin and Gore were apparently buried at sea. Usually, in preparation for burial, a dead man's arms, hands, and toes were bound together with strips of cloth to prevent rigor mortis from contorting the body. Franklin's body may have been. However, Gore's likely remained paralyzed in the position death had claimed him. The corpses were stitched tight in canvas and weighted at the foot with ballast. Covered by the Union Jack, they were carried onto the ice and services were held, salutes fired, and the bodies sunk in the fire holes.

In the next ten months, the ritual would be repeated with frightening regularity.

# CHAPTER 19

# Killer at Large

*We know that 3 of their men [young men] died in the first year, from which we may infer they were not enjoying perfect health. It is supposed that their preserved meats were of an inferior quality.*

—Captain Erasmus Ommanney,
HMS *Assistance*, 1852

At first, but for the numbing shock, the deaths of Franklin and Gore evidently changed little. The ceaseless routine of winter quarters continued. Navy discipline and procedure were faultlessly followed. Crozier assumed command of the expedition; it was the one thing he'd always hoped for, but now undoubtedly the last thing he wanted. Commander Fitzjames was made captain of *Erebus,* which he'd been all along except by title. Lt. VesContes took Gore's place. The ships remained fast-frozen. The lookouts in the mastheads continued to watch for any sign of a breakup and the crews went about their duties on reduced rations of food and coal. Nothing appeared much different than it had been before, but everything was.

A killer was aboard. Invisible. Opportunistic. Voracious. It didn't reveal its presence until after it claimed its victims. Ironically, it thrived in the one thing the expedition could not do without: food. And it filled the plate of every officer and man aboard three times a week—the approximate wintertime allowance of Goldner's canned food. The science fiction thriller *Alien* comes very close to depicting it. It was not a 9-foot-tall clawed creature bleeding acid, but an equally fantastic creature only a few microns wide, secreting toxins far more lethal. It did not inhabit and reproduce in the air ducts of a fictional twenty-first-century spaceship. It inhabited and reproduced in Goldner's canned provisions aboard a real nineteenth-century steamship. And it was every bit as adaptable and virulent and virtually indestructible.

Ironically, the Arctic cold not only hid it for the expedition's first two years in the ice, it may have made it increasingly lethal. Freezing largely prevents bacteria from multiplying but, as evidenced from the other type of *Clostridium* spores discovered in Private Braine's corpse 140 years later, it doesn't kill them. They go dormant, lying in a state of suspended animation until conditions are ripe for them to begin reproducing again. Indeed, those that survive may reproduce in thawing foods more rapidly, genetically sensing the narrow time frame available for survival and making the most of every microsecond.

Goldner's food cans, stowed on the unheated orlop decks and holds of the ships, froze and thawed repeatedly throughout the voyage. In the Arctic summers, as the cans thawed, the *Clostridium* in them awakened and multiplied. As the bacteria grew in number, they also secreted greater quantities of their toxic waste. During the Arctic winters, the cans froze again and the *Clostridium* in them, in uncountable numbers, surrounded by stunning concentrations of toxins, returned to dormancy.

By the summer of 1847, the food cans had undergone two deep freezes and three thaws. This repeated freeze-thaw dynamic produced massive bacterial colonies and quite enough *Clostridium botulinum* poison to kill every man on the expedition a million times over. Until that summer, however, even though the toxin was present in the expedition's canned food during the whole voyage, it had harmed no one at all. The reason was cruelly simple.

*Botulinum* toxin offers no clue to its presence. The poison itself is tasteless, colorless, and odorless. The food it has tainted, however, may smell rank or taste strange; yet aboard ship in the nineteenth century, virtually all food did after a few months at sea. The food in Goldner's cans probably appeared no more disagreeable than the 4-pound pieces of stinking, gray salt pork fished out of the brine casks or the moldy dried peas ladled out of rat-gnawed kegs. Brought up from the orlop deck, the cans were struck open with either a hammer and chisel or hatchet (the can opener had yet to be invented), the contents cooked and greedily eaten.

Unlike *Clostridium* spores, the toxic wastes they secrete as they reproduce and multiply are easily destroyed by heat. A few minutes of hard boiling is usually sufficient to rid foods of the poison. The expedition's cooks evidently were scrupulous about hard boiling or hard frying food. Both cooks—Richard Wall aboard *Erebus* and John Diggle aboard *Terror*—were veterans of the 1839–1843 Antarctic voyage. Their experience on that expedition had taught them the importance of keeping their galleys spotlessly clean and, perhaps intuitively, that cooking tainted foods at high temperatures "corrected" it and prevented illness. They knew plainly that hot food on polar voyages not only put starch in a sailor, but rid foods of "fellow-shipmates" like weevils, mold, and fungus. As much as, and probably more than, the ships' surgeons, their skill at food handling and preparation safeguarded the expedition's well-being. It was not altogether altruistic, however. Cooks routinely fried or boiled the fat out of the men's salt pork and beef, ostensibly to preserve it for other cooking tasks, but it was often also sold to hungry sailors on the side in exchange for coin, tobacco, or a part of their rum ration. This was known as the cook's "prerogative."

But when the ice didn't break up that summer, coal for cooking—the expedition's only defense against the undetected toxins—was among the first sacrifices. With all the other hardships they faced, it appeared trifling. Three hot meals a day may have been reduced to one. The crew fell back on a diet of ship's biscuit and salt meat straight out of the water cask in which it was soaked to make it palatable. This was no great hardship; many sailors preferred it raw—that way, the fat they craved (called *slush*) was not fried out and taken by the cook. They still got hot tea or cocoa, with hot oatmeal or barley mush, to warm them. Their issue of Goldner's canned provisions, usually given them in small quantities three times a week, had already been reduced and was not much missed. This and the fact that many of them refused to eat the stuff anyway, saved many of their lives.

By twist of fate, the officers were less fortunate precisely because they were more privileged. The stewards could not set the gentlemans' table with their monogrammed silverware, pewter plate, and leaded glassware and serve them hardtack and raw, stinking salt pork. With coal rationed so severely, hot baked bread and fried rashers of bacon were out of the question, but Mr. Goldner's canned provisions provided a proper alternative. Unlike the bulk foods aboard, Goldner's canned provisions were precooked, required no preparation beyond boiling and, since it was summer, were already thawed. Dumping them into the cook's kettle and bringing it to a boil took very little effort, time, or coal. Ladling out hot soup and boulli, preserved potatoes and ox cheeks was the answer to the stewards' prayer. The officers got a proper meal with their remaining claret, coal was spared, and the cook saved trouble.

The sledging parties, however, away from the oversight of the cooks and completely without coal, were at far greater risk. On a week's sledging trip, each man's ration included 5 pounds of hard ship's biscuit and 6 pounds of salt meat, which, though they were completely deficient of vitamins and caused scurvy, were not immediately fatal. The sledger's weekly ration of canned food, however—9½ pounds of meat, 3 pounds of vegetables, 1½ pounds of soup, and ⅔ pound of potatoes—could have been exceptionally deadly. If it was cooked at all, it was cooked on a feeble spirit stove, fueled by 1-pint glass bottles of what was labeled "pyroligneous" ether, a light, volatile, flammable liquid. Assuming none of the bottles leaked or had broken as sleds were jarred over pressure ridges in the ice, this fuel didn't burn hot or for very long. Considering the fuel inefficiency of these little spirit stoves, combined with Arctic cold and wind, it took an unbearably long time to bring anything to a boil. Most of the fuel, in fact, was probably used to melt drinking water for monstrously thirsty men. Each man, at minimum, would have required one gallon of water a day. This necessitated melting ice or compacted snow, which is such an effective insulator that aluminum cook pots have been known to burn through before it melts. A pint of ether may have yielded a gallon or two, drunk as soon as it turned to liquid or even slush. The thirst would have been too consuming to wait.

*Sledge Parties at Risk* Aboard ship, the toxins in the canned food were easily cooked away on coal stoves. Away from the ship, the sled parties were dependent on a feeble spirit stove, fueled by pint-sized bottles of ether. It's doubtful the canned food was heated long enough or hot enough to destroy any toxins they contained. (National Maritime Museum, Greenwich, England)

Rationed as it was, the fuel allowance was barely ample to rehydrate the sled parties. There was likely very little left for cooking provisions. This shortage of fuel for cooking probably did not concern the sledge parties too much. They had ship's biscuit, fat-rich salt pork eaten out of the cask, and, of course, Goldner's canned food. The canned meats and vegetables had, after all, already been cooked. Goldner's soups, however, were distinctly different. They were "concentrated," supposed to be diluted with water and then brought to a boil. They were also almost exclusively carrot soup and parsnip soup, and root vegetables are particularly susceptible to botulinum contamination. There was little water with which to dilute these soups and little fuel to bring them to a boil. But the 12-pound cans in which they were packaged (and insufficiently cooked during processing) were ideal for the sledge parties: each contained the exact 1½ pounds of soup allotted each man. Given this fact, it's scarcely imaginable the 12-pound cans were not routinely packed on the sleds. The ravenous sledge parties may have waited only for steam and a few bubbles to rise in the can before wolfing down the contents. This abundance of canned food and appetite, along with a shortage of fuel and a bare minimum of cooking time, left them more exposed to greater concentrations of *botulinum* toxins than anyone.

Sledging parties may, in fact, have been particularly subject to botulism poisoning outbreaks. If so, it may neatly explain the fact that (excepting Sir John) a total of eight officers and twelve men perished between June 1847 and April 1848. The numbers are revealing, since sled parties were typically composed of two officers and six men. Four sledging parties, had they eaten food laden with *botulinum* neurotoxins, not boiled or cold out of a can, suffering the mortality rate associated with botulism poisoning prior to modern treatment, would have accounted for the deaths of six officers and nineteen men—eerily near the eight officers and twelve men reported dead in that ten-month period.

There was, of course, a horrifying kind of Russian roulette going on. Some cans (the smaller ones, particularly) may have contained no *Clostridium botulinum* spores and therefore no toxins at all, providing Goldner had cooked them long enough and sealed them properly. Some cans may have contained an unequal distribution of toxin within the contaminated food, sparing some exposed individuals eating the contents while fatally poisoning others.

Brought to a rolling boil aboard ship, on the cooks' efficient Frazer's Patent coal stove, the canned food was made safe. Away from the ship, warmed fitfully over a spirit stove, or worse—ingested wholly uncooked—deadly concentrations of toxins would have remained.

But this deadly game of Russian roulette was even more complicated and random than that. Low-acid vegetables—potatoes, carrots, and parsnips—particularly concentrated in watery environments like canned soups—grow *Clostridium* more rapidly than others. These soups may have been chiefly responsible for what happened next, especially among the sledging parties.

The symptoms of botulism are pronounced and typically appear within twelve to thirty-six hours after the poison is consumed, generally depending on the amount of toxin ingested. Sometimes it's faster—cases have been reported developing in as short a period as two to four hours. At other times, its progression is slower; in one outbreak, an individual remained active and seemingly healthy for eight days after eating poisoned food before dying on the tenth day. Generally, however, persons with the early onset of illness (within twenty-four hours) will be more severely affected and more likely to die.[1] Once symptoms appear, they spread through the human body like fire through kindling.

These symptoms may have been manifest in the sledging parties, which would have been particularly active in the spring and summer of 1847, seeking any open water through which the trapped ships could escape. Within a day or so, sledgers who'd consumed concentrated and highly contaminated soups would have complained of stomach cramps and the "runs." The initial symptoms of foodborne botulism are usually gastrointestinal—including nausea, vomiting, abdominal cramps, and diarrhea—in about half of all cases. These were all common complaints that the officers leading the sled parties probably dismissed as indigestion or malingering. An officer suffering these symptoms would have been given lime water to settle his stomach and a dose of asafetida, a gum resin commonly used as an antispasmodic, to stop his heaving. A seaman would have been given a jolt of brandy. Both medications were contained in the medicine chests carried by the sledge parties.

These gastrointestinal symptoms are rapidly followed by alarming neurologic ones. The first to appear are dry mouth, blurred vision, and double vision (diplopia). Within a very short time, other

[1] *Botulism in the United States, 1899–1977;* Centers for Disease Control and Prevention; Handbook for Epidemiologists, Clinicians and Laboratory Workers; Atlanta, GA, 1998.

cranial nerve abnormalities are manifest. The victim's vocal chords are affected, resulting in a queer distortion of the voice (dysphonia), followed by difficulty in speaking (dysarthria) and swallowing (dysphagia). As the toxin is absorbed by the bloodstream, it's carried to the nerve endings of the peripheral nervous system. There it binds irreversibly to the nerve junctions, blocking the release of acetylcholine, a compound crucial to the transmission of nerve impulses. As it short-circuits these nerves, the body's peripheral muscles weaken and a symmetric descending paralysis commences, beginning with the body's upper extremities.

These symptoms would have quickly incapacitated officers and men alike. Out on the ice, far from the ships, unable to haul the sleds, panic probably set in. Those who by some quirk had not ingested the poison frantically pitched their brown Holland tent and tended their mates. To treat dry mouth and difficulty swallowing, they may have administered Syrup of Squills, a dried, sliced herb in a tannin solution, used as an expectorant, to lubricate the throat. To stimulate the victim's rapidly weakening motor muscles, Peruvian Wine of Coca (a mixture of wine and cocaine) or solutions of camphor or hartshorn (an ammonia-rich concoction made from the ground-up antlers of red deer) may have been used. These, of course, would have had no effect whatever in stopping the spread of neurotoxin throughout the body's muscles.

When the toxin reached the victim's respiratory muscles, the end was quick. As the lungs shut down, the caregivers may have administered Tincture of Lobelia, a solution of Indian tobacco consisting almost entirely of nicotine, which was a preferred respiratory stimulant at the time. But in almost all cases, it was hopeless. The victim, though still alert, was unable to draw a breath. Within a few minutes, he was dead.

The sledging parties may have been decimated in these outbreaks, especially if all the officers and men had eaten out of the same toxic can. But not all botulism poisoning outbreaks occur in such a regular, easily defined fashion. In Argentina in 1998, eleven bus drivers in Buenos Aires ate *matambre* (a traditional meat roll, prepared with meat, vegetables, and spices) at the same roadside home–restaurant over a five-day period. Nine of the eleven experienced botulism poisoning within two to eight days afterward. During that time, most of the drivers suffered neurologic and gastrointestinal symptoms, four of them extreme muscular weakness and difficulty breathing and one respiratory paralysis. The same incubation range and variety of symptoms may have occurred among the officers and men of the Franklin Expedition's sledging parties.

Some may have managed to make it back to the ships, hauling their sinking comrades. Others may, indeed, have perished to a man out on the sea ice, far from the vessels. Crozier and Fitzjames would have reckoned any parties that disappeared entirely had plunged through thin ice disguising open leads or fallen victim to cold and exposure. Of any survivors who managed to return to the vessels, from 60 to 80 percent would shortly die of respiratory failure, which the ship's surgeons could neither diagnose or treat.

It wasn't until fifty years after this tragedy was played out repeatedly in the ice that the cause of the disease was identified. In 1897, Dr. E. VanErmengem, investigating the outbreak of a similar disease in Ellezelles, Belgium, discovered its source in an innocuous-looking cured ham. In it, he found evidence of botulism neurotoxin and also isolated the microscopic organism that produced it. From this, he concluded the disease was foodborne, caused by anaerobic bacteria secreting minute but stunningly lethal poisonous waste. Beyond that, however, he had no idea how to defeat it.

Today, saving a botulism victim depends upon the swift isolation and identification of the seven types of *Clostridium botulinum* that produce neurotoxins, the prompt administration of antitoxins (stockpiled in readiness at major airports in the United States, at least, to respond to outbreaks), and the use of ventilators or bags to permit victims to breathe. Using these methods, the death rate of botulism victims has been reduced from approximately 60 to less than 15 percent—in the Western world, at any rate. According to the Journal of the American Medical Association, outside the Western Hemisphere there is still no reliable source of antitoxin elsewhere in the world.[2]

[2] *JAMA;* 8/06/97; Vol. 278; No. 5.

None of this was known, of course, in the summer of 1847, when the sledge parties would have been most active—scouring the pack for any means of escape, and eating Goldner's canned provisions largely uncooked. The horrible death scene was played out twenty-one times, the surgeons powerless to stop it.

Every month more men succumbed, most likely those in the sledging parties. The fitfully heated lower deck grew cold while the outside temperature plummeted to 35 degrees below zero. The polar night descended and grew longer and deeper until it was pitch black twenty-four hours a day. In the first throes of the illness, the sick vomited or suffered diarrhea, which fouled their clothing, blankets, and hammocks. Lacking fuel enough for washing, these could never be got clean. Those that sank into paralysis, drifted away suffocating.

At first the dead, like Franklin and Gore, were probably stitched in canvas and sunk in holes cut in the ice. But by midwinter, the pack was as much as 7 to 15 feet thick and could no longer be penetrated. The corpses were stacked in the hold, like logs, where they froze solid. There they accumulated in the dark, attacked by legions of rats to whom the frozen feast posed no obstacle.

Yet oddly, as some of the crew may have noticed, the rats feeding upon them—ingesting toxins secondhand—died just as swiftly.

# CHAPTER 20

# The Death March

*. . . and start on tomorrow, 26th, for Back's Fish River.*

—Captain F. M. Crozier

By early April 1848, Crozier could no more escape the escalating body count than he could the pack ice. In the ten months since Sir John's death, following another awful winter in the ice, twenty more men had died, eight of them officers. He had never seen anything like it; no one ever had. In his four voyages with Parry, he'd seen only two men die. In all the expeditions the Admiralty had sent in search of the Passage—eight of them by land and sea since 1818—there had been a total of seventeen dead. Franklin's expedition, Crozier's now, had already lost twenty-four and the dying went on.

Those were not the only numbers rocking him. It was now three years, less a month, since the expedition had sailed with provisions and stores calculated to last exactly three years. With the reduction in provisions, amplified by the dead men's rations, the food could be stretched to last another ten to eleven months. That gave him a chance. But on full allowance, the lemon juice would be gone in a month and once it was gone he would have two deadly plagues on his hands. Scurvy would doubtless return and the suffocating disease, which the surgeons could neither diagnose or treat, would continue.

The fuel situation was just as damning. It had been engines and coal that had gotten them so far into the pack in the first place; now the boilers' insatiable appetites and the ever-diminishing coal supply looked like they could never get them out. There was barely coal left for perhaps a week's steaming, even if the ice released the ships, which it yet showed no signs of doing. There was certainly not enough to heat the vessels another year if it didn't.

This grim arithmetic left Crozier with few options, all of them awful to contemplate. He could wait and gamble that this year the pack might break up in May or June or July. That would give him a month, maybe two, to press ahead or retreat the way they had come. But it was patently obvious that he couldn't go forward. With men dying wholesale, a pittance of coal, dwindling antiscorbutics, and half rations or less, finding and forcing the Passage—if it existed—was no longer a possibility. There was no time for that.

But going backward was largely an illusion. It depended wholly on the ice breaking up soon enough, staying out long enough, with winds favorable enough, to work the ships almost completely under sail through the narrows of Franklin Strait, Peel Sound, and Barrow Strait, the way they had come. Any one of these narrows might be blocked by ice, regardless of the season. Forcing all three in time to reach Lancaster Sound before freeze-up would be little short of a miracle. Then, of course, there was the very real possibility that the pack might not break up at all. It hadn't the previous summer. The ice masters saw no indication of it yet. All in all, waiting for it to do so looked little better than doing nothing at all, and Franklin had already played that game without success. Waiting any longer looked to be a slow death sentence.

The only other options, which involved abandoning the vessels, were straightforward and terrifying. If the ice did not release the ships, they must desert the ships and go out over the ice while there were still officers and men with strength and food enough to do it. There were only two ways to go: east to Baffin Bay in hopes of reaching the whaling fleet that summer, or due south to the Hudson's Bay Company outpost on Great Slave Lake.

Either route represented a desperate, all-or-nothing gamble and both required dragging heavy ship's boats. To get back to Baffin Bay meant traveling over the pack ice much of the way, through the tortured cordillera of pressure ridges that had already seemingly broken so many of the expedition's sledging parties. Hugging the coastline as they must, for the islands and peninsulas in between rose to 3,000 feet or more, it was a distance of over 1,200 miles. Once there, assuming they got there at all, they might or might not find the whaling fleet before its summer departure.

The journey to Great Slave Lake, some 850 miles to the south, was no less intimidating. Most of it involved going up the Great Fish River that Lt. Back had descended during his explorations fourteen years before. In his journal, which was among the volumes in *Terror*'s library, Back's description of it was horrendous. He described its length extending ". . . a violent and tortuous course of 530 geographical miles, running through an iron-ribbed country without a single tree on the whole of its banks . . . (with) no fewer than 83 falls, cascades and rapids." Still, the route was somewhat shorter and they would at least be traveling into summer—into lower, warmer latitudes, following the thaw.

Unlike the pack to the north, which would likely remain frozen and a barrier for several more months, it seemed probable that the river to the south, about 160 miles away, might be ice-free, if not at its mouth then certainly along its upper reaches. They would not have to drag the boats so far over the ice and could follow it most of the way. Crozier had Back's charts of the river. There would also be a greater chance of taking fish and game which, considering their dwindling provisions, was a necessity. There was also the positive assurance that the Hudson's Bay Company post, unlike the whaling fleet, was sure to be found at the eastern end of Great Slave Lake. Furthermore, the company had been notified by the Admiralty to be on the lookout for the expedition if it had not been heard from by the spring of 1848, so searchers might already be on their way downriver. These factors probably decided the thing for Crozier. They would make for Great Slave Lake before the disease aboard ship killed any more officers and crew.

If the escape plan was necessarily desperate, Crozier's preparations—in his first independent command—were seemingly careful, deliberate, and splendidly conceived. He appeared to have thought of everything. Before he had even contemplated deserting the ships, perhaps as early as the summer of 1847, he established a shore depot

*Escaping the Pack Ice* After deserting their ships in a desperate attempt to reach safety, the Franklin survivors would face this: ice pressure ridges as much as 60 feet high. Unlike Peary's 1905 party shown here, they had no dogs, light sleds, or fur clothing. Manhauling the ship's boats and provisions weighing almost two tons, they had to negotiate over 30 miles of this *before* they began the awful march south. (National Geographic Society)

near Victory Point on King William Island, some 25 miles from where the vessels were locked in the ice. A vast quantity of equipment, clothing, stores, and provisions were cached there. Hobson and M'Clintock, who first visited the site in 1859, estimated it amounted to over 10 tons but could not, for the life of them, figure out how or why so much had been hauled ashore simply to be abandoned. They interpreted Crozier's final message to mean, quite literally, that the ships were deserted on April 22 and the survivors had dragged everything ashore by April 25, only to leave it and set out southward the next day.

Obviously, that scenario was impossible. In 1846 it took Lt. Gore and seven other men five days to drag a comparatively lightly loaded sled the same distance. The 105 survivors who left the ships that spring could hardly have dragged sled-mounted ship's boats (each sled-boat weighing over 1,400 pounds), 20,000 pounds of gear and as much as 20,000 pounds of food ashore in three days. As the heavy rope, blocks, and tackle that Hobson found clearly suggest, everything had been quite systematically brought ashore earlier and a secure, land-based depot established. The reason was perfectly plain: Crozier off-loaded everything he could in case the ships were crushed in the ice during the winter of 1847–1848 and to make ready, if necessary, for the attempt to reach safety the following spring.

The abandoned stores later found by Hobson—all the expedition's heavy clothing, cookstoves, tools, even brass curtain rods and a lightning conductor—were laboriously carried there for a singular purpose. The slop (heavy) clothing was essential to remove; left aboard ship it was no good to anybody, but cached ashore it was safe. The four boat's stoves found were probably hauled ashore to bake the abundance of flour that remained into biscuit for the march south. No doubt they were heavy (all stoves at the time were made out of iron), but four boat's stoves could obviously bake biscuit faster than the single heavier, immovable stoves aboard ship which, in any case, were fully occupied cooking the crews' daily provisions.

Hauling brass curtain rods and lightning conductors ashore, while seeming ludicrous, also made eminent sense. King William Land is featureless and flat, and where Crozier landed and made camp, it's less than 30 feet above high tide, so especially vulnerable to lightning storms common in the spring and summer. During their surveys at the same spot in the 1980s, Beattie and Geiger were sore afraid their metal tent poles might attract lightning. Crozier was apparently aware of the same hazard and took precautions, in the form of improvised lightning rods.

Searchers later found thirteen stone tent circles at the same location, indicating that a good deal of prior thought and preparation had gone into building the place. There would have been no reason to build stout tent circles for a one-night stay. What's more, no large tents were listed in the ships' manifests, so they had to have been expressly sewn in advance. The thirteen of them made correspond almost exactly with the 105 survivors Crozier meant to house: eight men (one officer included) to a tent; organized, as might be expected, by messes.

The extent of Crozier's preparation did not end there. To get up the river, he needed enough boats to carry 105 men, all their equipment, and every ounce of food that was left. There were plenty of ship's boats aboard, eighteen in fact—cutters, pinnaces, whaleboats, jolly boats, dinghies, and ship's boats. But to get to the river at all, he would have to haul them and everything they contained over the pack ice around the west side of King William Land to Chantrey Inlet and then to the mouth of Back's River. Some of the boats were better suited for this service than others.

The expedition's four whaleboats, shallow-drafted and 30 feet long, were perfect. They were light but strong-built, and fast—pulling six oars—and double-ended like canoes. With no fixed rudder, steered by an oarsman at the stern, and equipped with a collapsible mast, they were ideal for river work. Even better, they were essentially sleds in or out of the water and could be easily dragged over the ice. The problem was that there weren't enough of them.

The expedition's four cutters were smaller—25 feet long—but deeper keeled, square-sterned, and steered by rudders, as they were primarily designed as sailing boats. But each pulled eight oars and was lug (gaff) rigged with two masts, so Crozier had no choice but to take them along. Each one could carry ten men and, with a proper wind and twice the canvas of the whaleboats, keep pace with them on the way upriver. But unlike the whaleboats, their deeper draft and keel prevented skidding them out over the ice. They would have to be mounted on sleds and these would have to be specially built. The collapsible sledges used by the traveling parties (made in the Woolwich Dockyards) were far too small and light. Thomas Honey and John Weekes, the expedition's carpenters, undoubtedly told Crozier they could build sleds large enough to haul the boats—they could build anything. However, the only wood aboard was oak and elm, which would make the sleds bloody heavy, but there was no alternative.

Likewise, the expedition's two jolly boats (each 30 feet long) and two pinnaces (each 28 feet long) had to be taken. These were heavier than the cutters and would have to be carried on sleds. The only other boats—four ship's boats (22 feet long) and two dinghies (12 feet long)—were too small and lightly oared. Neither of these types was sail-rigged or could carry as much and each would require a purpose-built sled to haul it.

While work on the sleds began, Crozier made other preparations. The boats' oars were cut down short, which he considered better suited for river work. Boat covers were fitted and sewn to shield the crews and cargo from bad weather. Each boat was equipped with a tool chest (saws, files, hammers, nails, sailmaker's palms, needles and thread) and adequate stores (spare canvas, sheet lead, twine) to make any repair. The men's shoes were cleated with screws for ice-work. Goggles were improvised from wire mesh to prevent snow-blindness. Bayonet scabbards were cut down to make knife sheaths. (All of these improvised modifications were found by searchers years later.)

The remaining flour was evidently baked down into hard biscuit, the salt meat dumped out of its heavy casks, covered anew with salt and packed into lighter sacks. What was left of the rum and, more especially the vinegar, which was considered their sole defense against scurvy once the lemon juice was gone, was decanted from casks into smaller kegs. Most of the rest of the provisions—chocolate wrapped in 1-ounce lead foil squares, canned food, rolled oats, barley, dried peas, tea, salt, and sugar—were removed from their wooden cases, barrels, and casks and dumped into light canvas sacks. In case of separation, each boat party carried its own, identical, store of provisions. It probably amounted to no more than 800 pounds of food per eight-man party—enough to sustain each, if severely rationed, for a maximum of three months. Any food that could not be hauled was left. Native Inuit, who ventured aboard one of the abandoned ships later, found—among other provisions—unopened cans of Goldner's preserved meat.

Together with the weight of the boats, sleds, and necessary equipage, this still constituted a hellish load of about 2,500 pounds: a bit over 300 pounds per man to drag. But Crozier had only Hobson's choices to make in these matters. The officers and men were clearly unfit to haul such loads, yet there was no option. They had to have the boats to reach open water—whatever direction they went—so they had to haul them on sleds over the ice to reach it. They had to have the boats' gear—oars, masts, sails, and tools especially—or hauling the boats was pointless. They had to take as much food as they could drag, but they couldn't drag all the food that was left. Crozier made the decisions and his crews, despite all they had suffered, carried them out with an energy and alacrity few other men, in similar circumstances, could have mustered.

In mid-April, Crozier—with only 15 officers and 90 men left—likely began sending the boats and their crews in relays to the shore camp to make everything ready. He and Fitzjames, along with skeleton crews, remained aboard ship until the last possible moment, perhaps still hoping for some sign of the spring thaw. On April 22, 1848, the ice as fast around them as ever, Crozier gave the order to desert the ships.

It must have been a wrenching parting for him. *Terror,* which had faithfully carried him so far and so long, was left in the ice. More than almost any other bond, that between a sailor and his ship is extremely strong, and that between a captain and his ship stronger still. There is a life-and-death dependency between them; neither can survive without the other. This affection, this love, may seem strange to those who have never gone to sea, but it is quite as real, perhaps more real, as other kinds of love. No ship is a mere inanimate object; it lives in wind and water and light, and it moves, murmurs, complains, or shouts like everything living.

Crozier knew every creak and groan in *Terror*'s timbers, every shriek and wail in her topsails, each comforting slap and wag of her halyards at anchor. The ship was the wife he'd never had, certainly the only enduring love of his life. To abandon *Terror,* still sound and willing, in the pack ice must have been the hardest thing he'd ever had to do. As he climbed over the ice-scoured sides, which had protected him so long, he may have thumped them like a well-loved hound. Until the mastheads were out of sight, he probably kept them in view. Then he turned his back, undoubtedly with tears in his eyes, and made for the thin horizon of King William Island.

There, at last, they would at least be free of the horrors of the shifting pack. They could leave the rats, foul smells, waking nightmares, and awful shipboard contagion behind. For all that had happened, they were at least alive and finally moving again, hopefully toward home. The boat crews dragged the last of the provisions with them. A portion of it consisted of Goldner's canned food.

On reaching the chill, stony shore, however, Crozier learned that yet another officer, sent ahead earlier, was dead. This death must have hit very close; it was Lt. John Irving, his junior-most lieutenant aboard *Terror.* Seemingly fit, he had apparently died like all the others. An American searcher, Lt. Frederick Schwatka, uncovered the remains in 1878. A medal, with Irving's name engraved on it, was lying in the shallow grave. He had apparently been buried with tenderness and care. According to Schwatka, "In the grave was found the object glass of a marine telescope and a few officer's gilt buttons stamped with an anchor and surrounded by a crown. Under the head was a colored silk handkerchief . . . and many pieces of coarsely stitched canvas, showing that this had been used as a receptable [sic] for the body when interred." Young Lt. Irving was among the last of the dead indulged such formality.

This raised the officers' death toll to ten out of twenty-four—over 40 percent. Whatever caused Irving's death had not been left behind. Barely ashore, Crozier seems to have decided to abandon everything that couldn't be dragged and make for the river as fast as he could, before he was left with no officers at all. M'Clintock later reported finding ". . . pickaxes, shovels, boats, cooking stoves, ironwork, rope, blocks, canvas, instruments, oar and medicine chest." The abandoned clothing alone was heaped in a pile 4 feet high.

It was here that Crozier dictated the last message ever found from the Franklin Expedition to his clerk-in-charge E. J. Helpman. It was almost certainly Helpman who wrote it; the handwriting on the message matches Helpman's handwriting in the muster books.

It consisted of just 158 words, obviously written in haste. The message is odd in several respects. Crozier had months to draft a more comprehensive report but, for some reason, did not. Most probably, he had planned to wait at the shore camp until the ice had melted sufficiently to float the boats and speed the journey south. But Irving's death, and perhaps the imminent deaths of others, changed his plans entirely. He apparently abandoned the well-built camp in a big hurry, indicating that he considered matters to have suddenly and unexpectedly reached life-or-death circumstances.

The message is puzzling in other ways. Its first two sentences are terse and well-written. In only fifty-three words, they identify the ships, dates, and position when they were abandoned, the period beset, number of survivors, and the latitude and longitude of their landing place. The next two sentences are wildly rambling, almost incoherent, and communicate no useful information:

> This paper was found by Lt. Irving under the cairn supposed to have been built by Sir James Ross in 1831, 4 miles to the northward, where it had been deposited by the late Commander Gore in June 1847. Sir James Ross' pillar has not however been found and the paper has been transferred to this position which is that in which Sir J. Ross' pillar was erected.

No part of this message makes sense. For some inexplicable reason, Crozier felt compelled to report who retrieved a sheet of paper (the dead Lt. Irving), where it was found (in a cairn 4 miles away), who had left it there almost a year earlier (the dead Lt. Gore), and the confusing notion that a 6-foot-tall cairn of stone (Ross' pillar) had somehow moved. To would-be searchers, this information was meaningless and Crozier's reason for relating it incomprehensible.

The last two sentences of the message were crystal clear, but incomplete. One relates Franklin's death and its date, as well as the total losses of the expedition. But maddeningly, it does not give a *cause*. If Franklin and the rest had perished of scurvy or starvation or typhus, why didn't Crozier say so? The only plausible explanation is that he did not know and could not say.

The final sentence, "And start on tomorrow $26^{th}$ for Back's Fish River," is particularly perplexing. The singlemost important piece of information—where they were going—was penned in almost as an afterthought. What's more, it was so vague as to be useless. Were they going to Back's River and west along the coast Dease and Simpson had charted? Up Back's River some 830 miles to Fort Resolution? To Back's River and then east to the whalers?

Crozier then had 105 survivors, was obviously intent on getting them out, yet left only the vaguest idea of his destination. Why didn't he plainly state it? The most probable explanation was that he didn't have a plan beyond reaching Back's River. Once there, he would make a determination on how best to proceed.

On April 26, 1848, Crozier quit the camp and led the survivors onto ice-packed Collinson Inlet toward today's Gore Point, some 6 miles south. Compared to the agonies of dragging a light-built, comparatively light-loaded (700 pounds) sledge through the Arctic, dragging heavy sleds topped by heavy boats crammed with provisions and gear was bone-crushing, mind-numbing, man-killing punishment. It must have been immediately apparent to Crozier that getting the boats to the river would take far longer than he ever imagined; far longer, in fact, than the food or many of the men would last.

Dragging the 6 miles over the ice to Gore Point likely consumed almost a week, perhaps more. Even for fit men, hauling boats across broken ice was snail-like. In his 1827 attempt to reach the North Pole, Sir William Edward Parry's crews (of which a young Lt. Crozier was a member) hauled two smaller (20-foot-long), purpose-built "troop boats" that featured metal sled runners as well as detachable wheels. Each was dragged by fourteen men. Even doubling the men in harness (twenty-eight to a boat), Parry calculated his progress at little more than a mile a day. In 1914–1917 Sir Ernest Shackleton's men, in far better condition than Crozier's, hauling similar ship's boats over the Antarctic pack, managed only one mile a day. It's unlikely that Crozier achieved more. Shackleton, in fact, calculated his progress in yards: "These boats were hauled in relays, about sixty yards at a time. . . . Every twenty yards or so they [the men] had to stop for a rest and to take a breath. . . . Thus the ground had to be traversed three times by the boat-hauling party." Hauling was only half the work: "The route lay over very hummocky floes, and required much work with pick and shovel to make it passable for the boat-sledges. . . . The first 200 yards took us about five hours to cross, owing to the amount of breaking down of pressure ridges and filling in of leads that was required."

The conditions Shackleton faced in the Antarctic spring of 1915 mirrored those Crozier encountered in the Arctic spring of 1848: ". . . at each step we went in over our knees in the soft wet snow. Sometimes a man would step into a hole in the ice which was hidden by the covering of snow, and had to be pulled up with a jerk by his harness." As Shackleton described it: "It was with the utmost difficulty that we shifted our two boats. The surface was terrible—like nothing that any of us had ever seen around us before. We were sinking at times up to our hips and everywhere the snow was two feet deep . . . [hauling] is killing work on soft surfaces." The cold and the wet soon hobbled many of Shackleton's men with frostbite, which his surgeons could treat only by amputating toes. They at least had chloroform; beyond rum, Crozier's surgeons had no anesthetics whatever. And while Shackleton's crew struggled to move three boats, Crozier's survivors dragged ten.

The weather Shackleton experienced ranged from "foggy and overcast, with some snow" to "abominably cold and wet underfoot" to "a howling south-westerly blizzard." The weather Crozier encountered negotiating the thawing yet still frigid ice foot fringing King William Island was likely quite as troublesome. Like Shackleton's men, who at first survived on "cold tinned mutton and tea" and "a quarter tin of bully-beef each, frozen hard," Crozier's crews were eating cold rations, perhaps including Goldner's toxic foods out of the can. The effect was gruesome. By the time they reached Gore Point, another officer and seaman were dead and buried in shallow graves there. More may have been left unburied or their graves simply never found.

Some 12 miles farther south, another officer died. At the point that today bears his name, the body of Lt. Henry LeVesconte, senior

*Manhauling Boats* This photo—of the Shackleton survivors dragging a sled-mounted ship's boat across the pack ice after the loss of the *Endurance*—is eerily reminiscent of the Franklin expedition's final fate. It took Shackleton's men, in far better condition, a week to drag two boats just seven miles. The Franklin survivors, laboring a month or more, managed to haul as many as thirteen boats more than 125 miles—a remarkable feat. Many dropped and died in harness before the boats were abandoned. (Underwood & Underwood and Royal Geographic Society)

lieutenant of the *Erebus* following Lt. Gore's death, was found by the American Charles Francis Hall in 1869. Other than Irving's, it was the only other skeleton from the Franklin Expedition positively identified—by means of a distinctive gold tooth filling. LeVesconte's death raised the officer's mortality rate to an appalling 45 percent.

How long it took Crozier to reach LeVesconte Point is anyone's guess: perhaps twelve days, perhaps two weeks. But when he left, his party had probably been reduced to thirteen starving officers and less than eighty men, and they were nowhere near the river and had made nowhere near the progress they had hoped to make. The survivors dragged the boats in harness, like Egyptian slaves harnessed to pyramid blocks. The boats represented their only hope, yet greatest curse. Without the boats, there was no hope of escape. To continue hauling them, however, growing weaker and weaker and making less and less progress every day, showed little chance of reaching the river at all.

Crossing the shore ice of today's Erebus Bay, an excruciating pull of 25 miles over pressure ridges and widening leads, likely consumed as much as three weeks. It was now early June. Six weeks had passed, a third or more of their scarce provisions were gone, and Crozier had managed to haul the boats less than 50 miles. Chantrey Inlet, which led south to Back's River, was still over 100 miles away; the mouth of the river itself was another 62 miles farther. At the rate they were going, it would take all summer and most of the fall to get there. Plainly, something had to be done, and quickly.

The crews had overcome incredible hardship, but a number had died since Lt. LeVesconte. Undoubtedly a significant number were too ill, malnourished, or simply too weak and frostbitten to haul. On the shores of Erebus Bay, Crozier seems to have divided the party. This is where the boat and remains Hobson discovered in 1859 were found, indicating such a split. Crozier apparently decided to take the strongest men and make for the river; the sick and lame would be left to make their way back to the camp near Victory Point, where the heavy clothing, the last of the coal, and some provisions had been left. If he could reach the river by midsummer, he might still get to Great Slave Lake and help. The men left behind would have to survive another winter as best they could until he came back for them; there was no other way.

The separation of the party must have been heart-rending. These men had trusted their lives with each other for three years; indeed their whole salvation had been laboring together. Taking leave certainly stunned them. Those left behind evidently gave their shipmates personal items to carry to their relatives, in case help did not arrive soon enough to save them. Those leaving, in turn, entrusted to their comrades' safekeeping items they could not carry—gold watches and the like. At least one officer, perhaps more, was left to command this forlorn party. Crozier pledged to return as soon as he could and, no doubt, told him to keep the men in good order and to lose no opportunity at taking game, especially the seabirds so abundant at that time of year. Shotguns, powder, and gooseshot were left for the purpose. The next day, Crozier's party took up their harnesses and commenced dragging the boats overland to the south.

The superhuman agony of this effort, and the superhuman courage required to undertake it, can scarce be measured. The forever halting march went on, hope going with it, under an anemic midnight sun. Crozier and the remaining officers dragged the boats in harness alongside the men, rank forgotten. The men left behind, the ships themselves, were soon only a faint, disturbing memory, like a nightmare recollected. The snow was soft, the shore ice slush, and the labor unrelenting: drag the boats forward 20 yards, then collapse, gasping for breath, in steaming, sweat-soaked duffle coats that were saturated with meltwater and, as soon as they got their wind, repeat the process. All day, every day, for as long as they could stand.

There was no way to keep their feet dry, no way of preventing frostbite which, in polar cold for men on foot, was a death sentence. Its onset was brutally swift. After a day's march during his 1899 expedition, the American who would later reach the North Pole, Robert E. Peary, complained of "a suspicious wooden feeling" in his feet. All his toes were found frozen. Seven of them were amputated on the spot. It was six weeks before he could walk again and then only in excruciating pain. On his desperate attempt to return from the South Pole in 1912, Robert Falcon Scott recorded the agony of frostbite that Crozier's survivors surely experienced. "My right foot has gone, nearly all the toes—[and] two days ago I was the proud possessor of best feet. These are the steps of my downfall," he wrote. A day later he recorded: "Today we started dragging [the sled] in the usual manner. Sledge dreadfully heavy. . . . All our feet are getting bad—Wilson's best, my right foot worst, left all right. There is no chance to nurse one's feet till we can get some hot food into us. Amputation is the least I can hope for now, but will the trouble spread? That is the serious question." Three days later, in one of his last entries, he wrote: "Wilson and Bowers unable to start [frostbite]—tomorrow last chance—no fuel and only one or two food left—must be near the end. Have decided it shall be natural—we shall march for the depot with or without our effects and die in our tracks."

At the same time, like Scott's doomed party, Crozier's frostbitten, starving survivors would have been tormented by thirst. Among Scott's last diary entries, he noted, "We have the last half fill of oil in our primus [stove] and a very small quantity of spirit—this alone between us and thirst." Crozier's much larger party had even less fuel for their tiny spirit stoves, if indeed any remained at all. There was not nearly enough water to drink and the suffering from thirst was almost beyond belief. The men lapped pools of meltwater like dogs, or ate snow. The more patient chipped ice into tin cups, carried them under their clothing and waited until it melted enough to provide a swallow or two. When the sun was high, it scorched their winter-whitened, pork-pale skin into blisters and forced them to wear their blindfoldlike snow goggles against the glare. When it dipped low on the horizon, never disappearing, their coats began to freeze as tight as straitjackets. It was exquisite torture of a kind devised by grand inquisitors; it was as if the Arctic was not only punishing them for entering its domain, but exacting vengeance on them by preventing their escape.

The brief night halts provided no real rest (Peary on his polar sledge trips, though exhausted beyond forbearance, managed only an hour of fitful sleep a night). The tents were raised by men stupefied with weariness, hunger, and thirst and made so clumsy with frozen fingers and rope-burned hands that tying the simplest knot took a godawful lot of time and concentration. The sole thing to look forward to was the cooks—Diggle and Wall—doling out the evening ration and the officers issuing each man some rum. It was a pitiful allowance. The last of the canned food, the meat they craved, was gone; but oddly, so too was the suffocating disease that had doomed so many of their shipmates. No one, not Crozier or the surgeons or the men, likely made the association. By that point, there was too much sickness from starvation, scurvy, and frostbite to distinguish one cause of death from another.

The men were bearded, sunken-eyed, skin-covered skeletons. They had been on two-thirds rations for almost a year when the ships were deserted, so they were painfully thin before the march even started. Idle, they would have required about 1,700 calories a day just to maintain their body weight. Dragging the boats on one-fourth rations, perhaps 500 calories a day, they were wasting away. Their bodies, in a process called autocannibalization, had quite literally begun to devour themselves. A starving human body at first consumes its fat, its principal fuel reserves, to keep functioning. When that is gone, the still hungry body begins to digest its muscles—its engine—resulting in drastic weight loss and a lowered immune system. As the muscles are sacrificed for survival, simply walking, much less hauling heavy loads, takes extraordinary effort. In its ravenous craving, the body next begins feeding on its organs. Stomach, kidneys, liver, eyesight, coordination, and mental faculties begin to fail. Body temperature and blood pressure drop. Glands go dormant or cease to function entirely. Physical collapse and cardiac arrhythmia are common. Without food, there is no stopping this process—the body will digest itself completely.

Crozier likely sent hunters out ahead of the main party to bring in any game they could find. The men, armed with shotguns and muskets with an effective range of no more than 25 to 70 yards maximum, may have succeeded in shooting some ptarmigan and Arctic hare. But however many they managed to bag were not nearly enough to feed the survivors. Seals, the mainstay of the native Inuit, may have been plentiful out on the sea ice, but the Englishmen likely avoided the treacherous sea ice they had escaped. What's more, hunting for seals took time and skills they did not have. Seals generally come up to breathe in open leads or holes in the ice, with their heads above water for only about 30 seconds. They do not venture onto the ice until May or June and then only occasionally. The patience required to find them, kill them, retrieve the carcass before it sinks, and drag a hundredweight or more of flesh back to the main party, were skills Crozier's emaciated sailors lacked. Even if they had them in abundance, it's unlikely to have done much good. There were simply too many mouths to feed. Inuit bands, well practiced in the art of seal hunting, consisted of no more than two or three families, ten to fifteen people at most, and they barely managed to survive.

Crozier's men may well have attempted to forage plants. One or more of the surviving officers had certainly read enough books on Arctic flora during the previous winters to distinguish Iceland moss and rock tripe, both of which are edible. But early spring, the season in which they headed south, is the most barren time for gathering plants. Most, including shoreside kelp, laver, and sea lettuce, had yet to germinate or were locked beneath ice and snow. Despite whatever efforts they made, the Arctic landscape yielded too little to account for the balance of their rapidly dwindling provisions.

The only thing that mattered now was food to return some kind of warmth to a man and give him strength enough to haul—to go on living—for another day. But there was precious little food left; dragging the boats had been too hard and the march had taken too long. At most, each man now got one ship's biscuit, a shaving of salt meat to go with it, a couple of one-ounce squares of chocolate, a palm-full of loose tea, a mouthful of sugar, and perhaps a tablespoon of rum. Nothing was cooked; there was no fuel left and a fellow was too hungry to wait for it to cook if there had been. It was wolfed down in a minute. For a brief while afterward, as the food and especially the rum, burned warm inside them, came their only respite. There was still a little tobacco and this was carefully broken up, tamped into clay-stemmed pipes, and gratefully smoked.

Crozier, on sore-frozen feet, likely visited each of the tent messes, encouraging the men, soliciting promises of better progress tomorrow in an exchange for an extra dram of rum. He'd had the foresight to pack extra shoes and boots in the boats, so a fellow could exchange soaking ones for a dry pair, if he could stand the pain of pulling them on over blackened, gangrenous feet. But their wet, freezing garments could never be got dry and these damped their blanket bags, which froze in turn. Consequently nobody, despite the half-hour's salvation after eating, rested soundly. The cramping hunger pangs and the shivering cold and the dread of another day's torture returned. As one English sledger, Lt. Sherard Osborn, laboring under far better circumstances, recollected: "Very few can possibly realize the utter wretchedness endured. . . . Inside the tightly closed blanket bag, it is too dark to read, too miserable to speak and woe to any who leaves the mouth open. For the whole interior of the tent is filled with snow drift—so fine and light as to be likened to the motes of a sunbeam—forever sifting gradually downwards and forming a thick and ever increasing deposit on the upper canvas stretched over the cramped men."

By some miracle—there is no other word for it—Crozier managed to reach the southwestern edge of King William Island sometime about mid-August; a distance of more than 80 miles. He still had a few of the boats, but by then the last of the food and even the strongest men were giving out.

M'Clintock found one of them in 1859, on a bare gravel ridge near the mouth of the Peffer River. "This poor man seems to have selected the bare ridge top, as affording the least tiresome walking, and to have fallen upon his face in the position we found him," he reported. The skeleton was wearing a steward's uniform with a pocketful of possessions: "a notebook, a small clothes brush . . . and a horn comb, in which a few light brown hairs still remained." The notebook belonged to Petty Officer Harry Peglar, captain of the foretop of *Terror,* leader of the picked topmen of the ship's company, who worked the dangerously high topsail and topgallant yards of the ship, the aristocrats of the lower deck. Peglar, starving, had either died on the march or been left at Erebus Bay and entrusted the book to the steward who, despite his own sufferings, tenderly carried it homeward, intent on delivering it to Peglar's relatives. In it—writing backwards—he left a cryptic note: "Oh Death whare is thy sting, the grave at Comfort Cove for who has any doubt how . . . the dyer sad."

Hope had, by that time, plainly begun to evaporate, though none of the men dared admit it, except to themselves. By writing backwards, the writer, whoever he was, didn't want to let his shipmates, still laboring south, to know his desperation. He was left where he lay; the living went on.

More than three months' tortuous labor left Crozier over 100 miles away from the mouth of Back's River. Even on starvation allowance, the food was about gone. The last crumbs of ship's biscuit had been eaten. Every particle of flour dust from the sacks, mixed with meltwater, had been made into a gruel and drunk. Nothing remained but chocolate, tea, and the leather uppers of their shoes. The men could keep down neither. Without something to eat, they could not continue to haul the boats. Without something to eat, they would never reach the river.

# CHAPTER 21

# Cannibalism

*(they were) carrying a number of skulls . . . there were more than four . . . also bones from legs and arms that appeared to have been sawed off.*

—Captain Francis M'Clintock,
reporting Inuit eyewitness accounts

At what is today Booth Point, with the men starving, weak, sick, and unable to drag the boats another yard, Crozier was forced to halt altogether. It was not mere exhaustion that stopped him in his tracks, but the crushing discovery of the last thing he expected to find. Beyond the point, the shore of King William Land, which had all along been leading southeast toward Back's River, suddenly bent back to the northeast as far as he could see. It was not part of the North American mainland at all, but an island; the ice-choked water now blocking the way south wasn't an inlet or a bay, but a narrow strait. It was still frozen, to be sure, but when the ice went out, it would open into an east-west road some 6 to 20 miles wide. He was looking—finally, incomprehensibly—at the fabled Northwest Passage. They had, in spite of everything, found it, found what men had been seeking for 300 years: the gateway across the top of the world.

He may have called for three cheers, but the men—doll-eyed and cadaverous—were beyond cheering, beyond caring. If he still carried his sextant, chronometer, and compass, he almost certainly fixed the position and inked it in his log. But his bitterness and despair may have been too great. All that had been risked, suffered, and endured was repaid with ashes. The news of their discovery would not survive if they didn't and it was of no earthly good to them now. At that point, he would have gladly traded the Passage for a cask of ship's biscuit.

As evidenced from more stone tent circles, the party encamped for some time, perhaps deliberating what to do next. The men left alive (dozens may have perished on the grueling march south) were barely alive and clearly incapable of going another step. They could certainly no longer drag the boats. They were paper-thin skeletons, moving painfully on scurvy-swollen legs and gangrenous, frostbitten feet, blinded by snow glare, tortured by thirst, shivering with cold, and, above all, tormented with hunger. Those with any strength left may have feebly foraged the shoreline or brought in some saxifrage, and the officers, with what little powder and shot remained, may have managed to shoot some seabirds; all of this would have been thrown into a kettle, heated over whatever could be found to make a fire, and doled out, in painstakingly equal measure, to each man. But it was not nearly enough to begin to feed ravenous men; indeed some men were so weak, they probably could not eat at all. They lay down in the snow and the mud, crying with hunger; the rest attempted to do their tasks, but something went out of them, too. By turns, they knelt, sat, or laid down and nothing Crozier did could move them.

One of these men, apparently a seaman suffering the last stages of starvation, scurvy, and exposure, soon died. His corpse, however, wasn't buried; it was left where it lay. One can only imagine Crozier at his ebb, his ragged greatcoat flapping in the wind, dying men collapsed all around him, the icy Passage mocking him. His eyes, like those of the men, may have gone blank with hopelessness. It had been his driving leadership, after all, that had carried them to a place from which it now seemed they could never escape. The survivors, who at every step of the awful march looked to him to sustain them, could not have helped but notice that Crozier too had reached his end. Something rather like an eclipse swept over them all. This is quite likely the moment when Crozier proposed the unthinkable. He may have asked the surviving surgeons point-blank: without food, how long could they live? The answer would have been obvious:

without something to eat, sooner or later, they would all die like the seaman lying before them, like so many others they had left behind.

Faced with certain death, Crozier was forced to make a horrible and repugnant decision, the only one left him. It was certainly Crozier who made it: he was the ranking officer and among the few officers the native Inuit later reported seeing alive. He apparently chose life. He may have put it to an officers' vote or perhaps a vote of the whole party, but at most this would have merely been a ratification. The decision had to have been Crozier's. The dead man, who had served so long and faithfully, could serve his shipmates again. With provisions exhausted, and still far from the river and with the crews broken beyond all forbearance, Crozier decided to cannibalize the dead.

Discoveries made by Beattie and Geiger in 1981 first revealed it. In one Booth Point tent site, they uncovered shell buttons, of the type worn by sailors, and broken clay pipestems that could only have come from Crozier's party. Scattered outside the stone tent circle were thirty-one human bone fragments, which forensic examination confirmed were the remains of a single individual: male, Caucasian, aged twenty to twenty-five at the time of death. The bones showed pitting and scaling consistent with scurvy, but they also showed parallel knife marks consistent with butchering. Near the entrance of the tent site were skull fragments, again of the same individual. Fracture lines indicated the skull had been forcibly broken. The face, both jaws, and all the teeth were missing. Evidence the body had been intentionally dismembered was further supported by the selective parts of the skeleton found. Besides the face, most of the skeleton was missing, including twenty-four ribs, breastbone, all twenty-four vertebrae of the back, the hips, collarbones, and shoulder blades.

More than likely, one of the surviving surgeons was deputed to butcher the corpse. Assistant Surgeon Harry Goodsir of the *Erebus* had trained as an anatomist, so was particularly qualified. Moreover, his surgical kit contained the tailor-made tools. A surgeon could have made quick work of this and, however repulsive it may have been to him, it was likely a comfort to the crew. The task would be done "proper," by a medical man, an officer and gentleman. The corpse was likely carried into one of the tents, out of sight of the rest and, attended by one or two men, the surgeon commenced.

From his medicine chest, Goodsir would have probably first selected a capital saw—a long, full-bladed saw, like a carpenter's. With this, he removed the head, sawed off the arms at the shoulder, and sawed through the pelvic bone to remove both legs. Switching to a metacarpal saw—a straight-bladed saw, about the size of a butcher knife—he divided the arms at the elbows and the legs at the knees and likely cut off the hands and feet. With catlins—long, thin, extremely sharp scalpels resembling filleting knives—he removed the meatiest portions first: buttocks, thighs, and the backs of the shins from the legs; deltoids, biceps, and triceps from the upper arms. Cut in thin strips, these were probably dropped immediately into a kettle set to boil over whatever barrel staves or planking the survivors could scavenge. The flesh from the trunk of the body—pectorals, shoulder blades, back, and sides—was next carved off and possibly laid in the sun to dry. In hours, they would brown into a stiff, uncured jerky unrecognizable as a man. Using tenaculum—slender, sharp-pointed instruments for holding—the sternum was cracked and the ribs removed one by one.

No part of the body, at this stage, was wasted. The heart, liver, and kidneys, all major organs, were probably extracted entire. More than likely the cooks, Diggle and Wall, chopped these up into tidbits with an axe and dropped them into the stew. As Goodsir knew, the intestines and the stomach, if well washed, were valuable food and the bone marrow especially. He would have used a Hey's saw—a long-handled, double-edged serrated saw—to open the abdominal sac. The guts were set aside, like the head, hands, and feet, for later. Then he may have used forceps to crack the long bones, and a raspator—a curved scraping tool, like a woodcarver's gouge—to remove the chunky, red marrow. The marrow was dumped straightaway into the kettle.

The dead man had been rendered from a human being into food. Goodsir probably retreated at once from the tent where this dismemberment had taken place and paced, ashamedly, back and forth in the snow. But before long, he began to smell the cook's fire and the indescribably wonderful aroma of fresh meat.

Undoubtedly that wasn't the end of it. There is overwhelming proof that the Franklin survivors practiced cannibalism on a far wider scale than that evidenced at Booth Point. In 1992, archaeologist Margaret Bertulli and anthropologist Anne Keenleyside made a particularly gruesome find in Erebus Bay (on the west shore of King William Island). The discovery of over 200 artifacts—wood fragments and nails from a ship's boat, buttons, glass, clay pipes, traces of leather shoes and cloth, wire gauze from snow goggles and percussion caps—clearly marked the site as one inhabited by Franklin survivors. More ominous was the recovery of almost 400 human bones, representing the remains of at least eight and as many as eleven individuals. All of them were estimated to be under the age of fifty at the time of death (consistent with the ages of the expedition's crew). A quarter of these bones, scanned under an electron microscope, showed cut marks characteristic of knives. What's more, the cut marks were "consistent with intentional disarticulation," indicating that the dead had been dismembered and the flesh meticulously carved away.

Located quite close to the "Boat Place" found by Lt. Hobson in 1859, this was probably another party laboring to return to the deserted ships. But at this point, they apparently stopped, desperate for food. Lacking a surgeon, they set about butchering the dead bodies with sailor's knives, as best as they knew how. The cut marks showed they had acquired experience. They cut through the joints and proceeded—quite systematically—to carve every ounce off the remains in a pattern Bertulli and Keenleyside concluded was "consistent with defleshing or removal of muscle tissue." Whether this propelled them any nearer to their goal is unknown. For a time however, it kept them alive.

In life-or-death situations, cannibalization is by no means uncommon. The living invariably choose life and the dead are, after all, dead—beyond all suffering and offering the sole remaining hope of life. It is never entered into lightly. Although practiced in the utmost extremity by the Inuit, Chippewyan, and other native American nations of the Arctic and sub-Arctic, it is considered the greatest taboo. But the more extreme the circumstances, the more extreme the choices. Most usually it begins with the survivors eating the dead; only later does it progress to survivors eating each other.

The experience of the infamous Donner Party, trapped by record snowfall in the Sierra Nevada in 1846–1847, at almost the same time Crozier's party was trapped on King William Island, is typical. So long as any food remained, it was divided equally. "The families shared with one another as long as they had anything to share," remembered a survivor. "Each one's portion was very small. The hides [of the last cattle] were boiled and the bones burned brown and eaten. We tried to eat a decayed buffalo robe, but it was too tough and there was no nourishment in it. Some of the few mice that came into camp were caught and eaten."

When every morsel of food was gone, real starvation set in. With the snow over 6 feet deep and the ground below hard-frozen, the Donner Party, like Crozier's, was unable to bury its dead. Their remains, according to an eyewitness, were "wasted by famine or evaporated by the dry atmosphere [and] presented the appearance of mummies." These mummified corpses, however, promised the only hope of salvation. The remains were butchered and eaten. Rescuers found "bodies entire, with the exception that the abdomens had been cut open and the entrails extracted. . . . Strewn about the cabins were dislocated and broken skulls, in some instances sawed asunder with care, for the purpose of extracting the brains . . . human skeletons, in short, in every variety of mutilation." Of the eighty-nine members of the Donner Party, only forty-nine—eating the dead—survived.

Arctic expeditions were particularly subject to cannibalism. Sir John Franklin's 1819 expedition down the Coppermine River was only the first. In 1881–1884, American Lt. Adolphous Greely's polar expedition, marooned three years in a makeshift hut far above the Arctic Circle, suffered the same horror. One of its members, Private Henry, was discovered eating its dead. Greely was revulsed and made short work of the matter. He penned a terse order: "Private Henry will be shot today, all care being taken to prevent his injuring anyone, as his physical strength is greater than any two men. Decide the matter of death by two balls and one blank cartridge. This order is imperative and absolutely necessary for any chance of life." Henry was summarily shot. But his execution didn't end the matter. When rescuers finally found Greely and seven survivors—the sole survivors among twenty-six men—they also found corpses from which the flesh had been stripped away and eaten. To hide the fact, the commander of the relief expedition suggested to the Navy Department that the remains of the dead be sealed in metal coffins.

The somber feast at Booth Point evidently went on for several days. After the meatiest portions of the body were consumed, the men likely slept sound. The flesh and marrow stew, though each got only a cup, rejuvenated them. For a time they would have felt invigorated. When they awoke, each man got an equal portion of the flesh that had been laid in the sun to dry. But there were still too many mouths to feed and great care and industry was taken to extract every scrap of nutriment from the corpse.

Dr. Goodsir likely hacked the jaws from the skull and removed the protein-rich brains. These, along with the stomach and intestines saved from the day before, went into the cook's kettle. The bones he had scraped of marrow earlier went into the pot as well, to boil out every particle of blood and fat. Sea water answered for salt and some seaweed thickened every man's cupful: it was enough for another hot meal, another night's sleep. The twenty-four ribs, breastbone, marrow-rich vertebrae, pelvis, collarbone, and shoulder blades were carefully stowed in the boats to eat later.

The effect of this meat must have been miraculous. The men were able to haul the boats once more and Crozier took them south across the ice of 23-mile-wide Simpson Strait. About this time, the survivors were startled to see people: the first other human beings they had laid eyes on in nearly three years. It must have caused a wild celebration: surely these were the rescuers sent down from Great Slave Lake to find them. They were saved.

But as the parties approached one another, Crozier could see they weren't Europeans, but fur-clad, tattooed Esquimaux (Inuit)—men, women, and children out on the ice in the strait, hunting seals.

For their part, the Inuit were just as shocked to encounter *kabloonans* (white men), coming from out of nowhere, dragging strange, monstrous contraptions over the ice. The encounter was surreal—and short.

Charles Francis Hall, the American who later searched for Franklin survivors, interviewed some of these Inuit nearly twenty years afterward. "Several native families," he reported, "provided an officer thought to be Crozier and a group of his men with seal meat. The Inuit then left, ignoring pleas for further aid." At the time, this was accepted as proof the native Americans abandoned Crozier and his pleading, begging men. In fact, that they shared what little seal meat they had was noble; that they stole away at the first opportunity is understandable. Imagine yourself on a family camping trip when, suddenly, a gang of fifty hairy, incoherent Hell's Angels appear out of nowhere. They're plainly starving, heavily armed with guns, knives, and hatchets—and openly carrying human body parts. The Inuit, thinking they might be next on the menu, were clearly terrified. They gave what seal meat they had and got away as fast and as far as they could.

The fat-rich seal meat, eaten raw, was like ambrosia to Crozier's men. It stilled, for a time, the bitter disappointment of the Inuit's departure and enabled them to drag the boats farther across the strait. But when they reached the mainland—at a place now called Starvation Cove—they were again starving, entirely broken, and unable to go on. At this bleak place, another seaman, whose remains were found by Schwatka in 1879, died and was eaten. Temporarily, starvation and scurvy were staved off. The mouth of Back's River, their goal, was only another 62 miles, but no more of the survivors died so conveniently to feed the rest.

The men left alive were, by this time, no strangers to the taste and life in human flesh. The strong may have looked at the weak, those who could no longer haul, not as shipmates but as food. At that point another, far more gruesome, decision confronted them.

The *taking* of human life for food, rather than just feeding on the dead, is the ultimate desperation. This is quite rare, but Crozier's men were apparently soon forced to adopt the practice. It's even more repulsive and psychologically damaging than cannibalizing the dead. One of the few clearly documented cases of this involved the wreck of the brig *Essex,* stove and sunk by an 85-foot sperm whale on Nov. 20, 1820. The ship went down in the most remote part of the Pacific Ocean.

Her twenty-man crew, most of whom were off hunting whales at the time, returned to find her sinking. In three whaleboats, they managed to get off all hands: seven in Captain Pollard's boat, six in the boat of First Mate Owen Chase, and seven in the boat of Second Mate Matthew Joy. Desperately, they retrieved some tools, one pistol, two compasses, two quadrants, and two books on navigation. The only provisions they could save were two casks of ships' biscuit, a half-dozen casks of water, and two live turtles they had taken on in the Galapagos Islands for fresh meat. What happened to them next—in all likelihood—happened to Crozier's survivors at Starvation Cove.

Steering for South America, each man was at first issued one ship's biscuit and a half-pint of water a day. In short order, they killed the turtles, drank the blood, and warmed the meat after a fashion over a fire built in the shells. When this was gone some flying fish, unfortunate to land in the boats, were devoured raw. Next, the barnacles were scraped off the bottoms of the boats and eaten. By sheer luck they struck Henderson Island, a minute dot of land in the mid-Pacific, and for four days scrounged crabs, clubbed nesting gulls and sucked down their eggs, and refilled their water casks from a tiny spring. But there was not enough food or water to sustain twenty men. A vote was taken: three men elected to remain; seventeen took to the boats again on December 27, 1820.

On January 12, 1821, Third Mate Hendrick's boat disappeared in a storm and was never seen again. On January 28, another storm separated the last two boats. Alone on the ocean, Captain Pollard sailed eastward. The only food was one and a half ounces of ship's biscuit per man a day and what rainwater they could catch in their sail. This kept them alive for nine weeks until both bread and water were gone. Four men remained barely alive: Pollard, his nephew Owen Coffin (a cabin boy), and two seamen—Charles Ramsdell and a free black man named Barzillai Ray. They were still over 1,600 miles from the nearest landfall. As captain, Pollard faced a horrible, inescapable decision: if any were to live, one had to die to feed the rest.

They drew lots. To Pollard's horror, his own nephew, young Owen Coffin, drew the short straw. They drew lots again to determine who would do the killing. Mortified, able-bodied seaman Ramsdell drew the short straw. There was nothing to stop the thing; they all understood the necessity and the love and regard for one another that made it a necessity. Coffin laid his head on the gunwale. Pollard gave his pistol to Ramsdell and turned away. He shot Coffin in the back of the head. The rest of the body was hauled into the boat. The still-hot blood was drunk, the quivering flesh sliced from the skeleton and eaten raw. The bones were later broken open, the marrow picked out and every fragment sucked clean. Coffin's corpse sustained them almost two weeks until Barzillai Ray died. Pollard and Ramsdell fed off his remains until February 23, 1821, when they were rescued by the whaler *Dauphin.*

The execution of his nephew, the cannibalization of Coffin's and Ray's corpses, haunted Pollard the rest of his days. He went to sea only one more time, was shipwrecked once more, and was never again trusted with command of a ship. He ended his life as a town watchman in Nantucket. Scorned and shunned, he hid biscuit and salt pork in the rafters of his house until he died.

Crozier now faced the same horror, but on a far larger scale. He still had as many as thirty or more men to feed and, other than what could be scavenged from the sterile shores around Starvation Cove (lichens mostly, perhaps some whelkfish), there was no food. The boats could not be moved. The men were too weak to hunt and, beyond gulls, there was nothing they knew how to hunt. It was September, the first snow began to fall, and they were still not yet to the river. If they were ever to make the 850-mile journey to Great Slave Lake, they had to begin at once, before the river began to freeze.

For a time, Crozier probably waited grimly. He had grown used to death. The dead were done with suffering at least. He was numb; the tears didn't come anymore; the twist in his stomach constricted no further; he felt everything less and less. He probably welcomed it; it was the mind and body shutting off, preparing him for what was to come. A few of the weakest might yet die in their sleep to feed the rest. Just a few more dead, a few more meals, would fuel the survivors long enough to drag the boats to the river. Once there, they could at last float the boats and, with a favorable wind, commence the journey south. On the river, they would surely find fish and likely game along its banks and, God willing, the Hudson's Bay Company coming downriver.

But the men that remained alive were survivors. Exposure and starvation dimmed their eyesight and devoured their bodies, but they hung on somehow, and soon Crozier could wait no longer. Some, not just one or two, would have to die to save the rest. None would survive otherwise. He could not ask any man to volunteer; that would be too much to ask of men who had already given everything. They would leave it in God's hands.

Courage was the only thing the expedition had left in abundance. Lots were likely drawn, every officer and man taking his chance. In the disastrous retreat of the British army from Kabul during the Afghan War of 1842, lots were drawn to determine who would remain behind with the sick and wounded, tantamount to a death sentence. On the shore of Starvation Cove, these were plucked one at a time by trembling, emaciated fingers. Who or how many may have sacrificed themselves is unknown. It could have been Francis Dunn, twenty-eight, the caulker's mate from *Erebus* or David Leys, forty, an able-bodied seaman aboard *Terror* or Sergeant David Bryant, thirty-five, head of the marine contingent on *Erebus*. By the same selfless token, it may have been Third Lieutenant George Hodgson of the *Terror* (whose custom-made sextant was found among the gear earlier abandoned at Victory Point) or John Cowie, thirty-five, a stoker from the *Erebus* or twenty-one-year old Thomas Evans, a midshipman from the *Terror*. How they were dispatched is, of course, unknown. Powder and shot would have been too precious to waste. Knives may have been employed instead. Their bodies were consigned to any of the surgeons who remained alive, or to their shipmates, who quickly rendered them into life for the survivors.

This food carried them to Montreal Island, near the mouth of Back's River. Searchers later discovered two iron barrel hoops, some other corroded pieces of metal, and the remains of one of Goldner's preserved meat cans (long before emptied of food and likely carried as a cookpot). Beyond that point, no more artifacts, skeletons, or boats were ever found. Most probably, those that were left finally floated their boats and ascended the river. It was their only chance. Ice, cold, and death had still not stopped them. Ironically, as long as they had each other for food, they went upriver.

Weakened and delirious, it's unlikely they got far. Some may have fallen victim to the river's treacherous rapids and drowned. Winter may have overtaken the rest. The very last survivors—coming out of the north, from the land of the Inuit, who had warred with the Chippewyans for centuries—may have been killed. More likely, in that rocky, treeless wilderness, they finally laid down and died. They could do no more. No men could.

Years later—as Rae, Hobson, M'Clintock, Hall, and Schwatka searched the area—it was rumored that Crozier had survived. He was said to have lived for a time among the Chippewyans, nomadic hunters of the far north. If true, it would make sense. Crozier had been a nomad in the north his entire life and, perhaps at last, had found a place where he was accepted for what he was; not for who he was born or where he came from. It was the place that Barrow, in first undertaking the expedition, had tried to make—an aristocracy of character, refined by adversity, sustained by courage and humanity, and undiluted by anything else.

# CHAPTER 22
# The Culprit's Footprints

*I have had the honor of supplying the Navy for the last 10 years. . . . This I confidently hope will be sufficient excuse for thus imploring one more trial before I am completely cut off.*

—Stephan Goldner,
to Comptroller of Victualling, Deptford

In 1847, six months before Franklin's death, Goldner won another polar victualling contract. He played the same bait-and-switch game. On December 3, 1847, he wrote: "I will undertake to deliver the whole quantity required within 3 weeks from this time. Great care shall be taken with the preparation of the articles, and due attention paid, that the sizes of the canisters shall not exceed 8-lbs. each."

A week later, he reneged: "I fear much delay would ensue were I obliged to manufacture such a quantity . . . to enable me to comply with the term of my letter, as regards the sizes of the canisters." It was the Franklin dodge all over again. He wagged the threat of delay under the Admiralty's nose, substituted larger cans for smaller ones and thus reduced the number of cans he'd contracted to produce by 25 percent. The savings went into his pocket.

In 1848, as Crozier's decimated survivors were engaged in their death march, Goldner won yet another handsome polar victualling contract. Ironically, it was to supply HMS *Enterprise* and HMS *Investigator* to go looking for Franklin. In the next years, these relief expeditions, dispatched after the man he had sent to his death, were to become Goldner's major source of income and a very lucrative one at that.

Again, he employed the bait-and-switch tactic, contracting to provide three sizes of cans—but supplying only one. Again, he held out the carrot of faster delivery: "Should you be pleased to grant my request [for larger cans], it would assist me much in the execution of the order." The Admiralty, desperate by this time to find Franklin, whose provisions were slated to run out by the end of the year, agreed to the request.

In 1849, supplying yet another Franklin relief expedition, Goldner contracted to fill the order in square, rather than round, canisters. The Admiralty, quite sensibly, decreed the change in the interest of saving space and more efficient stowage. Goldner, of course, provided nothing of the kind. Before the ink dried on the contract, he was at work violating it to his advantage. In two monumentally long, quasi-scientific sentences filled with double-talk, he convinced the navy that square canisters were more liable to rupture than cylindrical ones. "In reply [to the request for square canisters]," he wrote, "I beg to state that I have made sometime ago various experiments in pursuit of this object, but I have invariably found that the pressure of the atmosphere upon the canister, owing to there being a vacuum within, was so great as not only to collapse the canister so as to entirely destroy the shape of it, but also to endanger the safe preservation of the contents in consequence to the tin being liable to give way when the canister collapses to so great an extent." This was nonsense. The canisters were under the same atmospheric pressure, whether square, round, or oblong. Regardless of shape, there was a vacuum within. His sole motivation—profit—was transparently clear: "Under these circumstances, I think you will see it would not be advisable to adopt the alteration, especially as almost all of the articles ordered are already manufactured on the usual plan."

Again the Admiralty, by now frantic to find Franklin, accepted the explanation. Goldner escaped the terms he'd committed to, as well as the expense of retooling his factory, and furnished the order in round cans.

By 1849, however, the Admiralty had clearly begun to lose patience with Goldner. He was, more or less, continually late in his deliveries. Despite his contracts, he continued to furnish the navy cans that were neither manufactured to specification nor provided in the proper size. Worse yet, complaints about his goods had become more frequent. His canned meats were found to contain bone and offal; his canned vegetables "not clean of the soil"; and his "concentrated" gravy diluted. Numbers of his cans didn't stand up to rough handling at sea and routinely burst at the seams, spoiling the contents. These problems were regularly reported in the navy's "Returns reports," a listing of the quantity and quality of provisions remaining aboard ship upon their return to England. However, the purpose of these reports was not quality control, but pecuniary. The Admiralty returned any food that was still edible into its stores for reissue. It sold whatever was unfit for whatever the market would bear. In this, the Admiralty had as keen a palm for hard coin as Goldner.

The fact that it continued to do business with him and on a vastly expanded scale, knowing what it did, had nothing to do with confidence in his product. Far from it. Goldner was one of the few canned food contractors willing to commit to supply the Admiralty the vast quantities it demanded, in the short time frames required, at the lowest possible price. A considerable percentage of it might go bad, and invariably did. But Goldner's initial low prices (and the realization that whatever did go bad could probably be resold) excused other considerations.

Still, the navy took pains to protect itself. On May 2, 1850, Goldner signed a contract to supply the Admiralty 500,000 pounds of canned boiled beef. This was an enormous order—a windfall for Goldner—yet at his prices (3,000 pounds sterling at the time or about $202,000 U.S. today), a genuine bargain for the Admiralty. However, the riders the Admiralty wrote into the contract starkly revealed growing concerns. The terms prohibited Goldner from weighting cans with bone, labeling offal and intestines as boiled beef, supplying the beef in cans larger (and cheaper to make) than those specified, employing shoddy canning materials or workmanship (which might cause cans to "collapse and rupture"), or egregiously ignoring the plainly stated delivery deadlines. The contract further insisted that Goldner give notice, in writing, when and where he intended to process the beef, so Admiralty inspectors could "ascertain that the process is conducted in every respect in accordance with its [the contract's] conditions."

Not surprisingly, Goldner paid no more attention to the terms of this contract than any others. No notification was given to Admiralty inspectors. As much bone as boiled beef filled his cans. A significant percentage of the cans were delivered ruptured, and none of them were delivered on time.

Shockingly, the Admiralty favored him with another, even larger, contract only eight months later. On January 29, 1851, he was engaged to supply the Admiralty 800,000 pounds of canned boiled beef. Considering Goldner's dismal record, this seems incomprehensible. For the Admiralty, however, it made consummate sense. This enormous quantity of canned beef was bought "on the cheap," at a ridiculously low cost. Goldner quoted a price of but 4,000 pounds sterling (about $269,000 U.S. today) for the entire order—60 percent more beef than his 1850 contract at a price only 25 percent higher. On the ledger books, it appeared to be a purchasing coup.

But in return for this order, the Admiralty's bureaucrats held his feet to the fire. Goldner had to guarantee that the beef would "continue perfectly sound, sweet and good and fit for use" for five years. Goldner happily agreed (even though the shelf life of the U.S. military's latest Meals-Ready-To-Eat, or MRES, whose packaging is light years ahead of Goldner's, are warranted to last but five years). He was also contractually bound to guarantee all his cans. Any can "found collapse [sic] or bursting *from any cause whatsoever* and the Contractor shall pay back all such sums of money as he may have been paid for the same." Furthermore, the contract gave Admiralty inspectors ". . . the power to open as many Cannisters when delivered as they think proper . . ." for the purpose of examining them in detail—something that had *not* been done with the Franklin Expedition provisions.

The final terms were even more searing. Goldner was forced to post a bond in the amount of 4,000 pounds sterling, equivalent to the value of the contract itself. If he breached *any* clause in the contract, the money was forfeit to the Crown. Goldner willingly signed the bond.

By the end of 1851, however, matters came to a head. His preserved meats provided in the 1850 and 1851 contracts were found "in a pulpy, decayed and putrid state, and totally unfit for men's food." Over a thousand pounds of it was thrown overboard by HMS *Plover* in Bering Strait that year, as it set out to search for Franklin. This news, reported by Charles Weld, one of Franklin's relatives, found its way into the newspapers, along with the implication that the still-missing Franklin Expedition had been supplied with spoiled provisions due to lack of due diligence on the part of the navy. The Commander-in-Chief at Plymouth at once ordered a formal survey [investigation] of Goldner's products. Goldner was invited, but pointedly failed to attend. The survey was conducted without him.

The Admiralty discovered that the cans and foods delivered were markedly inferior to the samples they had been shown. The cans themselves were found not "to be made of Tin Plates of the best quality and of a substance sufficiently strong for securing their contents." A proportion of them were also far larger than those specified by contract: 9-pound, 12-pound, and some as large as 32-pound, versus the 6-pound cans the navy had ordered. Furthermore, the meats were not of the "best quality" and in many instances contained bone and cartilage. The results of the survey were forwarded to Parliament and a scandal erupted.

On February 5, 1852, the House of Commons launched a full-fledged investigation into the navy's dealings with Goldner. A Select Committee demanded returns "showing the Date and Terms of all CONTRACTS for PRESERVED MEAT for use of Her Majesty's NAVY with Goldner." It also demanded to know "whether these Meats were issued to the [Franklin] Arctic Voyagers." And, aiming plainly at uncovering any Admiralty responsibility, it demanded a full accounting of "Complaints when first made [against Goldner] and whether, after such complaints, further Contracts were entered into with the same Parties."

The committee's findings were shocking. Between 1845 and 1851, Goldner had supplied the navy 2,741,988 pounds of preserved meat.[1] Fully 12 percent of it was condemned and returned as "unfit for use." The actual figure was likely far higher, since the Admiralty admitted that "The examination which takes place upon delivery into store of the preserved meats in canisters must necessarily consist of a small percentage, as after opening a canister, the meat contained therein rapidly becomes useless." As much as 95 percent of Goldner's canned provisions—perhaps more—were never examined before they were loaded aboard ship, most especially those loaded aboard Franklin's vessels.

"It appears," stated the committee, "that the provisions so specially complained of were supplied by running contract, dated 28th December 1844, between the Government and Mr. Goldner, then manufacturing in London, at Houndsditch, as well as Galatz in Moldavia." The latter place, the committee investigation discovered, wasn't a food factory at all. It was "a tallow factory,[2] the production of tallow being the first and chief object, and that of the meat quite secondary, and that he [Goldner] was by this double trade enabled to furnish the supplies thus contracted for at a very low rate per pound." Goldner may well have worked the same double trade at Houndsditch. The committee found that, though the Admiralty contract gave it the power to enter his factories and inspect his process, "it was not generally acted upon." In fact, it wasn't until 1851, when the scandal broke, that an Admiralty inspector set foot into Goldner's factories.

But the committee's most damning conclusion for the spoilage of Goldner's preserved provisions wasn't cheaply made cans or the fact that they contained offal or unwashed vegetables. It was "imperfect

[1] Preserved meat encompassed all preserved provisions supplied by Goldner; soups, vegetables, and gravy included.

[2] A factory where old, not prime, cattle and sheep are rendered into soap and candles, not food.

cooking," particularly of the foods Goldner cooked in cans far larger than the Admiralty had ordered. One committee witness greatly familiar with Goldner's provisions, Royal Navy Captain Milne, testified "that decay is more in the nines and twelves [9-pound and 12-pound cans] than in the sixes [6-pound cans]" and "that the 6-lbs. and 4-lbs. canisters were always fit for use, and never one found bad." Goldner's larger cans—first supplied to the Franklin Expedition—were just as susceptible to spoilage. The reason assigned by the committee was straightforward, simple, and almost a recipe for *Clostridium botulinum* contamination. "In the larger pieces of meats [and cans]," they reported, "there is more cooking required, and there is greater difficulty getting at the interior of the meat from the larger extent of it." In short, foods in the larger cans were not heated long enough to effectively sterilize them. The resulting "cold spot" in the larger cans did not cook nearly long enough or hot enough to rid them of bacterial spores. In fact, the committee determined spoilage due to improper cooking was endemic in the larger cans: "The extensive condemnations [of Goldner's provisions] that have taken place are almost exclusively confined to the 9 lb. and 12 lb. canisters." According to the committee's findings, the sole reason these larger cans were used was that "the contractor could afford to supply the same quality of meat at a lower price when the larger canisters were used."

The gravity of these revelations into the shortcomings of his operations wasn't lost on Goldner. The navy contracts were the heart of his business and, though they had paid richly, he was badly overextended. He was not only faced with paying penalties under bond of 4,000 pounds sterling, a bankrupting sum, he was—by contract—obligated to pay back the navy for every can that had been condemned as well as to pay the navy for all meat they had been forced to purchase in lieu. This was absolute catastrophe for him. The country was perpetually short of minted coins and businesses, especially victualling firms like Goldner's which were loathe to part with cash, relied on elaborate chains of credit. If a link in that chain broke, debtors who could not meet their obligations went to prison.

On February 11, 1852, with a note of desperation, he wrote the Admiralty the only honest letter he ever sent them: "Should I be favored . . . I will pledge myself most solemnly: 1st—That every canister shall be of like quality to the samples now exhibited. 2nd—That every canister shall be expressly put up for this order, and under the immediate personal superintendence of the writer & that they shall contain no bones whatever. 3rd—That my manufactory shall be open at all hours for the purpose of allowing any person or persons appointed by their Lordships, to inspect the quality of the articles put into the canisters, as well as the canisters themselves. . . ." This was the first and only time that Goldner opened his Houndsditch and Galatz factories to Admiralty inspection.

But, for a change, the Admiralty didn't favor him with a reply. Two weeks passed. Goldner, desperate to secure the victualling contract for another voyage in search of Franklin, was not even asked to bid. He wrote again: "I take the liberty of once more entreating their Lordships to be allowed to compete for the supply of the whole or a portion of the order . . . that an opportunity may be afforded me of wiping off the disgrace under which I at present labor, the result of a combination of the most unfortuitous circumstances against me. I have had the honor of supplying the Navy for the last 10 years and not until the last few months have any material complaints been urged against my goods. This I confidently hope will be a sufficient excuse for thus imploring one more trial before I am completely cut off."

This was damning language in the extreme: "disgrace," "material complaints," "completely cut off." Even more damning was Goldner's final sentence: he pledged to "supply any preserved meats that may be required of the very best quality and entirely free from bone." He waited alone in his cramped, paper-filled office in Houndsditch for a reply; the February snow outside falling as silently and steadily as it was falling on his victims north of the Arctic Circle. The coals in his stove burned low, as they burned low aboard the *Erebus* and *Terror.* He waited, as they did, for an answer, a rescuer. It did not come. Like they, he watched the snow mount and the coals go out: but they

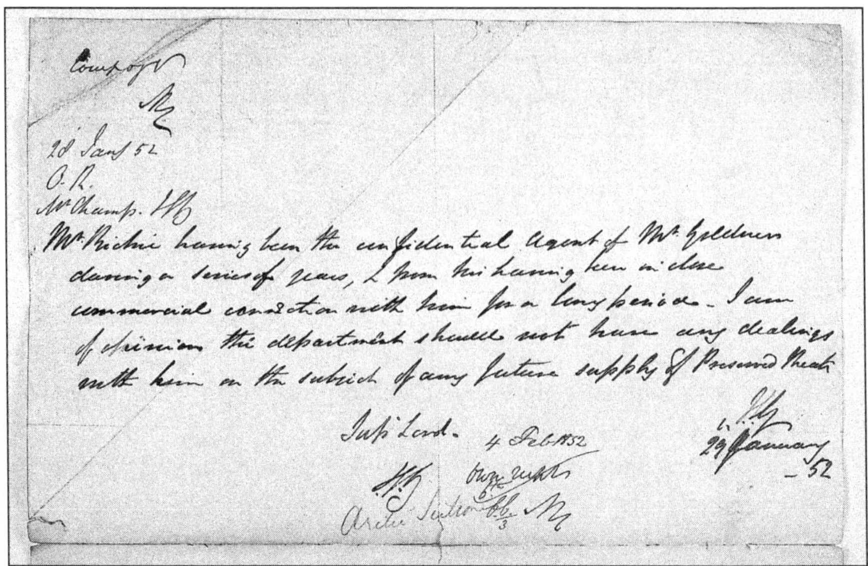

Compt.

28 Jan/52

O.R.

Mr Champ.

Mr Richie having been the confidential Agent of Mr Goldner during a series of years, & from his having been in close commercial connection with him for a long period – I am of opinion the department should not have any dealings with him on the subject of any future supply of Preserved Meats

Sup. Lord. 4 Feb 1852

29 January 52

Arctic Section

*Goldner's Doom* Informed upon by Mr. Richie, his former private secretary (then competing against him for navy contracts), the foul details of Goldner's operation were exposed. Days afterward, the Superintendent of Victualling wrote this note and ceased doing business with him, resulting in his ruin. (Public Records Office, London, England)

at least had each other; he had no one. In the dark and the cold, he sat alone.

In the end, the most compelling evidence against him came from perhaps the only man he ever trusted—his accomplice, co-conspirator, and personal secretary, Mr. Richie. Richie, who was by then competing himself for victualling contracts, apparently gave up his former employer with as little qualm as Goldner had sent brave men north to die. He told the Comptroller of Victualling at Deptford every foul detail about Goldner's operation. Three days after he did, the Comptroller put the final nail in Goldner's coffin: "Mr. Richie having been the confidential agent of Mr. Goldner during a series of years, and having been in close commercial connection with him for a long period . . . I am of the opinion the department should not have any dealings with him on the subject of any future supply of preserved provisions."

Goldner, whose greed had doomed so many, was doomed by it as well. He vanished, like Franklin's men, without a trace.

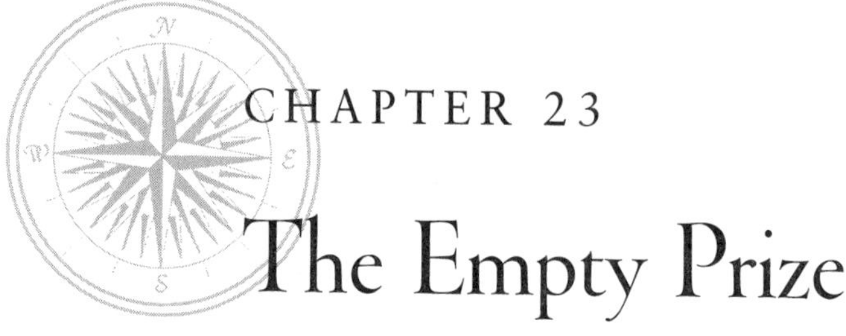

# CHAPTER 23

# The Empty Prize

*We bungled through zigzag as if we were drunk . . . it was just like sailing through an uncleared field.*

—Roald Amundsen,
on sailing through the Northwest Passage

The prize Franklin sought was more elusive than he, Barrow, or anyone else imagined. There is not one Northwest Passage; there are many—a half dozen serpentine routes through the Arctic Archipelago, routes that open and treacherously close at the whim of ice, wind, weather, and tide. All of them are forbidding.

No one actually completed a passage until 1906, some sixty years after Franklin's attempt. The prize did not fall to an Englishman, as Barrow intended, but to a Norwegian. It was not done in a single season, as Barrow had hoped; it took Roald Amundsen, who would later conquer the South Pole before the English, three years. Unlike Barrow, who could mount well-financed attempts employing large ships and hundreds of men, Amundsen was virtually penniless. His single vessel, the *Gjoa,* was a converted 70-foot fishing sloop of only 50 tons—a fifth the size of Franklin's ships. His crew numbered just six, fewer than the complement of eight officers' stewards Franklin embarked.

The voyage was so long and conditions so appalling that no others were made for thirty-four years. Only the outbreak of World War II warranted the attempt. In 1940, and again in 1944, the Royal Canadian police boat *St. Roch,* a two-masted, gaff-rigged steam schooner, navigated it in both directions. Each voyage took two years.

The only commercial use of the Passage occurred in 1969. The Humble Oil Company supertanker, USS *Manhattan,* set out to bring the first cargo of Alaskan crude oil to east coast refineries. It was a floating island—670 feet long, displacing 150,000 tons. Like Franklin's ships, *Manhattan* was refitted with the highest technology of the day. It carried a 125-foot, spoon-shaped, steel-armored bow weighing over 5,000 tons. Like an icebreaker, this was designed to lever the bow atop the pack ice, where the rest of the ship's massive weight would descend to smash it clear. The hull was sheathed with a protective steel belt 9 feet thick and 30 feet deep. The twin state-of-the-art propellers were replaced with specially strengthened ones and the dual rudders were reinforced with steel plating.

Unlike Franklin's vessels, *Manhattan* knew the way and the waters, thanks to computers, the latest satellite photographs, and hydrographic charts. Onboard helicopters conducted continuous aerial reconnaissance and two icebreakers accompanied the ship. Despite all these high-tech advantages, *Manhattan* was beset by ice in McClure Strait, just as countless square-rigged and steam-powered Royal Navy ships had been a century earlier. It was eventually freed by the icebreakers, but not before the Arctic exacted its vengeance. The ship suffered such crippling damage to the steel plating that it had to be docked for months for repair. It was the first, and last, commercial transit ever made.

The utter hostility of the Passage can only be judged in comparison. Humankind has made eight successful voyages to the moon. To date, it has traversed the Northwest Passage only seven times.

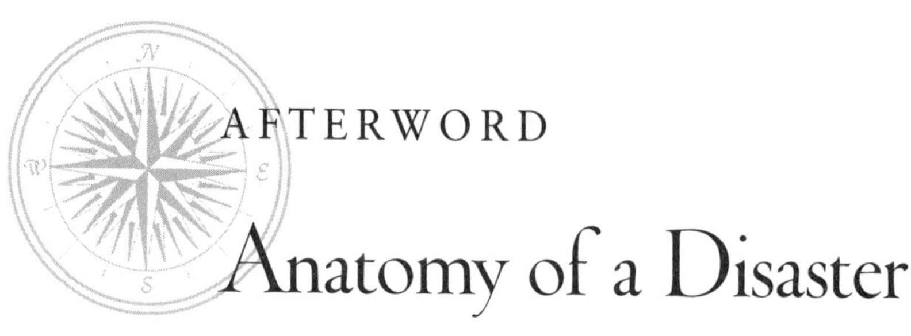

# AFTERWORD
# Anatomy of a Disaster

No disaster's a bastard. Most, in fact, have many fathers. Somehow they mature by circumstance into menace. There is no single thing that causes this, no one moment that makes it. Each disaster results from a highly individual, dynamic, but inseparable chain of events.

On the face of it, the cause of the world's other great polar tragedy is simply explained. Captain Robert Falcon Scott and his four companions froze to death in their tent after being beaten to the South Pole by Amundsen in 1912. But the choices and events that put them in that tent—within 11 miles of the supply depot that could have saved them—were more complex.

Scott's decision to use caterpillar-tracked motor sledges, advanced technology for the day, appeared a wise one at the time. The tracked machines could go anywhere, haul more than dogs, and required no rest. Underpowered, constantly breaking down, their fuel and lubricants hopelessly frozen, they proved useless. All three were abandoned. Today they remain just as they were left at Cape Evans on McMurdo Sound, mute testimony to technological hubris.

Scott's selection of Siberian ponies instead of sled dogs also seemed practical. They were bigger and more powerful than dogs and could drag heavier loads. Like Amundsen's dogs, they were bred to work in cold, harsh conditions. Had they been shod with *hestertrugers,* a kind of horse-snowshoe commonly used in Norway but rejected by the English, they may have stood a chance. But the Antarctic cold was orders of magnitude more severe than that of Siberia, and the conventionally shod ponies quickly went lame and died off before they did Scott much good.

Reduced to hauling—each man pulling 180 pounds apiece—Scott made another rational, yet fateful, decision. To speed progress, the party that made the final dash for the Pole would consist of not four men, but five. On the face of it, this made eminent sense. Yet the decision bore bitter fruit. Melting drinking water and cooking for five men consumed far more time and fuel than for four. The party, its progress more retarded than improved, was suffering exhaustion and dehydration long before it futilely reached the Pole on January 18, 1912.

To that point, the rapidly developing disaster had been shaped by good decisions gone bad. On the 800-mile return journey, it was accelerated by a series of unforeseeable accidents. A sealed biscuit box, when opened, was found half-filled, robbing them of a day's rations. This loss seems trivial, but in their now desperate circumstances it took on momentous proportions. In his journal Scott, usually stoic, scribbled "First panic."

A week later, Petty Officer Edgar Evans's hand—cut while he was repairing a sled—became severely infected. The wound festered, worsened by frostbite. His feet froze and he could no longer manage his skis. Stumbling, disoriented, he was unable to keep up. On February 17, dragged forward by his companions, he lapsed into a coma and died. A month later Captain Oates, the Guards officer who'd been in charge of the long-dead ponies, was so crippled with frostbite he could no longer walk. Bivouacked in a raging blizzard, knowing he could no longer continue and would only slow his fellows, he chose suicide. "I am just going outside," Scott recorded him saying, "and may be some time." No one stopped him. He never returned.

With but three men to haul the sled, progress slowed to a crawl. In March, the Antarctic winter overtook them. Reduced to two days' rations, feet and hands blackened and swollen huge by frostbite, they could travel only four miles a day. That left the all-important supply depot an agonizing three-day march away. But at this *"awful place,"* as Scott recorded, disaster came full term. A brutal blizzard, a cyclonic white-out with temperatures too low to measure, pinned them in their tent for a week. Scott, normally prosaic, wrote nothing in his journal the whole time. When he did, it was the final entry.

On March 29 he scribbled: "I do not think we can hope for any better things now. We shall stick it out to the end, but we are getting weaker, of course, and the end cannot be far. It seems a pity, but I do not think I can write more.—R. Scott. For God's sake, look after our people."

Eight months later the bodies, frozen solid in their sleeping bags, were found. The elements contributing to the disaster—motor sledges, ponies, man-hauling, shorted rations, a nicked thumb, frostbite, suicide, and pernicious weather—all came together to seal the expedition's fate.

On a vastly larger scale, similar assumptions, miscalculations, and sheer happenstance had overwhelmed Franklin sixty-seven years earlier. But, if anything, they were more varied, seemingly innocuous, incongruous, and thoroughly unexpected. To put them into perspective, each element must be examined in context.

Luck, the unfathomable ability to ride the wavelike synchronicity of events that favors an individual, is a singular quality of great commanders. Energy, intelligence, and integrity, sad to say, are no substitutes. One must have luck.

In taking stock, Sir John Franklin must be counted as one of the unluckiest lucky men ever born. Everything fate gave him fate robbed back, leaving him to survive on hope until it returned to play the same cruel trick on him again. Not just once, but over and over for his entire life. It's a tragicomedy, an epically sad one. He had the good fortune to learn naval surveying under a master hydrographer, Captain Matthew Flinders, and circumnavigate Australia. Yet this triumph—the nineteenth-century equivalent of the first Apollo flight to circle the moon—ended in shipwreck on the Great Barrier Reef. Fate placed him under the command of the incomparable Lord Nelson in two of the greatest naval battles of the age—Copenhagen and Trafalgar. While it miraculously spared him any injury, it recognized him not at all and abandoned him an unpromoted lieutenant.

The command of his first ship on Buchan's North Pole expedition swiftly dissolved into an unmitigated fiasco. Fortune again favored him with command of the 1819 Arctic expedition. But it deserted him at the very door of the Passage, causing the deaths of nine men and bringing him to within hours of his own. On his return, fate showered him with promotion, recognition, and a bride. Some seventeen months later, it left him a shattered widower.

Whatever began well for Franklin invariably turned out badly. He led the eminently successful 1825–1827 Arctic expedition. This brought him knighthood, fame, a new wife—and almost as suddenly unemployment and the "genteel poverty" of an existence ashore on half pay. Fate left him lingering in that state until he was near fifty, when it dangled the governorship of Van Diemen's Land in front of him. Governorships were ordinarily a good thing—positions of prominence and power, with the potential for making quite a sum of money. Franklin's wasn't. His post was not strategically located like Malta, nor rich like those in India or the West Indies. It was the worst, most corrupt prison colony in the Empire. But he had no choice but to accept it. Fate interned him there six years, exposing him to disease, cruelty, petty intrigue, and recall.

At fifty-seven, his luck—if it can be called that—had seemingly run out. That is when fate played its cruelest trick. After three other officers had refused the assignment, he was favored with command of the greatest expedition Victorian England ever dispatched in search of what he'd always sought—the Northwest Passage. To Franklin, it undoubtedly seemed the penultimate stroke of luck. What fate really had in store for him was unthinkable.

One wonders how the man weathered these professional disappointments and personal tragedies—why he didn't give up, retire ashore, and resign himself to comfortable memberships in the Royal Society and Arctic Council as other contemporary polar explorers of his stature, Sir Edward Parry and Sir James Clark Ross, did.

He is usually depicted as a well-intentioned but rather dull, bumbling fellow—a proper gentleman, of course, but certainly not a Nelson or a Hardy. By all accounts, he was nowhere near the charismatic or intellectual equal of the vivacious Lady Franklin. Polite society could not, in fact, imagine why she married him in the first place or why she remained so devoutly committed to him. He was by no means young, handsome, dashing, or brilliant. His career had been in decline for almost twenty years. But she saw something in him, something that all others who knew him invariably saw as well. He was that most misunderstood rarity—a genuinely good man. He wouldn't harm a fly on his sleeve, saying there was "room enough in the world for both." He did not flog his men, as Sir John Ross frequently did. He treated even his most junior officers as shipmates. He did not play politics or disparage others for his own gain, which slowed his advancement.

He was brave, not in the taking of lives but in doing what needed to be done without regard for his own, as he did when he continued to work signals at Trafalgar when nearly all his brother officers were cut down. Ahead of his time, he accorded women the same independence to think and to act as was accorded men, which exposed him to ridicule as a "man run by petticoats."

Modern historians typically take him out of context to judge him. "Franklin bashing" is commonplace in nearly everything written about him. He is lampooned for carrying his monogrammed silver, plate, and leaded crystal on the voyage. He had no choice; the Admiralty issued officers no eating utensils or dishes. Silver didn't corrode in salt air and plateware didn't break. The monograms weren't vanity, they merely identified the owner. Cook, Vancouver, Flinders, and Owen, who likewise traveled with their personal mess chests, do not come in for such criticism because their great voyages of exploration did not fail. Franklin's did, but not because of his silverware.

Vitriolics are hurled at him—from the safe distance of 150 years of hindsight—about his choices of ships, crews, provisions, and the like. The majority of these choices were Sir John Barrow's and the Admiralty's, not Franklin's. It's also in vogue for historians to cite "cultural bias" for the expedition's demise. It was comprised of Englishmen who, "secure in their artificial environment," disdained the ways of the native Inuit. It's quite true and utterly accurate, but Englishmen of the time disdained *any and all* peoples not English. Scots were "jocks," Irish "micks," and the French "frogs." Asians were "wogs," and blacks "niggers." Jews, Canadians, and Americans were similarly disparaged. Even fellow English officers, if they came from dubious families—or worse yet, were promoted from the ranks—were "common" and never accepted as gentlemen. It's quite true Franklin's expedition did not know how to build igloos (artificial environments themselves), hunt seals, use dogs, or "live off the land." No Royal Navy polar expedition did until Ernest Shackleton's 1914–1917 expedition was forced to. Even if Franklin's men had adopted Inuit ways, it would not have saved them. The expedition's survivors numbered 105, an enormous party to sustain by hunting or fishing. Shackleton managed to survive largely on seals, but he had only twenty-eight mouths to feed and still went hungry ("We have some biscuit crumbs in a bag, and that is all," one of his men wrote in his diary).

On his three voyages in search of the Passage, Sir William Parry spent four winters fast aboard his ships—not hunting seal, but contentedly growing mustard greens and watercress like an English gardener to ward off scurvy. He also had brought elaborate costumes for theatricals to keep up morale during the long polar nights, something Franklin did not do. Like Franklin, he took hymnals, books, writing desks, and school supplies. He greeted the native Inuit in full dress uniform. Yet he has not been maligned for "cultural bias," again because he succeeded. Even Captain M'Clintock, the navy's legendary sledger, refuted dogs and continued to man-haul sleds, as did Scott in the Antarctic well into the twentieth century.

Franklin, like all men, was a product of his time, but less so than many others. That he made mistakes, in retrospect, is irrefutable. Every explorer who "pushes the envelope" does, otherwise he is not pushing. But he came within a hair's breadth of success. And it is failure, inevitably, that's more intriguing to dissect, especially failure on a grand, tragic scale. But Franklin very nearly pulled it off. At an age when most men today are eyeing retirement—after a lifetime when more cautious and timorous men would have ardently sought it—he did not. Beneath his plain, pallid exterior, there was a core of Damascus steel in him somewhere and a perseverance made of English oak. Whatever his assignment, whatever cards fate dealt him, he played them out—life or death—to the end. The cards dealt him in his last hand were played as well as any gambler who ever lived. No one can deny him that.

The sole and only well-founded criticism that can be made of Franklin is that, in the end, he failed.

But the ultimate responsibility didn't reside with Franklin. Down to almost every detail, it was really Sir John Barrow's expedition, not Franklin's. Franklin was his surrogate. Barrow put his heart and soul, immense talents, and indefatigable energies into the enterprise. Unknowingly, and through no fault of his own, he was the chief architect of the disaster to follow.

In many ways, Barrow was like Scott. He did everything in a precise, orderly, modern, and scientific way. He acted on the very latest intelligence, his best judgement, the most advanced technology of the day, and the advice of the Arctic Council, which was composed of the world's most experienced polar explorers. But he was an unwitting victim of his own aptitude.

The ships he selected were thoroughly proven in the ice; if the Passage was to be forced in 1845, there were none finer. Every modification and state-of-the-art advance possible was made to give them the range, strength, and endurance to accomplish their mission. The ships' companies were filled—with considered calculation—from the best men that could be found. The fact that they persevered for so long under such horrible circumstances, with such discipline and courage, testifies to that in volumes.

He's often criticized for sending the expedition off without a plan for its rescue in event of emergency. If he's liable for such criticism, then so is NASA. As was painfully clear, there was no in-flight rescue plan for Apollo 13; the astronauts, through improvisation and grit, brought the ship home. In fact, any in-flight emergencies in the Mercury, Gemini, and Apollo programs necessarily had to be handled by their crews. There were never backup ships ready to assist them.

Lacking twentieth-century communications, navigation, and propulsion, any rescue plan for the Franklin Expedition was an utter impossibility. The Admiralty had no communication whatever with the expedition after it left Greenland. In fact, it did not learn that the ships had departed Greenland until a month afterwards. It was out of contact far longer and more profoundly than any spacecraft reentering the atmosphere or circling the dark side of the moon. In 1845, there was simply no way of knowing where Franklin was or whether he was in distress.

If Barrow had stationed ships in Lancaster Sound to the east and Bering Strait to the west—as many say he should have done—the exercise would have been pointless in any event. It would have taken months to get them word. They would have had no idea where to begin looking. Any search would have involved many months more (it took over fifty relief expeditions more than ten years to find Franklin). Any searchers would have been exposed to the same grim conditions that trapped Franklin. Even if, by some miracle, they managed to negotiate the pack ice and stumble upon his beset ships, it's likely they would have suffered the same fate, amplifying the tragedy.

To his credit, Barrow made the only contingency plans open to him. He notified the remote Hudson's Bay Company outposts to keep watch and render all assistance. He equipped the ships with more than enough boats to carry off the crews in event of mishap. His instructions directed the expedition to build cairns and cache messages along its way. For this purpose, he supplied Franklin over 200 airtight brass message canisters.

These plans, in retrospect, were hollow. The Bay Company posts were too far inland. Ships' boats were worthless in frozen seas. Cairns and messages, to this day, have proven impossible to find. But these plans, like all the others, were the best that could be laid.

If there's a valid criticism to be made of Barrow, it's that he tried to do too much too quickly. In expediting preparations for the expedition, little things with disastrous consequences went unseen.

The time element in preparing the expedition, indeed, played an insidious role in its doom. Barrow was eighty-two and running out of time to find the Passage. Practically speaking, Franklin was sixty and fully aware this was his last chance to do likewise. While all conceivable preparations were made, they had to be made in haste. Any delay endangered the government's backing of the whole enterprise—the last thing either Barrow or Franklin wanted. In the headlong rush to get to sea, decisions that would prove fatal weren't (or couldn't be) properly weighed. Expediency decided things.

The decision to fit the ships with bastardized railway engines, not marine locomotives, had grave consequences. The Royal Navy had far more powerful propeller-driven steamers available. HMS *Rattler,* which accompanied the expedition to Greenland, had an engine of 220 horsepower—ten times as powerful than those placed aboard Franklin's ships. But *Rattler* was twice as big as *Erebus* and *Terror* (880 tons vs. 372 tons), drew too much water, was far less maneuverable in the ice, and not nearly as strongly built. Politically, Barrow could not have cannibalized the navy's newest steam frigate for the expedition's sake. It wasn't feasible anyway. The engine and its fuel requirement were too large to be accommodated in either of the smaller bomb ships. If the expedition was to have auxiliary steam power—deemed a necessity to force the Passage—Barrow had to improvise. The railway engines could be hastily and cheaply procured. Better yet, they could be quickly installed.

Reinforcing thc vessels with tons of wood and iron was another fateful decision. There was no time to test the effect the added weight would have on the ships' handling and sailing abilities. And there was none whatever to test the strain it put on the engines, propellers, and drive shafts or the effect that it might have on coal consumption.

That the victualling was also rushed is patently clear. Goldner, recently engaged under running contract, was the lowest bidder for provisioning the expedition and the only contractor offering immediate delivery. The Victualling Department had no time to inspect his factory, indeed no time to inspect his goods. Most of them arrived only days before sailing. In fact, the whole expedition was outfitted for three years in little over sixty days.

On the face of it, the Admiralty achieved a miracle getting things ready in that time. In reality, it merely succeeded in setting the stage for the tragedy to follow.

But of all the parents of the Franklin disaster, the one who is least known played the most notorious part. There are no biographies or epitaphs of Stephan Goldner. He hovers in gaslight, a shadowy figure known for nothing but the catastrophe he fathered like a rapist, coldly taking his compensation and leaving behind the seed that caused it. The only justice is that, in the end, the act consumed him as well. In Latin, he was *felo de se*—literally an evildoer upon himself—one who dies from the effects of his own malicious deed. In double-crossing the Admiralty and betraying nearly everyone, he was himself double-crossed and betrayed by his accomplice, his personal secretary, Mr. Richie.

In truth, Goldner was probably no better or worse than many other victualling contractors. It was a dog-eat-dog business—winning military contracts usually is. He was, however, more of a dog than any others. He knew from the outset that he could never fulfill the terms of his contract; he committed to it knowing full well he'd default on all its particulars. That's the chief difference between Goldner and the other fathers of the Franklin disaster. The rest acted in the best of faith and made the most enlightened decisions of which they were capable, solicitous of the officers and men whose lives were at risk. Goldner alone did not. Goldner's only interest was Goldner. He knew how to play the victualling game for big stakes and he shrewdly played it to his advantage for ten years. Perhaps the only mistake he made was teaching Mr. Richie the same game. It was this that undid him.

He knew he was cheating the Admiralty. He didn't care. It was simply business the way it was done. If he didn't profit, someone else would. Cutting a few corners here and there was expected. A few sailors might go hungry for a time, but that was to be expected, too. They had, after all, volunteered. And they were, after all, just common sailors. At least they wouldn't die of scurvy. The officers, with their private stores, would be all right. In Goldner's mind, these rationalizations made perfect sense.

To be fair—which is more than he deserves—he had no idea the provisions he was canning contained *Clostridium.* Nobody knew. He also had no idea that his workers, returning from the factory's latrine, almost certainly carried infectious bacteria on their hands. He had no concept that his patented process almost certainly resulted in undercooking, which left millions of bacteria alive. But he most certainly knew he was sending men into the depths of the Arctic with provisions that—disguised in his brightly painted, cheaply built cans—were not what he'd contracted to provide. He was fully aware his meats were not "of superior description and quality." He knew that these, as well as his vegetables and soups, were not prepared "with utmost care." In the case of the Franklin Expedition especially, production was so hurried and rushed that no quality control whatever was practiced. His sole defense was the hope that his patented process—superheating the boiling water canners with the addition of calcium chloride—would somehow correct what was wrong with them. But even here he scrimped and cut corners. The unskilled laborers he employed to oversee the job were woefully ignorant of it. As Mr. Hogarth, a competitor of Goldner's called before the Select Committee to testify about proper canning and cooking techniques, put it: "Supposing any of your servants to be careless and allow the fires to go out, or the heat to fall below a certain pitch, if [the food] is not properly cooked, no matter what the vacuum [in the cans] were, it would not keep." Goldner knew this as well as Hogarth, yet exercised little, if any, supervision. Without doubt, he purposefully delayed delivery of his goods to Franklin's ships until the last possible moment to escape detection.

On long winter nights in England—while Franklin's crews suffered—Goldner sipped claret in front of a blazing hearth and counted his coin. When the expedition was posted missing, it did not deter him in the least. It was a boon to his business. He went after almost every victualling contract using the same modus operandi and won most or at least a portion of them all. Outfitting relief expedition after relief expedition, he raked in more money. He was solely devoted to the pursuit of profit. As a scam artist, he had no rivals. He stalled, obfuscated, lied outright—and got away with it. Ironically it was this success, this easy money, that brought Mr. Richie out of the woodwork like a cockroach.

Still, the blame is not entirely Goldner's. The Admiralty was not forced to accept his bid. It did so for the same reason that motivated Goldner—money. When deliveries fell abjectly behind schedule, it did not have to accept his excuses. Other contractors could have been retained to supply the shortfall before the expedition sailed. They were not because it would have cost more money. That the Victualling Department chose not to inspect Goldner's operations was plainly lack of due diligence. Yet mostly, the equation revolved around money—Goldner's desire to make it and the Admiralty's desire to save it. The lives of the expedition's officers and men weren't factored in.

But it was Goldner, with whatever conscience he had, who pocketed his profits without remorse. He never looked back. His mistake was playing the same hand again and again. He thought he'd never be caught. When he was, his demise was swift. He may have ended his life a wealthy man, but judging from his frantic final correspondence, it's unlikely. He was desperately in need of funds to pay his agents and creditors. He'd made too many enemies. Cut off from Admiralty business, shunned by his peers and done in by Richie, Goldner had condemned himself to bankruptcy and oblivion. The haggard faces of 129 men may have haunted him the rest of his days.

In the final analysis, all these parents of disaster had one thing in common. The Franklin Expedition was largely doomed by its overriding belief in technology. It believed in steam power and propellers to force the Passage. It believed in canned provisions to keep scurvy and disease at bay. It believed iron plate and marine engineering could best the ice. It believed instrumentation—Lloyd's instrument, a so-called "Robinson" instrument (for making magnetic observations), state-of-the-art chronometers, compasses, and "winterized" sextants—would reveal a Passage where the Admiralty said it would be. None of these beliefs were rooted in anything but the thin soil of hubris. Almost all of them, in fact, doomed the expedition from the outset.

Franklin's expedition, like Scott's, put its faith in state-of-the-art technology. At 25 and 20 horsepower respectively, *Erebus*'s and

*Terror*'s newly installed steam engines were too weak to propel their 372 and 326 tons at much more than a pensioner's walk in open water. Among the ice, it was probably far less. And, as with Scott's motor sledges, malfunctions and mechanical breakdowns could have been expected. The engines' inherent inefficiency gulped coal at a prodigious rate. It was lack of fuel for cooking, of all things, that left the expedition vulnerable to botulism. The propellers—designed wholly "by guess and by God," not scientific equation or model tests—were another inherent, perhaps fatal, weakness. Their retractability more so. No ships in the Royal Navy had employed such devices in polar ice.

The canned provisions—supposedly advanced—were a chimera. Like the fire-breathing she-monster in Greek mythology, they were compounded of incongruous, dangerous parts. The latest patented methods leached them of nutrients but left them tainted with bacteria and viruses. The canning process contaminated them with lead and arsenic. Soldered shut to prevent admittance of the "atmospherics" believed to cause spoilage, they were in fact death capsules packed with *Clostridium botulinum.*

The men who had to unwittingly bear these burdens were all volunteers. Critics later said there were far too many of them. But when the expedition embarked, it shipped a total of 130 men, 4 midshipmen, a dog named Neptune, and a pet monkey named Jacko. This was the standard complement for *Hecla* (67 men) and *Vesuvius* (67 men) class bomb ships. What was unusual was the disproportion between officers, seamen, marines, and so-called "idlers" (boatswains, carpenters, cooks, caulkers, stewards, and so on, who did not stand normal watches).

Officers alone numbered twenty-four—almost 18 percent of the whole expedition. This amounted to a ratio of one officer for every four men aboard, an unnecessarily high number. As a privileged class, they constituted quite a logistical burden. A total of eight stewards were embarked solely to serve them.

The preponderance of officers—all expecting promotion with the success of the enterprise—was eclipsed by the shortage of critical specialists. When it sailed from Disko Island in Greenland, the expedition carried but *one* sailmaker. Given the ferocity of Arctic gales, any severe damage to the ships' sails (still their primary propulsion system) would have been hard to remedy. There was *one* armorer to repair all of the ships' weapons. Stewards outnumbered critical carpenters by two to one. Though great hope was placed in the steam engines, there were but two engineers. The deaths of any of these specialists would have caused severe difficulties.

The thirteen marines—10 percent of the expedition's total complement—were largely superfluous. No resistance was expected and no mutinies had ever occurred on previous polar voyages. None of these men were hunters, nor were they equipped to hunt. Their sole purpose—and it may have proven useful for a time—was to enforce discipline.

Of all-important able-bodied seamen, the expedition took only thirty-nine—nineteen aboard *Terror* and twenty aboard *Erebus*. On these men fell the burden of working ship twenty-four hours a day when under way. In the best of circumstances, that meant standing a four-hour watch with an eight-hour rest. In the foul weather and icy conditions of the Arctic however, regular watches were meaningless. The men were called on deck night and day to climb ice-encrusted ratlines aloft. Perched perilously in the yardarms above the plunging deck—on a single, ice-glazed foot rope called a horse—they had to make or shorten tons of frozen sail and turn the yards with every course change of the ship. In so-called "winter quarters," when the ships were beset in the ice, their labors didn't lessen. Plunged into polar darkness, the topsides had to be regularly cleared of foot-thick ice and 10-foot drifts of snow. Like pack animals, they were tethered to sleds, hauling them and the ships' officers on excursions to make astronomical and magnetic observations. There were, in fact (as Crozier plainly stated in one of his last letters from Greenland), too many officers and too few "working men." And the brutal conditions, never-ending exertion, and ever-diminishing rations reduced them more. The manning of the ships followed standard Admiralty practice. But the Arctic proved anything but standard.

The weather, too, proved completely unexpected. As a pitcher plant admits an insect, the Arctic lured Franklin's expedition into its center. In the summers of 1845 and 1846 the weather was immoderately mild. The seas and channels were largely ice-free. Where they beckoned, Franklin followed, industriously using steam to force his way.

In September, 1846, however, when the expedition was in the heart of the Arctic archipelago, the weather reverted to menace. The ships, within a few hundred miles of completing the Passage, were frozen fast. Steam, black powder, ice saws, ice anchors, pickaxes, and chisels could not free them. Unknowingly, they were caught in the maw of the Beaufort Ice Stream, which pours off the Pole like an avalanche. Unable to move, they were assaulted by the worst the powers of Nature could hurl against them. Pack ice 10 feet deep. Inhuman temperatures of 50 to 60 below zero. Blizzards that lasted weeks and buried them in 20-foot drifts. Cyclonic gales that shook the ships to their keels and carried them helplessly back towards the Pole. It was here that coal, food, and hope—everything but courage—ran out.

Indeed, it was courage alone that sustained the expedition for so long. By any measure, Franklin, Crozier, Fitzjames, and the ships' companies proved an exemplary body of men. Isolated and totally alone, they bested the most horrendous Arctic conditions for three years. For two of those years, they were beset in the most awesomely powerful ice stream on earth. But the pack ice could not crush them. Disease and death did not intimidate them. They remained true to their ships and shipmates. The care, indeed the tenderness, with which they interred their dead was touching.

When they finally deserted their ships, it was in a disciplined, orderly fashion. No man was left behind. No contingency was overlooked. Veterans and "first entry men" alike held to their posts in the finest tradition of the Royal Navy. On the desperate march to Back's River, any hope of reaching safety almost surely evaporated. But the boat parties remained intact. They labored toward a horizon without promise as shipmates, with a courage and camaraderie almost impossible to comprehend. In the final extremity, they did what they had to do to survive. There can be no criticism in that. The expedition may have failed. The officers and men certainly did not.

# APPENDIX I
# Provisions

The Deptford Victualling Yard report for HMS *Terror*, dated March 11, 1845—eight days before it sailed—was typical of the food embarked on both ships. It carefully annotated the Admiralty's "DEMAND for PROVISIONS and VICTUALLING STORES for use of Her Majesty's Ship above-mentioned to complete her 3 Years for her Complement of 67 Men for Discovery Service."

The Admiralty's specifications are in italics, commentary follows.

Biscuit . . . . . . . . . . . . . . . . . . . . . . . . . . . . . . . . 16,884 lbs.
(*"All to be square biscuit to be packed in tin cases; 9,000 of varying size from 50 lbs. to 1 hundred weight."* Pre-made in the Admiralty yards, these were flat, hard cakes made with flour mixed with a minimum amount of water and slow-baked. This hardtack was a staple. Packed in tin cases, it was surprisingly free of the black-headed weevils that infested it when packed in casks or canvas bags. It kept practically forever—some baked in the 1800s was issued during WWI. Boiled up with salt meat and onions, the ship's cook made it into a hearty stew called "lobscouse." Oddly enough, the dish was a favorite of the crew.)

Flour In Lieu Of Biscuit . . . . . . . . . . . . . . . . . . . . . . . . 56,252 lbs.
(*"In casks to be watertight."* Usually mildewed, often rodent infested, this was enough to bake about 56,000 loaves of bread or over 100,000 biscuits. Along with hardtack, it was the crew's primary staple.)

Spirits, Concentrated . . . . . . . . . . . . . . . . . . . . . . . . . 2,288 gals.
(*"West Indian rum, 100 to 130 proof."* This was calculated to provide every man aboard with ¼ pint a day for three years. Mixed with ¾ pints water into grog, it made a full pint of very stout stuff. Sailors being punished were issued "six water grog," diluted with six parts water instead of three; ironically, this was no punishment at all—it simply made the rum last longer.)

Ale & Porter . . . . . . . . . . . . . . . . . . . . . . . . . . . . . 2,490 gals.
(*"In hogsheads."* Usually Burton's or Alsop's ale or porter. The ale was somewhat more authoritative than the porter, which had an alcohol content of only about 4 percent, but that was the navy's purpose. In "winter quarters," when the crews weren't actively manning ship, their rum ration was halved to ⅛ pint and supplemented with ½ pint of ale or porter per man per day. The captain of the *North Star,* one of the ships sent after Franklin, rated it "Very good and very important" to maintain morale among grog-deprived sailors.)

Salt Beef . . . . . . . . . . . . . . . . . . . . . . . . . . . . . . . 15,672 lbs.
(*"In 1,959 8-lbs. pieces, in casks to be watertight."* Typically stringy, horrendously oversalted, and of dubious origin; accurately labeled "salt horse" by the crew. The normal issue of this was 1¼ to 1½ pounds per man.)

Salt Pork . . . . . . . . . . . . . . . . . . . . . . . . . . . . . . . 15,672 lbs.
(*"In 3,918 4-lbs. pieces, in casks to be watertight."* This high-fat, salty portion was the sailor's favorite. Since it was fattier than the beef, a man got a ¾-pound portion instead of the larger issue of beef. Fried, or especially stewed with split peas, the lower deck seldom tired of it.)

Flour . . . . . . . . . . . . . . . . . . . . . . . . . . . . . . . . . . 10,452 lbs.
(*"In casks to be watertight."* This was somewhat higher-quality flour than that shipped "in lieu of biscuit." A good cook could make it into cake, pie, or pancakes, but it was most often used on Thursdays and Sundays—so-called flour days—for making Yorkshire pudding, duff, or bread pudding with raisins.)

Preserved (Tinned) Meat . . . . . . . . . . . . . . . . . . . . . . 15,664 lbs. (*"Boiled mutton 1,958 lbs., roast mutton 1,958 lbs., roast beef 1,958 lbs., boiled beef 1,958 lbs., seasoned beef 1,958 lbs., beef and vegetables 1,958 lbs., veal 1,958 lbs., soup and boulli 979 lbs., ox cheeks 979 lbs."* Goldner's mutton—the tough meat of old sheep—was not much improved by boiling or frying. The beef, by itself or mixed with vegetables or soups, likewise. Goldner's cans, shoddily made, often burst, spoiling the contents. If unspoiled, later officers who consumed his meats reported them "tremendously salty" and "tasteless.")

Preserved (Tinned) Soups . . . . . . . . . . . . . . . . . . . . . 10,452 pints (*"Vegetable soup 7,839 pints, Concentrated Gravy 2,613 pints."* Goldner contracted to supply all these in pint-size cans, but actually supplied them in much larger ones. Served hot in the freezing, but desertlike conditions of the Arctic, they were rehydrating and especially favored by officers and men alike. They were also—fatally—inhabited by *Clostridium.*)

Preserved (Tinned) Vegetables . . . . . . . . . . . . . . . . . . 7,839 lbs. (*"Carrots 3,136 lbs., parsnips 3,136 lbs., mixed vegetables 1,567 lbs."* According to later observers, Goldner's carrots tasted like "paste," the parsnips were universally disliked, and the "mixed" vegetables were found to be "too much of one kind.")

Preserved (Tinned) Potatoes . . . . . . . . . . . . . . . . . . . . 2,613 lbs. (*"In cases."* Pallid and resembling cucumbers, they were reported not "washed clean from the soil, the neglect of which gave them an unpleasant gritty taste." In this soil resided uncounted numbers of *Clostridium* spores. The potatoes were usually dipped in vinegar and consumed raw.)

Suet . . . . . . . . . . . . . . . . . . . . . . . . . . . . . . . . . . 1,467 lbs. (*"In casks to be watertight."* Beef or mutton fat, used for flavoring any number of insipid dishes.)

Raisins . . . . . . . . . . . . . . . . . . . . . . . . . . . . . . . . . . 492 lbs. (*"In casks to be watertight."* Considered to be an antiscorbutic, effective in fighting scurvy, they contained only trace amounts of vitamin C. Largely used in making puddings and duffs on "flour days.")

Peas, Split . . . . . . . . . . . . . . . . . . . . . . . . . . . . . . . . 72 bushels
(*"In casks to be watertight."* Anything green was welcome in the Arctic and peas were a great favorite. However, soaking and cooking them to any sort of tenderness took time, effort, and lots of fuel, so they were an occasional delicacy.)

Oatmeal . . . . . . . . . . . . . . . . . . . . . . . . . . . . . . . . . 82 bushels
(*"In casks to be watertight."* Mostly made into a largely tasteless mush and served for breakfast, or mixed into a hot drink called "skillygalee," sweetened with sugar and issued in place of cocoa. Often served to stokers, working in the boiler room, it was believed to prevent stomach cramps.)

Sugar . . . . . . . . . . . . . . . . . . . . . . . . . . . . . . . . . 6,859 lbs.
(*"In casks to be watertight."* The daily allowance was 1 ounce per man.)

Chocolate . . . . . . . . . . . . . . . . . . . . . . . . . . . . . . . 4,573 lbs.
(*"In one ounce squares, wrapped in lead foil, in tins."* Made into cocoa mixed with water or canned milk. This appears to be the only food the Franklin survivors did not consume in its entirety.)

Tea . . . . . . . . . . . . . . . . . . . . . . . . . . . . . . . . . . . 1,143 lbs.
(*"In cases."* Loose tea, caffeine its only benefit. With the exception of chocolate, it was also the only provision found from the Franklin expedition.)

Vinegar . . . . . . . . . . . . . . . . . . . . . . . . . . . . . . . . . 653 gals.
(*"In casks to be watertight."* Malt vinegar was used as an antiscorbutic, food preservative, and condiment.)

Tobacco . . . . . . . . . . . . . . . . . . . . . . . . . . . . . . . . 3,510 lbs.
(*"In casks to be watertight."* Consisting of both Virginia tobacco in "carrots" wrapped in twine, and Brazilian tobacco in smaller "twists" and "plug," for smoking and chew. Every man got 1 ounce per day. The nicotine, no doubt, suppressed the crews' craving for food and served its purpose.)

Lemon Juice ............................ 4,573 lbs.
(*"In 5 gallon kegs."* The 1 ounce of lemon juice issued daily—the yield of an average-size lemon—provided about 13 mg. of vitamin C, far short of today's 60 to 90 mg. RDA. Early in the voyage, it was so acid it was hard to choke down, even when well-sweetened with sugar. Later in the voyage, as it weakened, it got easier, but the men never liked it.)

Sugar for ditto ............................ 4,573 lbs.
(*"In casks to be watertight."*)

Soap ............................ 1,755 lbs.
(*"In casks to be watertight."*)

Pickled Cranberries ............................ 1,306 lbs.
(*"In 5 gallon kegs."* 3½ oz. of fresh, raw berries provide about 13 mg. of vitamin C; Goldner's had been stewed and largely leached of vitamin content.)

Pickles ............................ 4,573 lbs.
(*"In 10 gallon kegs; 1,143 lbs. mixed pickles, 1,143 walnuts, 1,143 lbs. cabbage, 1,144 lbs. onions."* These, packed in malt vinegar, were also leached of essential vitamins, but the variety they provided was welcome. As one officer testified: "Make no mistake; pickles cannot be made bad." The walnuts were typically reserved for "hardbake," a glazed mass of nuts baked in sugar or molasses. The cabbage was uniformly served up as sauerkraut or stewed with salt pork in lieu of peas. The onions however, were usually stewed with salt fish to make a dish called "salamagundi," which the crews universally disliked; not on account of the onions, but because of the relatively fat-free, cheap hake and codfish used.)

Scotch Barley ............................ 1,248 lbs.
(*"In casks to be watertight."* Barley mush was the mainstay of the poor and heartily disliked by the men.)

Cheese. ............................ 2,093 lbs.
(Like ale and porter, this was issued only during the winter months. It substituted for the quarter-pound reduction in the bread allowance,

a measure taken to reduce fuel consumption. Three times a week, each man got 2 ounces of cheese, typically long-lasting types like cheddar or double Gloucestershire.)

Butter . . . . . . . . . . . . . . . . . . . . . . . . . . . . . . . . . . 1,608 lbs.
(This was also strictly a winter allowance. Chiseled hard-frozen out of its container, every man got 1 pound per month, or about a tablespoon a day. Since it was high in fat—and it was fat the men craved more than anything else—it was highly prized.)

Macaroni . . . . . . . . . . . . . . . . . . . . . . . . . . . . . . . 1,200 lbs.
(*"In cases."* This was a largely reserved for the officer's mess. Most seamen, wedded to bread-and-beef or bread-and-pork, didn't favor it much and, in fact, likened eating it to eating "a gaggle of maggots.")

Pemmican . . . . . . . . . . . . . . . . . . . . . . . . . . . . . . . 500 lbs.
(This was made by the Admiralty itself at the Royal Clarence Dockyards and packed in cans especially for use by sledging parties as emergency rations. Made from rather expensive cuts of meat slowly dried, pounded fine, then mixed with fat and currants; it was high-protein, high-energy, and comparatively high in vitamins. Unfortunately, there was not nearly enough of it.)

Wine (for the sick) . . . . . . . . . . . . . . . . . . . . . . . . . 100 gals.
(This was very good quality white Tenerife wine, by no means as potent as the rum, but easier on a sick man's digestion.)

Brandy (for the sick) . . . . . . . . . . . . . . . . . . . . . . . . 100 gals.
(This was stouter proof than the wine, far less than the rum, and intended primarily to be used as an anesthetic.)

Mustard . . . . . . . . . . . . . . . . . . . . . . . . . . . . . . . . . 500 lbs.
(*"In glass bottles."* Good English mustard was issued as a condiment to the crew "when necessary." The longer the voyage, the more necessary it became. Slathered judiciously on aged salt beef, it could almost obscure the stink of it.)

Horseradish . . . . . . . . . . . . . . . . . . . . . . . . . . . . . . 50 gals.
(*"In glass bottles."* Likewise, this condiment was issued weekly to sauce up the endlessly bland diet of salt meat.)

Pepper . . . . . . . . . . . . . . . . . . . . . . . . . . . . . . . . . . . . 100 lbs.
(*"In cannisters."* Issued minimally as a condiment.)

Normandy Pippins . . . . . . . . . . . . . . . . . . . . . . . . . . . . . 55 lbs.
(These dried apples were a great luxury, reserved for holidays or use on "flour days.")

Portable Soup . . . . . . . . . . . . . . . . . . . . . . . . . . . . . . . 20 lbs.
(Like the pemmican, these dehydrated, concentrated soups were state-of-the-art for the time and reserved exclusively as emergency rations for the sledging parties. A handful of this "iron soup" would swell up in a kettle and feed eight men. Unfortunately, there was far too little of this, too.)

These were but the "official" provisions embarked for the crew. Sir John Franklin, Captain Crozier, and Commander Fitzjames all enjoyed the perquisite of a "captain's storeroom" where they could take almost anything they desired. The officers on both ships were free to bring whatever luxuries the limited space allowed.

In addition, each of Franklin's ships was furnished with several coops of "laying hens" to provide fresh eggs for the officers' mess. When they stopped laying, they were promptly dispatched as "stewing chickens."

To give an idea of what that officer's prerogative meant—and how far money went at the time—consider this. In 1848, the officers aboard HMS *Enterprise,* one of the ships fitting out to search for Franklin, placed the following order. For the sum of 157 pounds (roughly U.S. $706), the victualling firm of Wm. and Thos. Cooper provided the following to supplement the officers' mess:[1]

2 cases of corned beef
20 Westphalia hams
2 boxes of raisins
56 boxes of currants
50 boxes of "fine" tea
1 box of "fine" coffee
20 loaves of sugar
3 sides of bacon
10 jars of pickled tripe
12 kegs of salted cod

[1] Admiralty Records; Public Record Office.

18 cases of salted salmon
24 cases of "soup & boulli" (beef soup)
24 cases of oxtail soup
24 cases of mock turtle soup
24 cases of mulligatawny soup
3 bags of "best" South Carolina rice
1 case tinned potatoes
2 boxes of macaroni
1 box of vermicelli
10 boxes of tinned tapioca
3 barrels of "best" flour
24 cases of tinned carrots
12 cases of tinned "table vegetables"
12 quarts of "green pease"
24 cases of tinned parsnips
48 bottles of "pickled fruit"
18 jars of "assorted jams"
48 bottles of ginger
48 bottles of "assorted spices"
6 bottles of "chillies"
18 jars of table salt
1 case of yellow soap
24 casks of cheese
1 jar of bicarbonate of soda
8 cases of salted herring
5 cases of "seasoned beef"
24 bottles of "table vinegar"
18 bottles of "vegetable essence"
24 bottles of "assorted sauces"
2 firkins of butter (82 gallons)
1/2 firkin of lard (21 gallons)
30 bottles of mustard
9 bottles of cayenne pepper
18 bottles of black pepper
4 bottles of white pepper
6 bottles of capers
24 tins of curry powder
6 bottles of "assorted herbs"
360 bottles of Scotch ale
360 bottles of Barclay's stout
1 "mat" of salted cod
6 casks for "packing sundries"

APPENDIX II

# Northwest Passage Voyages: Mortality Rates

The Franklin Expedition suffered three dead (all crewmen) its first winter in the ice. Between June 1847 and April 1848, in just ten months, it suffered twenty-one dead (nine officers and twelve crewmen). None of the Royal Navy's previous expeditions in search of the Passage, either by sea or land, had experienced such catastrophic casualties.

To put the devastating effect of this swift, sudden die-off into perspective, an examination of mortality rates on the expeditions preceding Franklin's 1845 voyage bears scrutiny.

1819—PARRY'S 1ST VOYAGE (*Hecla* and *Griper*)
Duration: 17 months  Manpower: 94 men.
Mortality: (after 11 months) 1 dead of scurvy.

1819—FRANKLIN'S 1ST EXPEDITION (Overland)
Duration: 5 months (traveling)  Manpower: 21 men.
Mortality: 9 dead of scurvy, starvation, exposure.

1821—PARRY'S 2ND VOYAGE (*Hecla* and *Fury*)
Duration: 20 months  Manpower: 93 men.
Mortality: 1 ice master dead of scurvy.

1824—Parry's 3rd Voyage (*Hecla* and *Fury*)
Duration: 17 months Manpower: 93 men.
Mortality: no dead (*Fury* lost)

1825—Franklin's 2nd Expedition (Overland)
Duration: 4 months (traveling) Manpower: 32 men.
Mortality: no dead

1829—Ross's Voyage (*Victory*)
Duration: 48 months (beset) Manpower: 23 men.
Mortality: 1 dead of scurvy.

1833—Back's Expedition (Overland)
Duration: 6 months (traveling) Manpower: 20 men.
Mortality: no dead.

1836—Back's Voyage (*Terror*)
Duration: 15 months Manpower: 64 men.
Mortality: 3 dead of scurvy.

In the eight expeditions the Royal Navy (Barrow) dispatched to search for the Passage over seventeen years (1819–1836), only seventeen men died. Franklin's first disastrous expedition accounted for eleven of them (over 64 percent). Since the latter was the exception, not the rule, the mortality rate for the approximately 513 men involved in the other seven expeditions was 1.16 percent. All six of these deaths were attributed to scurvy. Only one fatality (an ice master) was an officer.

By contrast, when the Franklin Expedition quit its ships in 1848 nine officers and fifteen men were dead—a mortality rate of 18.6 percent!

From autopsies Beattie performed on the three men who died in the winter of 1846, the most likely causes of death were identified. Lead Stoker Torrington died a lingering death from tuberculosis contracted before he sailed. Able-bodied seaman Hartnell died in but four days of a virulent respiratory disease, most probably viral or bacterial pneumonia. Pvt. Braine, weakened by tuberculosis and scurvy, was likely doomed by supervening pneumonia.

For the next fifteen months, nine of them beset in the Beaufort Ice Stream, the expedition suffered *no* deaths whatever. The next recorded was that of the expedition's commander, Sir John Franklin, on June 11, 1847, followed soon afterward by the deaths of eight officers and twelve men. Once the expedition deserted its ships and reached King William Island, the death toll mounted. Between the landing site and Starvation Cove, from twenty-two to as many as seventy others may have perished, at least three of them officers (Lt. Irving and Lt. VesConte, who were identified, and a third, supposed an officer by his "fine quality blue cloth coat and gilt buttons.")

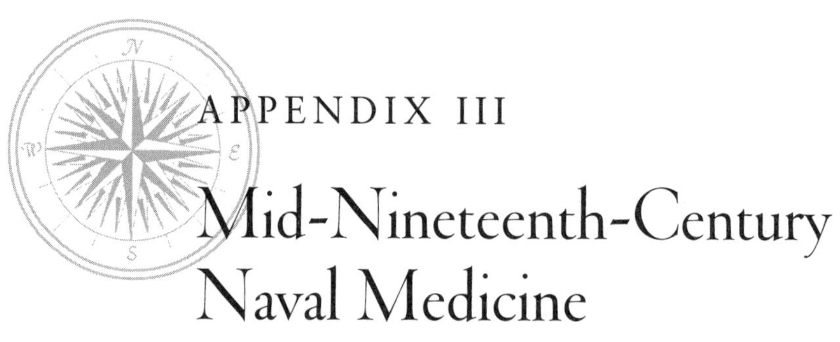

# APPENDIX III

# Mid-Nineteenth-Century Naval Medicine

The botulism that savaged the ships of the Franklin Expedition, forced their desertion, and cast the survivors out upon the ice to their ultimate doom was unidentifiable and untreatable to nineteenth-century medicine. There was no knowledge of infectious diseases, much less foodborne ones. Even primitive diagnostic tools like stethoscopes were a novelty, and clinical thermometers were unknown.

In many ways, the worst place for a sick sailor to be was in sick bay. Closely confined in poorly ventilated quarters, he was exposed to a host of infectious diseases. Even today, after over 150 years of radical medical advances, the same holds true. The Centers for Disease Control and Prevention (CDC) estimates 2 million Americans develop hospital-acquired infections annually.

A botulism-poisoned Franklin seaman suffered far worse. He was not only exposed to infection, but treatment from physicians and surgeons trained in many, stupendously uninformed schools of medicine. If he fell under the care of a simple navy surgeon, he was comparatively fortunate. He was excused from duty and fed a diet of rice and only rice. He was dosed with medicinal wine or brandy and allowed to rest.

If he was a patient of a physician—even one trained at the renowned Edinburgh Royal Infirmary or Hunter's in London (which few were)—he was unfortunate indeed. Doctors trained in the *Cullenist* method thought infectious disease was caused by an "excess or deficiency of nervous energy," so the poor man may have been forced to exercise. *Brunonian-schooled* physicians, on the other hand, believed illness was caused by "weakness or inadequate stimulation of the organs involved." Both schools followed roughly the same regimen of treatment. They administered massive doses of laudanum, opium, and morphine to quiet patients. If patients sank into unconsciousness, they copiously administered calomel (a poisonous compound of mercury) or Tincture of Lobelia (pure nicotine) as a cathartic. In many cases, they administered rhubarb, Rochelle salts, and dogwood bitters (all laxatives). *Humoralists* attributed all disease to an "imbalance of bodily fluids" and favored bloodletting, enemas, and emetics. *Counter-Irritationalists* believed diseases could be overwhelmed with electric shock, arsenic, strychnine, and prussic acid.

The result of this physicians' "art" was horrendous. The botulism patient, his respiratory tract paralyzed, was drugged, dosed with poison and nicotine, and given purgatives that dangerously dehydrated him. The cure did nothing to stop the neurotoxin paralyzing the peripheral muscles.

Dr. Oliver Wendell Holmes Sr., a professor at Harvard medical school at about this time, was unequivocal in his opinion of medical practices of the day. "If the whole materia medica, as now used, would sink to the bottom of the sea," he wrote, "it would be all the better for mankind and all the worse for the fishes."

Until botulinum antitoxins and ventilators were perfected, the expedition's surgeons relied on the medicines of the day to fight botulism. These consisted of an amazing variety of poisonous, addictive, or altogether worthless concoctions. Most were used to purge the patient of disease and included enemas, emetics (to induce vomiting), diuretics (to heighten urination), and laxatives. In almost all cases, the treatment was probably more harmful than the illness. The list is ghoulishly instructive.

**For Purging**

Calomel (a poisonous mercury solution)
Syrup of Squills (a powdered herb in pure alcohol)
Oil of Turpentine (a solvent approximating PineSol)
Castor Oil (essentially a lubricant)
Tincture of Jalap (made of hallucinogenic morning glory seeds)

**For Stimulants**

Peruvian Wine of Coca (cocaine)
Tincture of Lobelia (a solution of Indian tobacco, pure nicotine)
Hartshorn (powdered red deer horn in ammonia, a caustic bleach)
Camphor (a nauseating, vomit-inducing compound, now widely used in insect repellent)

**For Sedatives**

Laudanum (tincture of opium, highly addictive)
Opium (narcotic, highly addictive)
Morphine (principal alkaloid of opium, highly addictive)

**For Pain**

Dover's Powders (powder of ipecac and cocaine)
Mandragora (a narcotic, made from the roots of mandrake herb)

**For Disinfecting Wounds**

Sulphate of Copper & Lead (a solution of soluble salts capable of killing bacteria—and humans—in concentrated doses)
Sugar of Lead (a poisonous soluble salt)
Chloride of Lime (caustic bleach)
Spirits of Ammonia (yet another bleach)

**For Spasms**

Asafetida (a noxious gum resin)

# APPENDIX IV
# Expedition Muster

The officers and men who persevered through the ordeal of the Franklin Expedition bear remembrance for their sublime courage and gallantry. Only two bodies were ever returned from the Arctic to England. The crews' ages, ranks, and postings previous to the expedition are given.

**HMS *Erebus* (Complement: 68)**

Officers "Commissioned to draw bills" (13):[1]

Sir John Franklin (59) . . . . . . . . . . . . . . . (Captain, Half Pay)
James Fitzjames (33) . . . . . . . . . . . . . (Commander, Half Pay)
Graham Gore (?) . . . . . . . . . . . . . . . . . . (Lieut., HMS *Cyclops*)
H. T. D. LesVesconte (?) . . . . . . . . . . . . . . . (Lieut., Half Pay)
James Fairholme (?) . . . . . . . . . . . . . . . . (Lieut., HMS *Superb*)
Robert Sargent (?) . . . . . . . . . . . . . . . (Mate, HMS *Excellent*)
Charles DeVoeux (?) . . . . . . . . . . . . . . (Mate, HMS *Excellent*)
Edward Couch (?) . . . . . . . . . . . . . . . . . . (Mate, Actg. Comm.)
Henry Collins (?) . . . . . . . . . . (2nd Master, HMS *Sheerwater*)
James Reid (?) . . . . . . . . . . . . . . . . (Ice Master, Actg. Comm.)

[1] ADM 38/672 and ADM 38/1962; Public Record Office. The ages of most ship's officers were not recorded in the muster; they were gentlemen and above such practice. Franklin's and Fitzjames's ages are noted because the discrepancy between the two was much publicized at the time.

Stephen Stanley (?) . . . . . . . . . . . . . . . . . (Surgeon, Half Pay)[2]
Harry Goodsir (?) . . . . . . . . . . . (Asst. Surgeon, Actg. Comm.)
Charles Osmer (?) . . . . . . . . . . . . (Paymaster/Purser, Half Pay)

Warrant Officers (3):

John Gregory (?) . . . . . . . . . . . (Engineer/1st Class, Woolwich)
Thomas Terry (?) . . . . . . . (Boatswain/3rd Class, HMS *Ocean*)
John Weekes (?) . . . . . . . . . (Carpenter/2nd Class, HMS *Eagle*)

Petty Officers (23):

John Murray (43) . . . . . . . . . . . . . . . . (Sailmaker, Woolwich)
William Smith (28) . . . . . . . . . . . . . . (Blacksmith, Woolwich)
Thomas Burt (22) . . . . . . . . . . . . . . . . . (Armorer, First Entry)
James Brown (28) . . . . . . . . . . . . . . . . . (Caulker, First Entry)
Francis Dunn (25) . . . . . . . . . . . . (Caulker's Mate, Woolwich)
Thomas Watson (40) . . . . . . . . (Carpenter's Mate, Woolwich)
Samuel Brown (27) . . . . . . . . . (Boatswain's Mate, Woolwich)[3]
Richard Wall (45) . . . . . . . . . . . . . . (Ship's Cook, Woolwich)[4]
James Rigden (32) . . . . . . . . (Captain's Coxswain, Woolwich)
John Downing (34) . . . . . . . . . . . . (Quartermaster, Woolwich)
William Bell (36) . . . . . . . . . . . . . (Quartermaster, First Entry)
Daniel Arthur (35) . . . . . . . . . . . . (Quartermaster, Woolwich)
Robert Sinclair (25) . . . . . . . (Capt. of the Foretop, Woolwich)
John Sullivan (28) . . . . . . . (Capt. of the Maintop, Woolwich)
Phillip Reddington (28) . . (Capt. of the Forecastle, Woolwich)
Joseph Andrews (35) . . . . . . . . (Capt. of the Hold, Woolwich)
Edmund Hoar (23) . . . . . . (Capt.'s Steward, HMS *St. Vincent*)
John Bridgens (26) . . . . . . (Sub. Officer's Steward, Woolwich)
Richard Aylmore (24) . . . . . . . (Gunroom Steward, Woolwich)
William Fowler (26) . . . . . . . . . . (Purser's Steward, Woolwich)

[2] Stanley, Goodsir, and Osmer, while officers, belonged to the Civil Branch, not the Military Branch; they were not expected to command.

[3] Brown had previously served aboard HMS *Erebus* on its 1840–1843 Antarctic voyage.

[4] Wall had been cook aboard the *Erebus* in the Antarctic.

James Hart (33) . . . . (Leading Stoker, First Entry)
John Cowie (32) . . . . (Stoker, Woolwich)
Thomas Plater (?) . . . . (Stoker, HMS *Wm. & Mary*)

Able-Bodied Seamen (20):

John Morfin (25) . . . . (ABS, First Entry)
Charles Coombs (28) . . . . (ABS, Woolwich)
George Thompson (27) . . . . (ABS, Woolwich)
John Hartnell (25) . . . . (ABS, Woolwich)
Thomas Hartnell (23) . . . . (ABS, Woolwich)
John Strickland (24) . . . . (ABS, Woolwich)
William Orren (34) . . . . (ABS, Woolwich)
William Closson (25) . . . . (ABS, First Entry)
Charles Best (23) . . . . (ABS, First Entry)
Thomas McConvey (24) . . . . (ABS, First Entry)
Henry Lloyd (26) . . . . (ABS, First Entry)
Thomas Work (41) . . . . (ABS, First Entry)
Robert Ferrier (29) . . . . (ABS, First Entry)
Joseph Greater (32) . . . . (ABS, First Entry)
George Williams (35) . . . . (ABS, Woolwich)
Thomas Tadman (28) . . . . (ABS, Woolwich)
Abraham Seely (34) . . . . (ABS, Woolwich)
Francis Pocock (24) . . . . (ABS, Woolwich)
Robert Johns (24) . . . . (ABS, Woolwich)
William Mark (24) . . . . (ABS, Woolwich)

Royal Marines (7):

David Bryant (31 & $^{6}/_{12}$)[5] . . . . (Sergeant, Woolwich)[6]
Alexander Paterson (30) . . . . (Corporal, Woolwich)
Robert Hopcroft (38 & $^{8}/_{12}$) . . . . (Private, Woolwich)

[5] For some reason, the marines' ages were recorded in exacting detail.

[6] Sgt. Bryant had been a marine for 17 years, enlisting at age 15. The others had similarly long service records: Corp. Paterson (11 yrs.), Pvt. Hopcroft (16 yrs.), Pvt. Pilkington (11 yrs.), Pvt. Braine (12 yrs.), Pvt. Healey (11 yrs.), Pvt. Reed (10 yrs.). The term of enlistment was 7 years, so all were on their second or third tours.

William Pilkington (28 & 4/12) . . . . . . . . . (Private, Woolwich)
William Braine (31 & 3/12) . . . . . . . . . . . . (Private, Woolwich)
Joseph Healey (29 & 10/12) . . . . . . . . . . . . (Private, Woolwich)
William Reed (28 & 8/12) . . . . . . . . . . . . . (Private, Woolwich)

Volunteers 1st Class (2):

George Chambers (18) . . . . . . . . . . (1st Class, HMS *Vesuvius*)
David Young (18) . . . . . . . . . . . . . . . . . . (1st Class, Woolwich)

(Two midshipmen were "discharged with disgrace" prior to sailing. Their offense was not noted. In the Muster Book, under the category of "Quality," they were marked as having "None.")

**HMS *Terror* (Complement: 65)**

Officers (11):

Francis Crozier (49) . . . . . . . . . . . . . . . . . (Captain, Half Pay)
Edward Little (?) . . . . . . . . . . . . . . . . . (Lieutenant, Half Pay)
George Hodgson (?) . . . . . . . . . . (Lieutenant, HMS *Excellent*)
John Irving (?) . . . . . . . . . . . . . . (Lieutenant, HMS *Excellent*)
Frederick Hornby (?) . . . . . . . . . . . . . (Mate, HMS *Excellent*)
Robert Thomas (?) . . . . . . . . . . . . . . . . (Mate, HMS *Mastiff*)
Giles MacBean (?) . . . . . . . . . . . . (2nd Master, HMS *Mastiff*)
Thomas Blanky (?) . . . . . . . . . . . . . . . (Ice Master, Woolwich)
John Peddie (?) . . . . . . . . . . . . . (Surgeon, HMS *Wm & Mary*)
Alexander MacDonald (?) . . . . . . . . (Asst. Surgeon, Half Pay)
E. J. Helpman (?) . . . . . . . . . . (Clerk-In-Charge, HMS *Herald*)

Warrant Officers (3):

James Thompson (?) . . . . . . . . (Engineer/1st Class, Woolwich)
John Lane (?) . . . . (Boatswain/2nd Class, HMS *Wm & Mary*)
Thomas Honey (?) . . . . . . (Carpenter/3rd Class, HMS *Ocean*)

Petty Officers (23):

James Elliott (20) . . . . . . . . . . . . . . . . (Sailmaker, First Entry)[7]
Samuel Honey (22) . . . . . . . . . . . . . . (Blacksmith, First Entry)

[7] Elliott was sent home from Greenland aboard the *Baretto Junior.*

Robert Carr (23) . . . . . . . . . . . . . . . . . . (Armorer, First Entry)
Thomas Darlington (29) . . . . . . . . . . . . (Caulker, First Entry)
Cornelius Hickey (24) . . . . . . . . . (Caulker's Mate, First Entry)
Alexander Wilson (27) . . . . . . . (Carpenter's Mate, First Entry)
Thomas Johnson (28) . . . . . . . (Boatswain's Mate, Woolwich)[8]
John Diggle (36) . . . . . . . . . . . . . . . (Ship's Cook, Woolwich)[9]
John Wilson (33) . . . . . . . (Captain's Coxswain, HMS *Blazer*)
David McDonald (45) . . . . . . . (Quartermaster, HMS *Perseus*)
William Rhodes (31) . . . . . . . . . (Quartermaster, HMS *Rattler*)
Henry Peglar (37) . . . . . . . . (Capt. of the Foretop, Woolwich)
Thomas Farr (32) . . . . . . . . (Capt. of the Maintop, Woolwich)
Reuben Male (27) . . . . . . (Capt. of the Forecastle, Woolwich)
William Goddard (39) . . . . . . . (Capt. of the Hold, Woolwich)
Thomas Jopson (27) . . . . . . . . . (Capt's. Steward, Woolwich)[10]
William Gibson (22) . . . . . (Sub. Officer's Steward, Woolwich)
Thomas Armitage (40) . . . . . . (Gunroom Steward, Woolwich)
Edward Genge (21) . . . . . . . . . . (Purser's Steward, First Entry)
John Torrington (19) . . . . . . . . (Leading Stoker, First Entry)[11]
Luke Smith (27) . . . . . . . . . . . . . . . . . (Stoker, HMS *Terror*)[12]
William Johnson (45) . . . . . . . . . . . . . . . . (Stoker, Woolwich)

Able-Bodied Seamen (19):

George Cann (23) . . . . . . . . . . . . . . . . . . . . (ABS, First Entry)
William Strong (22) . . . . . . . . . . . . . . . (ABS, HMS *Belvidera*)
David Sims (24) . . . . . . . . . . . . . . . . . . . . . (ABS, First Entry)
John Bailey (21) . . . . . . . . . . . . . . . . . . . . . (ABS, First Entry)
William Jerry (29) . . . . . . . . . . . . . . . . . (ABS, HMS *Terror*)[13]

---

8 Johnson had served with Crozier in *Terror* on the Antarctic expedition.

9 Diggle had been cook aboard the *Erebus* on the Antarctic expedition.

10 Jopson had been Crozier's steward throughout the Antarctic expedition; as soon as he became available, Crozier dismissed Robert Nixon, the steward he'd recruited earlier.

11 Torrington, new to the navy, new to the Arctic, was the first of the expedition to die on Jan. 1, 1846.

12 Smith had served under Crozier in *Terror* on the 1839–1843 Antarctic expedition.

13 Jerry had served under Crozier in *Terror* on the 1839–1843 Antarctic expedition.

Henry Sait (23) . . . . . . . . . . . . . . . . . . . (ABS, HMS *Belvidera*)
Alexander Berry (32) . . . . . . . . . . . . . . . (ABS, HMS *Perseus*)
John Handford (28) . . . . . . . . . . . . . . . . . . (ABS, First Entry)
John Bates (24) . . . . . . . . . . . . . . . . . . (ABS, HMS *President*)
Samuel Crispe (24) . . . . . . . . . . . . . . . . . (ABS, HMS *Poitiers*)
Charles Johnson (28) . . . . . . . . . . . . . . . . . (ABS, First Entry)
William Shanks (29) . . . . . . . . . . . . . . . . . . (ABS, First Entry)
David Leys (37) . . . . . . . . . . . . . . . . . . . . . (ABS, First Entry)
William Sinclair (30) . . . . . . . . . . . . . . . . . . (ABS, First Entry)
George Kinniard (23) . . . . . . . . . . . . . . . . . (ABS, First Entry)
Edwin Laurence (30) . . . . . . . . . . . . . . . (ABS, HMS *Ariadne*)
James Walker (29) . . . . . . . . . . . . . . . . . . . (ABS, First Entry)
William Wentzell (33) . . . . . . . . . . . . . . . . . (ABS, First Entry)
Magnus Manson (28) . . . . . . . . . . . . . . . . . (ABS, First Entry)

Royal Marines (7):

Solomon Tozer (34) . . . . . . . . . . . . . . . . (Sergeant, Woolwich)
William Hedges (30) . . . . . . . . . . . . . . . (Corporal, Woolwich)
William Aitken (37) . . . . . . . . . . . . . . . . . (Private, Woolwich)[14]
Henry Wilks (28) . . . . . . . . . . . . . . . . . . . . (Private, Woolwich)
James Daly (30) . . . . . . . . . . . . . . . . . . . . . (Private, Woolwich)
William Heather (35) . . . . . . . . . . . . . . . . . (Private, Woolwich)
John Hammond (32) . . . . . . . . . . . . . . . . . (Private, Woolwich)

Volunteers 1st Class (2):

Robert Golding (19) . . . . . . . . . . . . . . . (1st Class, First Entry)
Thomas Evans (18) . . . . . . . . . . . . . . . . (1st Class, HMS *Lynx*)

(A third midshipman, William Eaton, signed on with the expedition on April 8 and was discharged "From the Ship per order of Commander Collier KCB" three weeks later.)

[14] Discharged and sent home on HMS *Rattler* at Disko Island.

# Bibliography

## Books

Amundsen, Roald. *The Northwest Passage.* London: Constable, 1908.

Beattie, Dr. Owen, and John Geiger. *Frozen In Time.* New York: Dutton, 1987.

Berton, Pierre. *The Arctic Grail: The Quest for the Northwest Passage and the North Pole.* New York: Penguin Books, 1988.

Bradford, William. *The Arctic Regions.* London: Sampson, Low, Marston, Low & Searle, 1873.

Cherry-Garrard, Apsley. *The Worst Journey in the World.* London: Chatto & Windus, 1965.

Craig, W., J. Hughes, and M. Scheld. *Emerging Infections.* Washington: ASM Press, 1998.

Cyriax, Richard. *Sir John Franklin's Last Arctic Expedition.* London: Methuen, 1939.

D'Urville, Jules Dumont (translated by Helen Rosenman). *Two Voyages to the South Seas.* Honolulu: Univ. of Hawaii Press, 1992.

Editors, Reader's Digest Assoc. *Everyday Life Through the Ages.* London: Reader's Digest Assoc., 1992.

Farwell, Byron. *Queen Victoria's Little Wars.* New York: W. W. Norton, 1972.

Francis, Clare, and Warren Tute. *The Commanding Sea: Six Voyages of Discovery.* London: British Broadcasting Corporation and Pelham Books, 1981.

Franklin, John. *Narrative of a Journey to the Shores of the Polar Sea.* London: John Murray, 1823.

Franklin, John. *Narrative of a Second Expedition to the Shores of the Polar Sea.* London: John Murray, 1828.

Gilder, William. *Schwatka's Search.* New York: Abercrombie & Fitch, 1966.

Goetzmann, William. *The Atlas of North American Exploration.* New York: Prentice Hall, 1992.

Hill, J. R. *The Oxford Illustrated History of the Royal Navy.* Oxford: Oxford Univ. Press, 1995.

Holland, Clive. *Farthest North: A History of Polar Exploration in Eyewitness Accounts.* New York: Carroll & Graf, 1994.

Kane, Elisha Kent. *Arctic Expeditions in Search of Sir John Franklin.* London: T. Nelson & Sons, 1898.

Keay, John. *Exploration: Classic Accounts of the Great Stories of Human Endeavor.* New York: Carroll & Graf, 1993.

Kemp, Peter. *Oxford Companion to Ships and the Sea.* Oxford: Oxford Univ. Press, 1976.

Lawrence, R. D. *Natural History of Canada.* Toronto: Key Porter Books, 1988.

Lewis, Edward, and Robert O'Brien. *Ships.* New York: Time, Inc., 1970.

Ley, Willy. *The Poles.* New York: Time-Life Books, 1961.

Lyon, David. *The Age of Nelson.* Annapolis: Naval Institute Press, 1996.

Maxtone-Graham, John. *Safe Return Doubtful: The Heroic Age of Polar Exploration.* New York: Barnes & Noble, 1998.

M'Clintock, F. L. *Narration of the Discovery of the Fate of Sir John Franklin and His Companions.* London: John Murray, 1859.

Mowat, Farley. *Ordeal By Ice.* Salt Lake City: Gibb-Smith, 1973.

Mowat, Farley. *Tundra.* Salt Lake City: Gibb-Smith, 1989.

Mowat, Farley. *The Polar Passion.* Salt Lake City: Gibb-Smith, 1973.

Neatby, L. H. *In Quest of the Northwest Passage.* Toronto: Longmans, Green & Co., 1958.

Newman, Peter. *Company of Adventurers.* Markham, Ontario: Penguin Books, 1985.

Nikiforuk, Andrew. *The Fourth Horseman: A History of Epidemics, Plagues and Other Scourges.* London: Fourth Estate, 1991.

North, Dick. *The Lost Patrol.* Edmonds, Washington: Alaska Northwest Publishing Co., 1978.

Osborn, Sherard. *Stray Leaves from an Arctic Journal: or Eighteen Months in the Polar Regions in Search of Sir John Franklin's Expedition in the Years 1850–51.* London: Longman, Brown, Green & Longmans, 1865.

Parker, Steven. *Medicine.* New York: Dorling Kindersley, 1995.

Parry, William Edward. *Journal of a Voyage for the Discovery of a North-West Passage.* London: John Murray, 1821.

Rosenfeld, Dr. Isadore. *Symptoms*. New York: Bantam Books, 1990.

Ross, John. *Narrative of a Second Voyage in Search of the Northwest Passage and of a Residence in the Arctic Regions*. London: A. W. Webster, 1835.

Sebrell, William, and James Haggerty. *Food and Nutrition*. New York: Time-Life Books, 1967.

Shackleton, Ernest. *South*. London: Heinemann, 1919; Century, 1983.

St. Louis, M. E. *Bacterial Infections of Humans: Epidemiology and Control*, second edition, A. S. Evans and P. S. Brachman, eds., New York: Plenum Medical, 1991: 115–131: chapter: "Botulism."

Stefansson, Vilhjalmur. *Hunters of the Great North*. New York: Harcourt Brace Jovanovich, 1922.

Stonehouse, Bernard. *North Pole, South Pole*. London: Prion, 1990.

Toussaint-Samat, Maguelonne. *History of Food*. Translated by Anthea Bell. Oxford: Blackwell Publishers Ltd., 1992.

Ware, Chris. *The Bomb Vessel*. Annapolis: Naval Institute Press, 1994.

Weems, John E. *Peary: The Explorer and the Man, Based On His Personal Papers*. Boston: Houghton Mifflin, 1967.

Wilkinson-Latham, Robert. *The Royal Navy 1790–1970*. London: Osprey, 1977.

## Papers, Articles, Reprints, and Web Sites

Centers for Disease Control and Prevention Web site: http://www.cdc.gov/ncidod/dbmd/diseaseinfo/botulism_g.htm

Farrer, K. T. H. "Lead and the Last Franklin Expedition." *Journal of Archaeological Science*. 1993. No. 20, 399–409. Glen Ebor, Hampshire: Academic Press Ltd.

Keenleyside, Anne. "The Final Days of the Franklin Expedition—New Skeletal Evidence." *Arctic Magazine*. March 1997. Vol. 50, No. 1.

Laing, E. A. M. "Introduction of Canned Food Into the Royal Navy 1811–1852." *The Mariner's Mirror*. 1964. Vol. 50. London: Cambridge Univ. Press.

Shapiro, Roger L., Charles Hatheway, D. L. Swerdlow. "Botulism in the United States: A clinical and epidemiologic review." *Annals of Internal Medicine* 1998: 129: 221–28.

Shapiro, Roger L., J. Becher, D. L. Swerdlow. "Botulism surveillance and emergency response: A public health strategy for a global challenge." *Journal of the American Medical Association* (JAMA) 1997: 278: 433–35.

Trafton, Stephen. "Did Lead Poisoning Contribute to Deaths of Franklin Expedition Members." *Information North*. Nov. 1989. Vol. 15, No. 9. Calgary: Arctic Institute of North America.

*U.S. Dept. of Health, Education and Welfare*. "Botulism in the U.S. 1899–1977." Atlanta: Reprinted by U.S. Public Health Service, U.S. Centers for Disease Control and Prevention.

Villar, R. G., Roger L. Shapiro, S. Bustos, C. Riva-Posse, G. Verdejo, M. I. Farace, F. Rosetti, J. A. San Juan, C. M. Julia, J. Becher, S. E. Maslanka, D. L. Swerdlow. "Outbreak of type A botulism and development of a botulism surveillance and antitoxin release system in Argentina." *Journal of the American Medical Association* (JAMA) 1999: 281: 1334–40.

## Government Records and Documents

Records listed are drawn from the Public Record Office (UK), Home Office Records (UK), Parliamentary Papers of Great Britain (House of Lords Library), and others. Key information is indicated in parentheses. The following abbreviations are used. ADM: records of the Admiralty, Naval Forces, Royal Marines, Coastguard, and related bodies; HO: records created or inherited by the Home Office, Ministry of Home Security, and related bodies; J: records of the Supreme Court of Judicature and related courts.

ADM 38/1962 (Final Muster Book, HMS *Terror*)

ADM 38/672 (Final Muster Book, HMS *Erebus*)

CS4/12507 (Goldner's 1841 patent application, for preserving animal and vegetable substances)

HO 1/21/306 (Goldner's 1845 naturalization application)

ADM 114/17/1 (1845 Franklin Expedition: victualling tenders, bids, correspondence w/victuallers; final ships' provisioning returns; clothing/stores returns)

J 110/29 (Goldner's running Dec. 1844 contract for preserved provisions, including Franklin Expedition)

ADM 114/2 (Goldner correspondence re: preserved provisioning contract for 1847 Franklin relief expedition)

ADM 114/21/2 (Goldner bids on preserved provisions for 1850 Franklin relief expeditions)

J 117/33 (Goldner's 1850 contract)

J 117/2 (Goldner's 1850 contract particulars: specifications mandating he guarantee food quality, proper preparation, and canning)

ADM 114/17/4 (Goldner correspondence re: preserved provisioning contract for 1850 Franklin relief expeditions)

ADM 114/21/1 (Goldner's correspondence re: discrepancies in provisions ordered vs. provisions delivered for 1850 Franklin relief expeditions)

J 117/34 (Goldner's 1851 contract: requiring him to post a bond of 4,000 pounds, manufacture tins to specification, guarantee his meats to be free of bone, and open his factory to Admiralty inspection at any time)

ADM 114/20/4 (1852 report requested by the Admiralty on processing/canning procedures and costs at the Royal Clarence Yard, apparently for purposes of comparison with Goldner's)

ADM 12/544 (Returned & Condemned report: condemning Goldner's preserved meats, charging him for same, scheduling and informing him of a survey of his products, noting he failed to attend; survey results forwarded to Parliament)

ADM 114/19/2 (Report of 1,000 lbs. of Goldner's preserved meats aboard HMS *Plover* on 1852 Franklin relief expedition found putrid and dumped overboard; Capt. Inglefield's returns report re: quality of provisions supplied HMS *Isabel* on 1852 Franklin relief expedition)

Parliamentary Papers, 1852. House of Commons. Sessional papers, accounts, and papers 30 (59) (Parliamentary investigation into Goldner's provisions)

Report from the Select Committee on Preserved Meats (Navy). House of Commons. May 3, 1852. (Findings of Parliamentary investigation into Goldner's provisions)

ADM 114/18/1 (1852 correspondence from Superintendent of Victualling recommending the Admiralty have no more dealings with Goldner)

ADM 114/17/4 (rationing plan/sledging parties Parry's 1824 expedition; rationing plan/shipboard Penny and Stewart's 1850 expedition in search of Franklin)

ADM 114/16/3 (Parry's 1820 correspondence to Commissioners of Victualling re: quality of canned provisions)

ADM 114/19/4 (returns report on quality and quantity of provisions of Inglefield's 1853 expedition in search of Franklin)

ADM 114/22/1 (Goldner correspondence regarding provisioning contract/specifications for Austin's 1850 expedition in search of Franklin)

ADM 114/18/1 (Capt. Austin's 1852 correspondence: recommendations for provisioning future Arctic voyages)

ADM 114/22/3 (correspondence regarding quality of preserved provisions for 1852 expedition in search of Franklin)

ADM 114/16/2 (general polar provisioning plans previous to and following Franklin Expedition)

ADM 114/16/4 (polar provisioning plans, HMS *Hecla* 1823–1826)

ADM 114/19/5 (victuallers' bids, HMS *Assistance* 1852, in search of Franklin)

ADM 114/18 (reactions/recommendations of Capts. Ommaney and Austin on quality of polar provisions 1850; winter rationing plans)

ADM 114/19/1 (original provisioning and returns reports from Capts. Penny and Stewart 1851)

ADM 114/16/1 (quantities/costs of provisions for HMS *Erebus* and HMS *Terror* on 1839–1843 Antarctic expedition)

ADM 114/17/3 (equipment and provisions for boat parties on 1847 Franklin relief expedition; Franklin's boats would have been similarly equipped)

# Index

Page numbers in *italics* indicate illustrations.